THE
CHURCHILL
SISTERS

THE CHURCHILL SISTERS

The Extraordinary Lives of Winston and Clementine's Daughters

RACHEL TRETHEWEY

ST. MARTIN'S PRESS
NEW YORK

To my sister, Becky, with love.

First published in the United States by St. Martin's Press, an imprint
of St. Martin's Publishing Group

THE CHURCHILL SISTERS. Copyright © 2021 by Rachel Trethewey.
All rights reserved. Printed in the United States of America. For
information, address St. Martin's Publishing Group, 120 Broadway,
New York, NY 10271.

www.stmartins.com

Library of Congress Cataloging-in-Publication Data

Names: Trethewey, Rachel, author.
Title: The Churchill sisters : the extraordinary lives of Winston and
    Clementine's daughters / Rachel Trethewey.
Other titles: Extraordinary lives of Winston and Clementine's
    daughters
Description: First U.S. edition. | New York : St. Martin's Press, 2021. |
    Includes bibliographical references and index.
Identifiers: LCCN 2021027555 | ISBN 9781250272393
    (hardcover) | ISBN 9781250272409 (ebook)
Subjects: LCSH: Churchill, Winston, 1874–1965—Family. |
    Children of prime ministers—Great Britain—Biography. |
    Churchill, Clementine, 1885–1977—Family. | Churchill family. |
    Churchill, Diana, 1909–1963. | Churchill, Sarah, 1914–1982. |
    Churchill, Marigold, 1918–1921. | Soames, Mary. | Sisters—
    Great Britain—Biography. | Women—Great Britain—Biography.
Classification: LCC DA566.9.C5 T74 2021 | DDC 941.084092/
    2[B]—dc23
LC record available at https://lccn.loc.gov/2021027555

Our books may be purchased in bulk for promotional, educational,
or business use. Please contact your local bookseller or the Macmillan
Corporate and Premium Sales Department at 1-800-221-7945, extension
5442, or by email at MacmillanSpecialMarkets@macmillan.com.

Originally published in Great Britain under the title *The Churchill Girls*
by The History Press

First U.S. Edition: 2021

10 9 8 7 6 5 4 3 2 1

Contents

Introduction

Winston Churchill is portrayed as the man who stood alone against Nazi tyranny during the Second World War until the United States came to Britain's aid. Yet in his private life, he was a world leader who never stood alone; by his side at many of the most crucial moments in the conflict was one or other of his devoted daughters. They were eyewitnesses at some of the most important events in world history: beside him at Tehran, Yalta and Potsdam and with him when he met Roosevelt, Stalin and de Gaulle.

Nor was this purely a wartime phenomenon. Throughout Winston's political career, he liked to keep his daughters close. When he was Chancellor of the Exchequer in the 1920s, his eldest daughter, Diana stood beside him outside No. 11 Downing Street before he presented his Budget. After the war, Sarah was his chosen companion on holidays to Italy, Morocco and the South of France, while Mary was there to support him at Chequers and Chartwell in his final years as prime minister.

Thousands of books have been written about Winston Churchill, but this is the first focussing on his four daughters: Diana, Sarah, Marigold and Mary. *The Churchill Sisters* brings them out of the shadows to discover who they really were, and by telling their story adds to our understanding of 'the greatest Englishman'. Looking at him from their perspective, we see him in a new light as not just a great war leader but a father.

Building on the now widely accepted argument that Churchill could not have achieved what he did without his wife, Clementine, my book shows that he also depended on his daughters. The women in his family worked as a team to help him fulfil his destiny. Clementine was the most important person in his life, but when she was unavailable, one of his daughters stepped in to support him. During the Second World War, as his health deteriorated, they acted as a human shield, travelling with him when he met world leaders and protecting him whenever necessary. Together, they helped to create the stable domestic life he needed to be able to fight on. In those crucial days, when the future of Britain hung in the balance, there were few people Winston could trust and his wife and daughters were among the faithful few he knew would never let him down. As the pressures mounted, Clementine also relied on her girls to give her the strength to keep calm and carry on.

Despite touching on the great events of history, this is not a story set on the battlefields or in Parliament. It is an intimate family saga, which gives a behind-the-scenes insight into the Churchillian world. It recreates the atmosphere of what it was like to live in one of the most powerful families in England at a pivotal period in our history, and while there is plenty of country-house colour, this is far from a superficial chronicle of upper-class life. The Churchill girls were never just social butterflies and from an early age they were motivated by a profound sense of duty.

Drawing on hundreds of previously unpublished family letters, including those from the recently opened Soames archives, this book delves into the complex dynamics of the family.[1] Although Winston was self-centred and his vocation came first, he was always very loving to his daughters. As I read their letters, I was impressed with the intimacy and informality of his relationship with his girls. At moments of crisis, they confided in him and sought his advice. They felt that he was the one person who could always make them feel better. As Sarah said, he created in his children the same emotions he inspired in people during the war: 'It's a feeling that no matter how grim things are, if you hold on, and do your best, all will be well in the end.'[2]

Churchill's relationships with his daughters are a fundamental part of the story, but they are only one aspect of a multifaceted narrative. Clementine's relationships with her daughters and their interactions with each other lie at the heart of it. The way one personality played off another shaped the people they became. Bright, attractive and well connected, in any other family the girls would have shone. But they were not in another family, they were Churchills and neither they nor anyone else could ever forget it.

The girls were born into a cast of larger-than-life personalities. It was their fate to be overshadowed and it was not just their famous father who expected to take centre stage; there were plenty of other flamboyant characters waiting in the wings. Their only brother, Randolph, was next in the pecking order. At first, he was the golden boy, then the *enfant terrible* who undermined family peace with his erratic behaviour. Even their more distant relatives stole the limelight; who could compete with their glamorous cousins, the Mitford girls?

In fact, the Churchill girls could and *did*. Their lives were just as full of drama, passion and tragedy as their Mitford rivals. There was an elopement, affairs with powerful characters and a series of suicides. It is a story of extremes which takes the reader from Hollywood to Holloway Prison, from the peaks of power to the depths of despair.

Theirs was a double-edged sword. Being Winston's daughters opened up a world of privilege and opportunity, but it also raised expectations. Their positions as handmaids to the great man were the easy part of their role; establishing meaningful lives of their own away from their charismatic clan was harder. Sadly, Marigold died too young to achieve her potential, but Diana, Sarah and Mary coped in very different ways with the demands of living up to their famous name.

Like so many women of their generation, their lives were limited by their gender. Until his daughters' sterling war work changed his attitude, Winston had a Victorian view of women's roles; they were expected to be dutiful wives and mothers. Their brother Randolph, purely because he was male, was treated as the star. Arguably, the girls had greater potential, which they fought in varying degrees to fulfil.

Although Diana was very political, she chose a traditionally female role, acting as a supporter of first her father and then her husband. She only found her true vocation at the end of her life. Similarly, after a brilliant wartime career, Mary put her family first. It was only in later life that she became a public figure in her own right. In contrast, Sarah was the least conventional of her sisters and always the rebel. She became an actress and pursued her career in America. It was not an easy choice, but as she wrote to her father, 'I have in me, as strong an instinct, as most women (as Mary for instance) as powerful an instinct to be alone and free, as they have to find a true mate and found a family.'[3]

In a less sexist era, it might have been Sarah rather than Randolph who became Winston's heir apparent. She was the one who inherited a touch of her father's genius. Always on the cusp of success, she was almost a great beauty, nearly a famous film star, but she never quite made it. Her self-destructive streak sabotaged her talent.

In such a dynamic family there was never a dull moment, but there is a point in their story when the drama takes a darker turn. The issue of mental health runs like a deep vein through this book. Both Diana and Sarah fought poignant battles against personal challenges which threatened to overwhelm them. Drawing on the Churchill girls' candid letters, doctors' reports and friends' memories, this book pieces together what happened.

Most people know about the legendary courage Churchill showed in the war, but fewer know about the adversity he faced in private. Over the years his family endured more than its fair share of problems, but the lasting image of the Churchill girls is not one of tragedy; they are heroic rather than tragic figures. Like their father and mother, Diana, Sarah and Mary were resilient and courageous.

This book is an extraordinary love story – not in the conventional sense, but in the true meaning of the word because Winston's daughters' deep love and loyalty to their parents and each other was exceptional. Their relationships are inspiring because they were so compassionate; they accepted human frailties and forgave past failures. Tested to the limits, the bond between them was indestructible. In later life, as they remembered all they had been through together, Mary wrote to Sarah, 'I cling to our loving bond of sisterhood – and know that is one of the most precious things in my life.'[4] Sarah agreed, 'Out of it all comes a shining light for me – we were really sisters.'[5]

Part One

The Early Years

Part One

Poisoned Arrows

1

Diana
The Gold Cream Kitten

When Winston Churchill's first child, Diana, was born, he wrote to his wife, Clementine:

> I wonder what she will grow into, and whether she will be lucky or unlucky to have been dragged out of chaos. She ought to have some rare qualities both of mind and body. But these do not always mean happiness or peace. Still I think a bright star shines for her.[1]

Winston firmly believed in destiny, but was it really written in the stars what life would be like for his daughters? Were they predestined to follow a course charted for them by fate, step-by-step to its inevitable conclusion, or did a unique combination of characters playing off each other have consequences none of the main protagonists could have foreseen? Did nature or nurture turn the Churchill girls into the women they became? Piecing together what shaped their ends involves tracing their stories from the beginning, and that started when two exceptional people met and fell in love.

When Winston Churchill married Clementine Hozier at St Margaret's, Westminster, on 12 September 1908, it was the most important political wedding of the decade. Politicians from across Parliament joined the congregation as Winston's former headmaster,

Dr Welldon, told Clementine that her role and the influence she exerted in her husband's future public life would be so important it would be 'sacred'.[2] Never off duty for long, during the signing of the register in the vestry the groom discussed politics with David Lloyd George. Afterwards, Winston's Cabinet colleague told a friend he had 'never met anyone with such a passion for politics'.[3]

Winston never hid his ambition and it seems that, when Clementine married him, she understood what she was signing up to. Like her husband, she believed he was a man of destiny and she saw her role as supporting him to achieve his potential.[4] However, Clementine was never just some flimsy, submissive wife. Intelligent and strong-willed, she was special too. Her husband loved her deeply, but he also respected her and realised how lucky he was to have her. She was her own person, and was a shrewd judge of character with her own political views. She challenged him and her emotional intelligence made her worth listening to.

As well as mutual respect, an emotional neediness brought them together. Neither Winston nor Clementine had ever come first with anyone before they met and the knowledge that they were at last the centre of another person's world gave them the stability they both craved.[5] The closely bonded couple had much in common. They both had unhappy childhoods and complicated relationships with their parents and, inevitably, their lack of positive role models was to affect their parenting.

Clementine's father, Sir Henry Hozier, was from a wealthy brewing family while her mother, Lady Blanche Ogilvy, was the daughter of the 10th Earl of Airlie. The couple had four children, Kitty, Clementine and the twins, Bill and Nellie, but it was rumoured that none of them were fathered by Henry. Apparently, Blanche had at least nine lovers, so the paternity of her children was hard to pinpoint. There were various candidates for Clementine's biological father, but it seems most likely to have been Bertie Mitford, the 1st Lord Redesdale.[6] As Bertie was married to Blanche's younger sister, it was a liaison which verged on the incestuous even by her promiscuous standards.

After Clementine's parents separated in 1891, she had an insecure childhood. Blanche was always short of money, so in a quest to make economies she moved her family to Dieppe in France. She could not have chosen a worse place. As she was a gambler, the lure of the local casinos soon attracted her, and she was often in debt.

Although Clementine had inherited her mother's strong features, they had little else in common. Blanche favoured her vivacious eldest daughter, Kitty, and showed little affection to her serious-minded second child. However, despite their mother's blatantly divisive behaviour, the two sisters became inseparable.

The most formative moment in Clementine's early life came in 1900 when Kitty developed typhoid. She watched as, in just a few weeks, her vibrant sister was transformed into a wraith. The memory of the person she was closest to dying at the age of nearly 17 would haunt Clementine when she had children of her own. She had seen for herself that the worst thing possible could happen and fate could be cruel. Rather than deal with the complex emotions triggered by Kitty's death, both Clementine and Blanche just kept a stiff upper lip and carried on. Although they were both bereft, rather than consoling each other, Blanche turned all her attention on to her youngest daughter, Nellie.[7]

Clementine grew up to be very different from her mother. Rather than inheriting Blanche's spendthrift tendencies, she was always careful with money. Perhaps in reaction to her mother's decadence, Clementine had a puritanical streak and she was to be a faithful wife throughout her long marriage to Winston. No doubt she also intended to be a very different mother from Blanche, but sadly, she repeated many of the same mistakes with her own children.

Winston's relationship with his parents was equally problematic. His recent biographer, Andrew Roberts, describes his mother and father's treatment of him as 'verging on the abusive'.[8] His father,

Lord Randolph, was always a harsh critic of his eldest son. When Winston was 20, Lord Randolph died from a rare brain disease. For the rest of his life, the younger Churchill wished they had known each other better and been closer. Winston hero-worshiped his father and wanted to emulate his career to prove his underestimation of his potential wrong. He dreamed of having a son who would one day enter Parliament with him and form a political dynasty.

Winston's high-spirited American mother, Jennie Jerome, was no more nurturing than his father. When he was a child, she neglected him to pursue her all-consuming social life. Winston was abandoned at a school he hated.[9] Despite his begging letters, Jennie rarely visited or even wrote to her lonely little boy.[10] So, lacking maternal love, Winston turned to his nanny, Mrs Everest, who gave him the emotional support and devotion he needed to thrive. He was determined not to repeat the mistakes his parents made with his own children. He did break the pattern by being a very loving father, but his over-indulgence of his only son was to be as detrimental as his own parents' neglect.

Deprived of a stable home in his childhood, Winston could not wait to start a family. When Clementine became pregnant shortly after their wedding, he was delighted. The couple moved into a town house at 33 Eccleston Square, London, and prepared for the arrival of their baby. Winston's younger brother Jack's wife, Goonie (Gwendoline), was also expecting and the two young wives became firm friends. After Goonie gave birth to their first child, John George (known as Johnny), Winston wrote to Clementine telling her what an easy time her sister-in-law had, hoping this would reassure his nervous bride. He added that he did not like to think about her having to go through such a painful experience but that it would be worth it for the joy the baby would bring.[11] Fortunately, the birth was straightforward and on 11 July 1909 Diana was born.

Drawing on a combination of the pet names Clementine and Winston used for each other – 'Kat' or 'Cat' for her, and 'Pug' or

'Amber Dog' for him – their baby daughter was soon known as 'the Puppy Kitten' or, because of her auburn hair, the 'Gold Cream Kitten'.[12]

From the start, Diana looked more like her father than her mother. When David Lloyd George asked Winston, 'Is she a pretty child?', he replied proudly, 'The prettiest child ever seen.' To which his friend responded, 'Like her mother, I suppose.' Winston answered, 'No. She is the image of me.'[13]

Setting a pattern which would continue throughout her children's childhood, shortly after the birth, Clementine went away. While she convalesced in a cottage near Brighton, Diana was left in the care of Winston and her nanny in London. Showing her priorities, Clementine wrote to her husband saying that she missed them both, but especially him.[14]

Although leaving her baby daughter sounds strange to modern readers, Clementine's behaviour was not unusual for her era. Many upper-class Edwardian mothers spent much of their time apart from their children, delegating their care to nannies. For some, it enabled them to pursue a hedonistic existence, but for Clementine the reasons were far less frivolous. Self-preservation rather than self-indulgence made her go away. Throughout her life she suffered from anxiety and frequent holidays seemed to be the only way she could cope with her demanding husband and motherhood. Over the years, Winston accepted that she needed to get away. He understood that it was her way of regaining her emotional balance. It also allowed her to reassert her own identity which was in danger of being crushed by living with such an egocentric husband.[15]

With Clementine away, Winston became a surprisingly involved father for his generation. Whenever she was absent, he happily stepped in, displaying an enthusiasm for everyday experiences that she lacked. He enjoyed officiating at bath times and reading Beatrix Potter's *Peter Rabbit* to his first-born at bedtime. Admittedly, he was not expected to shoulder the same responsibility as his wife and could opt in and out of family life as he pleased, but he relished being a father. Even when he was particularly pressured at work, he took his duties seriously. In between making important political decisions, he spent time carefully choosing just the right present for his daughter.[16] It seems that he found involving himself in family life a way to switch off from his work.

Refreshed after her convalescence, Clementine collected Diana and took her to stay with her Stanley relatives at Alderley Park, Cheshire. Diana was a particularly pretty baby, which pleased her competitive mother. She reported with pride to Winston about how their daughter compared with the six other infants who were visiting. She wrote, 'None of them are fit to hold a candle to our P.K. or even to unloose the latchet of her shoe.'[17] She was delighted when the staff at Alderley considered Diana to be 'the finest specimen' ever to visit.[18]

However, during their stay, Clementine became concerned that her baby daughter seemed unwell. Understandably, after the tragedy of her sister's death, she became anxious when her baby showed the slightest signs of illness, and naturally inclined to worry; as a first-time mother she lacked confidence and preferred to rely on their nanny's judgement rather than her own.[19] Throughout her children's childhood, when she was with them she fussed about their health.[20] She veered between being over-protective in some ways and then strangely under-protective in others. As she was unable to strike an equilibrium, it seems that she could only escape her anxieties by handing the responsibility to someone else and getting away from it all.

However, the threats to her children's well-being were not just in Clementine's imagination. As the daughter of one of the country's leading politicians, Diana grew up in a privileged but high-pressured environment. It was a turbulent political period and Winston was a controversial figure at the centre of the action. In 1910, he became Home Secretary. As he was known for his opposition to giving women the vote, he became a target for the suffragettes.[21]

When Diana was only 16 months old, it was rumoured that the most militant campaigners might try to kidnap her. For her protection, a detective was assigned to accompany Diana and her nanny on their walks in Hyde Park.[22] This was to be the first of several times during Diana's childhood that there would be a threat of violence against her father or his family. Although Diana was too young to understand what was happening, it is likely that she would have picked up on the tense atmosphere.

It was not a happy time for the whole Churchill family. Winston's depression, which he called 'the Black Dog', reared its head during his period at the Home Office. In a letter to Clementine in July 1911 he told her that his cousin Ivor Guest's wife, Alice, had seen a doctor in Germany who had cured her depression. He felt the man might be useful if his 'black dog' ever returned, adding that it was a great relief that he did not feel that way any longer.[23]

It seems his role as Home Secretary had put a strain on his mental well-being. A distinguished psychiatrist, Anthony Storr, believed Winston was affected because he had the imagination to empathise with the distress of others. He identified with the underdog and showed genuine concern for prisoners.[24]

Winston found it particularly onerous making the ultimate decision on whether criminals condemned to death should live or die. One particularly gruelling case, which worried him so much he mentioned it to Clementine, concerned a woman who murdered her 2-year-old illegitimate child 'under very bad circumstances'. He described it as 'a very disagreeable Death Sentence'.[25] Perhaps it weighed particularly heavily on his conscience because his own daughter was the same age. He knew Clementine also found motherhood challenging but the childcare and support she had was in striking contrast to the situation of the woman whose life he held in the balance. The woman was due to be executed, but on Winston's advice she was given a reprieve and the death sentence was commuted to penal servitude for life.[26]

Just a few days after Winston wrote to his wife about his dilemma, the difference in the two mothers' worlds was highlighted. Clementine was mourning the loss of her trusted nanny, Nurse Hodgson, who had left to work elsewhere. Being unprepared to shoulder the responsibilities of motherhood alone, she recognised how dependent she was on good staff. She told her husband that she missed their old nanny very much and she was concerned because the new nursery maid was careless when left in charge of Diana.[27] Winston promptly advised Clementine to sack her.[28] Finding suitable staff to care for their children was to be a major problem for the Churchills throughout this decade.

Diana's rule as sole heir was short-lived. In 1911 Clementine gave her husband his longed-for son, Randolph. Nicknaming him 'the Chumbolly', Winston immediately treated him as a young crown prince. Although there is no doubt that Winston loved all his children deeply, as a man of his era, he believed that a son could achieve more than his daughters.

A good-looking, extrovert child, Randolph seemed to have the potential to fulfil his paternal dreams. From his first years, Randolph was spoilt by his father. In a letter to his wife, Winston rather guiltily expressed a preference for his more outgoing son over his self-conscious, enigmatic daughter.[29]

After Winston became First Lord of the Admiralty in 1911, the family moved into Admiralty House, overlooking Horse Guards Parade. As Winston advanced up the ministerial ladder, the demands on Clementine became even greater. As chatelaine of a grand house, she entertained his colleagues with style, while behind the scenes offering sound advice. Clementine always put her husband's needs above her children's, and Randolph and Diana were far down her list of priorities. As she later told her youngest daughter Mary, after she had given her all to her husband there was nothing left over.[30]

The children's care was delegated to nannies. In many ways it was a challenging job to be a nanny to the Churchill children. As they grew older, Randolph and Diana were partners in crime who delighted in devising childish pranks and, always rebellious, Randolph was the ringleader while the more docile Diana followed his lead. Their nannies rarely lasted long and when they left the mischievous duo would chuck their bags down the stairs, chanting, 'Nanny's going, Nanny's going. Hurrah! Hurrah!'[31]

At this period in her life, Clementine gave even less attention to her children because she was unwell. The year after Randolph's birth she suffered a miscarriage. It was an unpleasant experience which left her physically and emotionally drained. To recuperate, Clementine went with Goonie and their children to stay at a friend's house at Sandwich.

Throughout their childhood, Clementine always tried to take her family on a summer holiday by the sea. These breaks were some of the happiest, most relaxed times she spent with her children. However, to her frustration, Winston was less keen, preferring more glamorous destinations. The attraction of British seaside resorts could never compete with the French Riviera for him. He rarely joined family holidays for long, usually just popping in for part of the time. Annoyingly for Clementine, who invested so much time and effort in these breaks, his intermittent visits were often the highlight of the holidays for his children. While he was there, he focussed his full attention on them and made every moment fun.

When Winston finally visited his family at Sandwich, as usual he brought drama with him. The suffragettes had tracked down where their adversary was staying. As he arrived at the holiday home, two women on bicycles blocked his car. A few days later, a larger group of campaigners tried again to interrupt his journey, but this time he had left before they arrived. After these incidents, he warned Clementine to be careful not to open any suspicious parcels in case they contained explosives.[32]

As when Diana was a baby, the most militant suffragettes were once again targeting the Churchill children. They sent letters threatening to kidnap them,[33] and these were not just idle threats. Back in London, when Randolph and Diana were having their daily walk in the park with their nanny, Randolph recalled being pulled out of his pram by a would-be kidnapper. Thanks to his nanny reacting quickly, catching hold of him and putting him back into the pram, the half-hearted attempt failed.[34] According to her brother's account, Diana witnessed this frightening incident. Secure children grow up feeling the world is a safe place; for the Churchill children that comforting myth was shattered early.

2

Sarah
The Bumblebee

At the beginning of 1914 Clementine discovered she was pregnant again. When she was expecting she always felt vulnerable, but this pregnancy was particularly difficult. Her miscarriage had made her even more nervous of giving birth. Adding to her anxieties, she worried about Winston, who was learning to fly.

Her fears were not irrational. In the early days of flying the death toll was high and several of the pilots her husband flew with were killed.[1] In April, Winston nearly became a casualty when engine failure forced the pilot on his plane to make an emergency landing.[2] Clementine pleaded with him to give up but she admitted that trying to persuade him was pointless.[3]

In May she went to stay with her mother in Dieppe. For once, she focussed her attention on Diana and Randolph rather than on Winston. As she spent time playing with them, Clementine felt that she was really getting to know her children for the first time. However, she still seemed to be observing them rather than really engaging with them. Her letters to her husband show a detachment which seems odd to a modern mother. Revealing her insecurity about her place in their affections, she told Winston that he would be surprised to hear that they were becoming quite fond of her.[4]

There was a poignancy in her remarks, as if she longed to be closer to her children but did not know how to be intimate. She loved them very much, but her reserved nature created a barrier which made it hard for her to express it. She was not unusual in her class or generation; her cousin David Mitford's wife, Sydney, seemed to have a similar inability to show her children affection. The Mitford girls, like the Churchills, grew up wanting more from their mother than she could give.[5]

While she was in Dieppe, Clementine had a nightmare that the baby she was expecting was born 'a gaping idiot'. She asked the doctor to kill her child, but he refused and took it away. Unable to cope, in the dream Clementine went mad. When she woke up, she felt on edge, and each time she saw a telegram she thought it would say that Winston had been killed flying.[6] After Clementine's disturbing dream, her husband reluctantly agreed that he would not fly again, at least until she had recovered from having their baby.[7]

Relieved that Winston was no longer taking unnecessary risks, Clementine returned to England with the children and, once again, they joined Goonie and her children for a summer holiday. The two families stayed in neighbouring seaside cottages at Overstrand, near Cromer in Norfolk. Winston visited occasionally, but as tensions with Germany grew, he was busy preparing the Royal Navy for war.

When he did come, he threw himself into family life and, switching off from the demands of his position, organised expeditions to the beach with military precision. Trouser legs rolled up, cigar in his hand, Winston built a fort from sand with the children. As Fortress Commander, he led them in a battle against the incoming tide. They were not allowed to abandon their posts until the last vestige of the sandcastle had been demolished by the waves.[8]

During his visit, he received urgent phone calls from the Admiralty which made him decide to return to London.[9] With a combination of anticipation and trepidation permeating the atmosphere, Diana and Randolph picked up on the excitement as their father rushed back to his post.[10]

As war became imminent, Clementine wished that she was back in London with Winston. On 4 August 1914 the ultimatum to Germany expired and Britain declared war. Clementine remained in Norfolk with the children until the end of the month, but Winston became concerned about them being on the east coast in case there was a raid by the Germans.[11]

Rather than being afraid, Randolph and Diana enjoyed the drama. Every morning they looked out to sea, expecting enemy ships to loom on to the horizon. When the only change in their life was that their father did not come down from London, they were disappointed.[12]

For the final stage of her pregnancy Clementine moved back to Admiralty House with the children. Her anxiety levels reached new heights when Winston travelled to Antwerp in early October to take charge of British troops supporting Belgian resistance in the beleaguered city. Clementine was worried about her husband's safety and thought his intervention would harm him politically.[13] She also resented being left behind when she was at her most vulnerable.[14]

On 7 October 1914 the Churchills' second daughter, Sarah, was born. A few hours after her birth, she was introduced to her father who had just returned from Antwerp. A tired but relieved Clementine wrote to Jennie, 'The Baby is so sweet – another little Winstonia with fiery hair – It is a very pronounced type!'[15]

News soon spread of Sarah's striking resemblance to her father. When Lloyd George met Winston in the House of Commons, he teased his friend, 'I hear the baby looks like you, but then all babies look like you.'[16]

Demonstrating Winston's family pride, his second daughter was named after his most famous female ancestor, Sarah, Duchess of Marlborough, who had been Queen Anne's favourite and had done so much for the Churchill family fortunes. Like her siblings, Sarah was soon given a nickname and, because she had a shock of fuzzy red hair, she was called 'the Bumblebee'.

During Sarah's first years, Winston had little time for family life because he was fighting his own battles. A few days after Winston's return, Antwerp fell to the Germans. Clementine's intuition was right: his intervention was seen by many as an 'escapade' and he was portrayed as an adventurer.[17] Even more detrimental to his reputation was the failure of the Gallipoli invasion in 1915. As the Western Front was stuck in stalemate, an alternative strategy was developed to open an Eastern Front. As First Lord of the Admiralty, Winston became one of the main promoters of the idea of forcing the Dardanelles Straits between the Turkish mainland and the Gallipoli Peninsula, with the aim of capturing Constantinople. However, the naval expedition to bombard and take the Gallipoli Peninsula did not go to plan.[18]

Once again, public events intruded into the children's private lives. Aged 5, Diana was aware of a feeling of 'impending disaster' permeating the atmosphere in their home.[19] Every night she prayed, 'God bless the Dardanelles – whatever they might be.'[20] When the Gallipoli invasion ended in disaster, resulting in a large loss of life, Winston was one of the men blamed for the fiasco. It was the low point of his career and he became so depressed that Clementine feared he would die of grief.[21] The attacks made on Winston were vicious and upsetting for Clementine and the children to witness.

Winston's demotion from First Lord of the Admiralty to Chancellor of the Duchy of Lancaster also affected the family financially. When Winston's ministerial salary was more than halved, they had to economise. No longer living at Admiralty House, Winston and Clementine rented a country house, Hoe Farm near Godalming, Surrey. Here, away from the stresses of work, Winston discovered the pleasure of painting. It became a lifelong safety valve for him which he could turn to in times of trouble. The hobby completely engaged his interest and made him temporarily forget his worries.[22] He also relaxed by playing 'Gorilla' with his children. Dressed in his oldest clothes, he would crouch behind the bushes until one of them came close. To their delight, he would spring out, growling, with his arms swinging by his sides and chase them to the trees. Pounding his chest with his fist and baring his teeth, he then climbed up after them.[23]

In some ways, Winston was childlike himself and so he always found it easy to get down to his children's level. Clementine was the opposite: serious and sophisticated, she could never understand how a child's mind worked. Their parenting styles could not have been more different. While she was formal with her children, he was spontaneous. Clementine was the strict parent who lay down the rules and Winston was the fun one who broke them. He expected to be adored, she did not, and it became a self-fulfilling prophecy. While the children developed a tactile relationship with their father, they saw Clementine as a goddess on a pedestal.[24]

When they were in London the Churchills shared Goonie and Jack's house in Cromwell Road, South Kensington. The five cousins became a self-contained unit, who were more dependent on each other than their parents.[25] Goonie and Jack's youngest son Peregrine and Sarah became particularly close as they were only eighteen months apart in age. When they were lying in cots next to each other they held each others' fingers through the bars.[26]

As their new home was almost opposite the Natural History Museum, the older children often spent afternoons there. They showed minimal interest in the exhibits, preferring to charge along the corridors playing hide and seek.[27] More exciting were the German Zeppelin raids on the city. Rather than being scared, the children considered it to be 'a wonderful midnight party'.[28] They enjoyed being bundled up in blankets and taken to the basement where they would join the grown-ups who were dining and drinking champagne.[29]

In November 1915, Winston temporarily left politics to fight in France. Clementine missed him but firmly believed it was the right thing to do. While he was away, she wrote to him that she was having her breakfast with baby Sarah, who 'fills your place and does her best to look almost exactly like you'.[30] As they were old enough to understand what their father was doing, every morning Diana and Randolph asked anxiously after him.[31] Aged 6, Diana delighted Winston by writing a formal letter to him. He found it a strange sensation writing back to her and signing himself for the first time 'your loving father'.[32]

Clementine was busy with her war work running canteens for munitions workers. She was soon in charge of nine restaurants, each feeding up to 500 munitions workers.[33] She worked long hours, but it seems she found it less emotionally demanding than caring for her growing clan. Preferring to regale her husband with political news, Clementine rarely wrote to Winston about their children. Her brief updates revealed her preoccupations as she informed him about their health and looks.[34] Apparently, Diana's new haircut made her look like Peter Pan and was a great success. After a society children's party Clementine wrote that Randolph and Diana were more beautiful than the other children and she felt very proud to have produced 'two such delicious beings'.[35] They were very grown up and intelligent and were becoming good companions.[36]

Reading Clementine's enthusiastic descriptions of her children you get the feeling that she would have found motherhood easier if she had lived in our age rather than a century ago. With her surfeit of nervous energy, which needed channelling, perhaps being a modern career woman would have suited her. She got a taste of what we now take for granted during the First World War. When she was fully stretched and fulfilling her own potential, she thrived. It was when she felt most positive about herself that she saw the best in her children and was able to relate to them as she wished. When she was less happy with herself, she picked fault with them.

However, Clementine had only a vague idea of what was really going on in their lives. Some of the nannies she left them with were unkind. Admittedly, Randolph often goaded them into reacting harshly, but on at least one occasion, his nanny overreacted and completely lost control of her temper. One lunchtime Randolph kept asking her to allow him to have some mustard on his food. Eventually, worn out by his nagging, she seized the mustard spoon, thrust it in his mouth and rattled it against his teeth until they nearly fell out. Shocked, Randolph shrieked with pain and fury.[37] Neither he nor his sisters and cousins would ever forget the shocking incident.

The others also experienced petty punishments, although they were less extreme. When Sarah 'stole' a chocolate, she found their nanny had substituted the cream filling for mustard to deter her.[38] On another occasion, Diana was locked in a cupboard all day for some minor misdemeanour.[39]

Although these punishments were cruel and unacceptable, they were far from unique. Upper-class memoirs of this era are littered with anecdotes about callous carers. For several years, the Prince of Wales (the future Edward VIII) was pinched until he was bruised black and blue by his sadistic nanny. The Mitford girls' 'unkind nanny' banged Nancy's head against the wooden bedpost as a punishment.[40] It does not make such abuse right, or negate the effect it had on the victims, but it was common. The Churchill children themselves, in later life, seemed to minimise the impact these incidents had on them. In her memoirs, Sarah wrote that no physical force was ever used against the Churchill children, except by one or two nurses, when they were very small.[41] As soon as Clementine became aware of a nanny overstepping the mark she dismissed them. Nor were all the nannies at war with the children; while most of them found Randolph a trial, at least one of them 'idolised' Diana.[42]

In later life, Sarah claimed that she had a happy, sheltered childhood. This could be dismissed as her usual positive spin on events, but it appears in her private diary as well as her many interviews for public consumption. As she grew older, she saw her childhood as a halcyon era that she wanted to return to. She explained that she had grown up in 'a gentle world' in which she had been 'completely shielded from evil'. She had been taught right from wrong and not to tell lies or be unkind, but 'Nobody ever raised a hand in our house with hate – or a wish to destroy'.[43] In an era when corporal punishment was common, Winston and Clementine were unusual. If their children misbehaved, they banished them to their rooms or stopped their pocket money. They believed that reason, rather than physical force, would stop them doing it again.[44]

In May 1916, Winston came back to England and was later made Minister of Munitions. At the end of the year the family moved back into 33 Eccleston Square, but they also wanted 'a country basket'. They found what they were looking for at Lullenden, a Tudor stone-and-timbered manor house with a small farm and 60 acres of fields and woodland, near East Grinstead in Sussex.

With London still under threat from air raids, the children and their Churchill cousins decamped to Lullenden. As Winston was busy with ministerial duties and Clementine was running her canteens, they often did not see their parents for weeks. When the adults did visit, they stayed in the main house while the children lived in a converted barn.

The children's time at Lullenden has been likened to a life of young savages.[45] However, reading Sarah, Randolph and Johnny's accounts, it sounds far less dark. The children were not without adult supervision or a routine. At home they were cared for by local staff and for half the day the oldest children were looked after by teachers at school in the nearby village of Dormansland. Their morning lessons finished with a short religious service and the hymn 'Oh God Our Help in Ages Past'. Then they were taken home for lunch in a pony and trap.[46]

The only time they were completely left to their own devices was during the afternoons when they enjoyed a free-range existence roaming through the countryside. It was perhaps feral by today's very different parenting standards, when health and safety take precedence and children are supervised every hour of the day. But by the standards of their era it was far from unusual and it seems they enjoyed their freedom.

The overgrown garden fired their imaginations. Sarah wrote that it 'seemed full of mystery and imagined dangers for children'. With Peregrine by her side, she would lie for hours in the long grass watching the cows, which seemed like dinosaurs to their childish eyes.[47]

Admittedly, Randolph dominated his gang and could be a bully. His forceful nature subdued less robust characters like Diana and Peregrine, but one biographer's description of him as 'diabolical' is perhaps going too far.[48] He was only 7 years old and we should be careful not to read back into this period what Randolph later became. His behaviour at this stage was more like a naughty schoolboy with an irreverent sense of humour than a juvenile delinquent. Anyone who has read the *Just William* children's books will already be acquainted with a dominant lad leading his gang in a series of misguided escapades.[49] Much of what Randolph did was pure *Just William*. As an experiment, he and his cousin Johnny pushed a miniature caravan down a hill with Peregrine and Sarah in it, but luckily no one was hurt. On another occasion, they leaned out of an upstairs window and tipped the contents of a chamber pot on to Lloyd George's head as he was talking outside. They thought it was 'screamingly funny', and who would disagree?[50]

However, to see the Lullenden experience in proportion is not to pretend that no harmful seeds were sown for the future. Randolph's bad behaviour was not curbed at a time when it would have been relatively easy to keep him in check. Although Clementine was critical of their only son, with his father he could do no wrong. Rather than being reprimanded, he was treated as a star. When important guests visited, Winston invited him to stand on a stool and recite a poem to them.[51]

No equivalent honour was granted to his eldest daughter. As she grew up, Diana was made to feel that boys were literally worth more than girls. When the wealthy financier Sir Ernest Cassel came to stay, she was called down to see him first and given a £1 note, but when it was Randolph's turn, he came back brandishing £5.[52]

Winston was not the only father to treat his son differently from his daughters. Like so many men of their generation, Clementine's cousin David Mitford had the same attitude. He loved his daughters dearly, but when his eldest, Nancy, badgered him to let her go to school, complaining it was not fair because her brother Tom was allowed to, David replied, 'Tom's a boy.'[53] Winston's favouritism followed the same principle but, as with everything Churchillian, on a larger, more public scale.

While Diana's self-esteem was undermined, Sarah's health was affected by their time at Lullenden. After drinking unpasteurised milk from the cows, she developed tubercular fever. She was transformed overnight from an exuberant toddler to a 'listless little old lady'.[54]

Unfortunately, after misdiagnosing her condition, doctors decided to remove Sarah's adenoids and tonsils in a makeshift operating theatre in a Lullenden bathroom. The operation traumatised both Sarah and Clementine. When the chloroform mask was put over the little girl's face, she became hysterical and fought off the medics like a wild animal,[55] and trying to run away, she had to be pinned down. The operation left lasting scars both physically and mentally on Sarah, and for the rest of her life she would have a fear of being restrained.[56]

Looking back over those crucial first years of their childhood, the Churchill children's upbringing was far from ideal – but then whose childhood is perfect? Parents do their best, but their personalities and circumstances sometimes make that not good enough to meet their children's individual needs. Looking back through the prism of what happened to Diana, Randolph and Sarah in later life can distort the picture. Many of the memoirs written by family or friends were penned decades later with hindsight, while looking for clues as to what went wrong.

Examining the facts with a fresh eye, the Churchill children's childhood was very similar to many of their upper-class contemporaries. At this point, there was no single element that was so traumatic that it could explan the problems the three siblings faced in later life. Even Clementine's absences were not unusual in mothers of her class and generation.

However, although their early experiences were not that different from their family and friends, the personalities involved were unique. Their father was outstanding and both they and everyone else recognised it. It was not easy to grow up in his shadow. Their mother was also exceptional and someone, particularly for her daughters, to measure themselves against. It is hardly surprising that each of the Churchill children was also a heightened version of the norm; this was partly innate, but it was also magnified as they reacted to each other and bid for attention from their busy parents. Underlying their very different personalities was a sensitivity which, although at times concealed, was there in them all. Throughout their lives this quality heightened their experiences, but it also meant that they could hurt more deeply.[57]

3

Marigold
The Duckadilly

The First World War began and ended with Clementine giving birth. When she discovered that she was pregnant for the fourth time she did not relish the thought of another child. She was worried about family finances, and as the lease on 33 Eccleston Square had expired, the Churchills no longer had their own London home. Clementine had to move from spare rooms in one friend or relative's house to another. She became increasingly stressed by the situation and was particularly concerned about where the baby would be born.

Four months into the pregnancy her ambivalent feelings about having another child were made clear. In June, Winston and Clementine stayed with the former military commander Sir Ian Hamilton and his wife, Jean.[1] During the visit the two wives confided in each other. Lady Hamilton was desperate for a child and explained that she was intending to adopt an abandoned little boy called Harry.[2] Clementine advised her not to and said if she had twins Jean could have one of her babies. Lady Hamilton readily agreed and offered to let her new confidante stay at her house because Clementine had been complaining that she could not afford to stay in a nursing home.[3]

When taken at face value, Clementine's offer seems extraordinary, even for such an unmaternal woman. When it was drawn to the attention of her daughter Mary, more than eighty years later, she considered it curious. However, as she pointed out, we do not know the 'tone of voice' of the conversation between the two women.[4] It seems most likely that it was only a fleeting thought when Clementine was emotionally overwrought and never a proposition which either woman seriously considered.[5] Certainly, no aspect of the conversation was taken further.[6]

After this outburst, Clementine resigned herself to the inevitable. A few weeks later, she wrote to her mother-in-law, Jennie, 'I am beginning to look forward to the event. I was rather dreading it.'[7] Finally, it was decided that Clementine would stay at Winston's aunt, Lady Wimborne's house for the birth. On 15 November 1918, just four days after the Armistice was signed, Marigold was born.

Whatever feelings Clementine experienced beforehand, from the moment Marigold was born she was adored by the whole family. Soon known as 'the Duckadilly', she was a beautiful baby with red-gold curls and a sweet nature. However, she was a fragile child whose health was always a worry to her parents. In the influenza epidemic of her first winter, Marigold's Scottish nanny Isabelle suddenly went down with the illness. While delirious, the young woman had taken the baby out of her cot and into bed with her and Clementine had to prise her child out of the dying woman's arms. She then spent an anguished night, running up and downstairs between her daughter and her seriously ill nanny.[8] The epidemic was so widespread that no doctors were available and without medical help Isabelle died early that morning. Fortunately, Marigold did not develop flu, but afterwards she frequently suffered from coughs and colds.

Family life was now focussed in London. The Churchills leased Lullenden to the Hamiltons and moved into a town house in Sussex Square near Hyde Park. Marigold was so full of energy that she brought the house alive. She would sing her favourite song, 'I'm forever blowing bubbles', and run at full speed around the dining room table while the adults had lunch.[9] She was a very loving child, and made a great impression on their friends. The society hostess Ettie Desborough described her as having something 'special about her of radiance'. She was sure that a bright future lay before her.[10]

Once they were settled in their new home, the other children started school. Randolph was sent to Sandroyd Preparatory School, near Cobham in Surrey, while Diana and Sarah were day girls at Notting Hill High School in London. Educating upper-class girls at school rather than at home with a governess was an unusual move in this era and it reflected the pleasure Clementine had gained from her own education at Berkhamsted School for Girls. She had been an exceptionally bright pupil and she would have liked to have gone to university, but her mother blocked her ambitions.[11]

Neither of her daughters were as studious as Clementine. Sarah's teachers had already noticed a rebellious streak and commented that she was 'impertinent' and inclined to 'resent authority'.[12] Always competitive, Clementine wrote to Winston with delight when Sarah came top in arithmetic. She enthused, 'She is such a pet.' In contrast, although Diana's conduct was good her examination marks were 'catastrophic', and being a conscientious pupil, Diana was unhappy about her lack of success. Clementine tried to console her, but she expressed her true feelings to her husband, writing, 'She is a goose but a very sweet goose.'[13]

Although Clementine did not mean to be unkind, this casual remark shows how she was beginning to compare and label her daughters. She was a perfectionist, which was not always easy for herself or others. Jock Colville, who knew Clementine well in later years, explained that her standards were always exceptionally high for her children, husband and staff. If they fell short, she could 'display an acidity of tongue before which the tallest trees would bend'.[14] Diana was far from the tallest of trees. She could not have known what her mother wrote to her father, but as a sensitive child she would have been well aware of what her mother thought.

While Clementine cast a critical eye over her children, Winston always saw the best in them. He described Diana as turning into 'a very beautiful being', while Sarah was 'full of life and human qualities'.[15] Wanting to capture their youthful essence, he employed the portrait artist Charles Sims to paint the two girls together. They look like flower fairies in their short white dresses and the portrait is pretty, but lacks sparkle. Winston was disappointed with the result. He complained that the picture focussed on their least attractive aspects. Diana looked priggish and lacking in charm, while Sarah's image displayed some of her beauty and vivacity, but it made her look rather impudent and vulgar.[16] It was hard for Winston to accept that not everyone saw his daughters as he did.[17]

Both Winston and Clementine expected their children to be the best. However, they rarely witnessed their success. They were too busy with their own lives to attend sports days, prize-giving or plays. Even in the school holidays, the children's needs were not a priority, and although Clementine made sure enjoyable expeditions were arranged to entertain them, she rarely went with them. In later life, Clementine recognised this shared time had been a 'missing factor' in her relationship with her children.[18]

The year 1921 turned out to be an *annus horribilis* for the Churchill family. It started promisingly, when Winston inherited a substantial estate from a distant relative, and for the first time Winston had a private income of about £4,000 a year and more than £20,000 in the bank.[19] The windfall took the financial pressure off the family, but money could not solve the problems they were to face during the rest of the year.

Still suffering from her nerves, Clementine was away from her children for the first three months of the year. In January she went on holiday to Nice with Winston and when he returned to England, she stayed on to enjoy the sunshine and tennis. Back in London, Winston sent updates on the children to his wife. Diana and Sarah had been ill, so they were sent to recuperate by the sea at Broadstairs. As he liked to have at least one of his children to keep him company, Marigold stayed with him. He even took her to Chequers, the prime minister's country house, when he visited Lloyd George.[20] Although she had several colds and a cough and had to see a doctor, her father was not unduly worried as she was fit enough to march into his bedroom every morning and pay him her formal visit.[21] On returning from their holiday, Winston gave Diana and Sarah the choice of visiting Randolph at school or going to the zoo. When they chose seeing their brother, he was so impressed by their loyalty that he took them to the zoo too.[22]

In March Clementine joined Winston at Marseilles. They went on to a conference in Cairo together and then spent a few more weeks travelling. They finally arrived back in England on 10 April.[23] Only a few days later, Clementine's younger brother, Bill Hozier, shot himself in a hotel bedroom in Paris. He was just 33 years old but, like his mother Blanche, he was a gambler. However, there was no evidence that at the time of his death he was in debt or had been gambling so his death remained a mystery.[24]

The year of unrelenting tragedy continued when, just weeks later, Winston's mother Jennie suffered a fatal accident. While wearing vertiginous high heels, she had fallen down some stairs and broken her ankle. Unfortunately, gangrene set in, so her leg had to be amputated and she died from a haemorrhage on 29 June. Winston grieved deeply for his mother.

While his parents were coping with their bereavements, 10-year-old Randolph was dealing with his own traumatic experience. At Sandroyd School, one of his teachers had invited him into his room and asked him to touch him sexually. Although Randolph claimed to be unaffected emotionally, he was puzzled and worried by the experience. Being closest to Diana, during the summer holidays he confided in her about what had happened. A nanny overheard the conversation and reported it to Clementine, who then told his father. Winston was furious and drove a 200-mile round trip to the school to see the headmaster. He discovered the paedophile teacher had already been dismissed on other grounds.[25]

The greatest tragedy of this devastating year occurred later that summer. While Clementine visited the Duke and Duchess of Westminster at Eaton Hall in Cheshire and Winston was in London, the children were sent for a seaside holiday at Broadstairs. They stayed in lodgings with an inexperienced French nursery governess, Mlle Rose. At first all went well, the children had fun sailing in a little rowing boat, catching shrimps for tea and getting sunburnt. When Marigold developed a cold and sore throat Mlle Rose failed to alert the Churchills, although hints of her illness appeared in the children's letters to their mother.[26] Rather than improving, Marigold's condition deteriorated and it was only at the landlady's prompting that her parents were contacted and told that their daughter was seriously ill. By the time Winston and Clementine arrived their little girl was dying; the sore throat had developed into septicaemia.

The other children continued with their planned holiday and were sent to Scotland. They kept in touch by post. Taking her elder sisterly role seriously, 12-year-old Diana wrote a mature letter to her mother, 'I was very sorry to hear poor little Marigold is so ill. We have had a very unlucky year […] I do wish you could be here but it is impossible.'[27]

Both parents stayed with Marigold to the end. One of her last acts was to ask her mother to sing her favourite song, 'I'm forever blowing bubbles'. Somehow, Clementine managed to do this to comfort her dying daughter, but before she had finished Marigold put out her hand and whispered, 'Not tonight […] finish it tomorrow.'

Nothing could save the little girl. Marigold died on 23 August 1921 aged 2 years and 9 months. Winston recalled that at the time of her death Clementine let out a series of wild shrieks like a wounded animal.[28] Three days later, the little girl was buried quietly after a simple religious service at Kensal Green Cemetery in London. After the funeral Winston and Clementine joined their other children in Scotland.

A fortnight later, Clementine returned to London with them while Winston joined a house party at Dunrobin Castle. Once again turning to painting to deal with his grief, he wrote to his wife, saying that he kept on feeling the pain of their daughter's death.[29] He told a friend that it was so sad that Marigold's beautiful and happy life had ended when it was just beginning.[30] Clementine was numbed by the irreparable loss and guilt combined with grief as she blamed herself for being away when Marigold became ill and leaving her with an inexperienced nanny.[31]

A month later, Clementine took the children to see Marigold's grave. There was a poignant moment when, as they knelt around it, a white butterfly fluttered down and settled on the freshly planted flowers. The children were silent all the way home.[32] Trying to make life as normal as possible for them, the next day Clementine hired a car to take Randolph back to school and, on the journey, the family had a picnic and played hide and seek. The following day Diana and Sarah also returned to school.

It will be surprising to a modern reader how little was done at the time to help Marigold's siblings deal with their grief. There seems to have been no recognition of how traumatic it must have been for them to lose their sister so suddenly. One week they were playing happily on the beach with her, the next she was dead. Clementine must have been able to identify with their feelings as she had gone through a similar experience when Kitty died and no doubt the loss of her daughter was made even more agonising by the memory of her sister's death twenty years before. However, if she had tapped into those feelings, they might have engulfed her. Instead, she decided they should all just carry on. This 'stiff upper lip' approach was characteristic of the era. A generation of young men had been annihilated in the First World War and many of their mothers, wives and sisters had coped with a silent stoicism.

Even though Clementine tried to suppress her grief, it occasionally broke through. After Christmas, while Winston was on holiday in Cannes, Diana and Randolph and several of the staff developed flu and had high fevers. Clementine employed two nurses to help care for her household. To protect Sarah from the illness, her mother sent her to a nearby relative. The influenza epidemic was the final straw for Clementine at the end of a tragic year and she became confined to bed with nervous exhaustion. Following a desperate day that she dubbed 'Black Monday', she wrote to Winston on 2 January, describing her 'deep misery and depression […] after one of the most dreary and haunted weeks I have ever lived through'. She added that during her week in bed all the sad events of the last year, particularly the death of Marigold, kept 'passing and repassing like a stage Army thro' my sad heart'.[33]

The youngest Churchill girl, Mary, believed that her mother never completely got over the loss of Marigold. She rarely talked about it to anyone. When Mary was about 12, she asked Clementine about a picture she kept on her bedroom desk of a little girl wearing a sun hat on the beach. Her mother told her that it was Marigold and the photograph had been taken shortly before her death. Clementine regularly made solitary pilgrimages to her daughter's grave. It was only many years later, when Mary was writing Clementine's biography, that her mother finally told her the whole tragic story.[34]

4

Mary
The Chartwell Child

The death of Marigold was a turning point for the Churchills. In the years afterwards there was a marked change in how the family lived. It did not happen overnight, but gradually, brick by brick, Winston and Clementine built a more secure world for their children. The frenetic early years where they lived a nomadic existence ended as they moved into a permanent family home. Out of tragedy came new beginnings.

Less than six months after Marigold's death, Clementine was pregnant again. She discovered that she was expecting a baby while on holiday in the South of France. In a letter to Winston, she speculated whether the child would have red hair like him or black like her.[1] Although the wound left by Marigold's death was still raw for both parents, Clementine admitted to Winston that she was excited about the birth of a 'new kitten'.[2]

Winston was also thrilled to be starting their nursery again but, as always, he was preoccupied with his career. He had been one of the signatories to the treaty which would eventually lead to the independence of Southern Ireland. As he was now Colonial Secretary, he had responsibility for Ireland, which had descended into civil war. At risk of assassination by the Irish Republican Army, Winston slept with a revolver under his pillow.

Although the children did not understand the political intricacies of the situation, they could not avoid being aware of the consequences. One day, Randolph and Diana returned from roller skating in Holland Park to discover their home surrounded by police. Inside, policemen were running up and down the stairs, looking in every room, searching for any would-be assassins. The children were informed that one of their father's colleagues had been shot by an Irish gunman on his doorstep earlier that afternoon. There were fears that Winston would be next on the hit list.[3] Yet again, as it had been with the militant suffragettes, the security of their world was shaken by outside events.

Clementine decided to escape the threats of London and took the children for a summer holiday at the fashionable resort of Frinton-on-Sea in Essex. For most of their stay, Winston was elsewhere, staying with his grand friends but when he did visit, three detectives went along to protect him. They were put to good use, helping the children dam streams on the beach.[4]

As the anniversary of Marigold's death approached both Clementine and Winston relived her final days, but they were determined to focus on the future rather than the past. Relaxing with her children, Clementine suffered from none of the anxiety of her previous pregnancies and, looking forward to having another child, she wrote to Winston, 'Only five weeks now and a new being – perhaps a genius – anyhow very precious to us – will make its appearance.'[5]

On 15 September 1922 Mary was born. She would be known as 'Baby Bud', and was to be the Churchills' last child. Her childhood was so different from her older sisters' and brother's that it seems like a different story. Writing about the older children's upbringing, there is a rather dark and chaotic feel to it, whereas when it comes to Mary's it feels like entering the sunlit uplands. There was a large age gap between Mary and her siblings; Diana was 13, Randolph, 11, and Sarah nearly 8 when she was born. In many ways, Mary was brought up like an only child. She was treated by her brother and sisters as alternately a 'cuddly toy' or a 'real little bore'.[6]

The most crucial difference between her upbringing and that of her siblings was that she had one person in her life who was totally dedicated to her care. Having learnt a harsh lesson from the death of Marigold, Clementine knew she could never risk leaving her children with inexperienced staff again. She found the perfect nanny in her cousin, Maryott Whyte.[7] Known in the family as Nana or Moppet, Maryott became to Mary what Mrs Everest had been to Winston. She devoted her life to bringing up her protégée. She also instilled the Christian values which were to give Mary firm foundations for the future.[8]

Moppet was no ordinary nanny. She was a confident woman who expected to be treated as an equal by her cousin, and when Clementine went on her frequent holidays, Moppet naturally became a substitute parent. During one absence, Mary commented that her mother had gone away because she was bored with her, but with her nanny around, she never lacked security.[9] Mary reckoned that her mother was a little jealous when she deferred to her cousin rather than her about decisions, but on balance Clementine valued her freedom too much to disrupt the arrangement.

A new baby was not the only symbol of a new era for the Churchills. For a long time, Winston and Clementine had wanted 'a country basket' in which to raise their growing children. Winston dreamed of an estate where he could create an idyllic family home and he found just what he was looking for at Chartwell Manor in Westerham, Kent.

The dilapidated, red-brick Victorian mansion was built around a much older house. Instantly, Winston could see past the dry rot and damp to the house's potential. It was unlived in and the garden was wild, but there was an air of enchantment about the place. Set in 80 acres, on a hilltop looking over the Weald of Kent, Chartwell cast its spell on him. The seed had been planted long ago, as his beloved nanny, Mrs Everest, had come from that county,[10] and with its ancient houses and unspoilt rural landscape Kent encapsulated England for Winston.

When Clementine first saw Chartwell, she liked it and believed they would be happy there. However, as she began to consider the practicalities, she was not so sure; always the more cautious one with money, she realised that the house and gardens needed so much work done to them that it would be a drain on their finances. In an act which Clementine saw as one of the few betrayals by her husband in their long marriage, Winston went ahead with buying the house without asking her. Shortly after Mary's birth, he took Diana, Sarah and Randolph down to see Chartwell and asked them whether he should buy it. Excited to be with their father and at the thought of a new home, they enthusiastically encouraged him.[11]

In fact, he had already bought it. Clementine was very annoyed but there was little she could do once the purchase was completed. The house needed a great deal of work done to it, so the family was not able to live in it for nearly two years. After extensive and expensive rebuilding and landscaping Chartwell was ready. In spring 1924, when the family eventually moved in, Clementine signalled her displeasure by going away to visit her mother.[12] It was left to Winston and his children to set up home. They worked hard all day and thoroughly enjoyed getting filthy.

Perhaps to appease Clementine, she was given the best bedroom, and lying in her four-poster bed beneath a spectacular vaulted ceiling she could look out at panoramic views of the Kent countryside. This room was her inner sanctum, where she could retreat when the pressures of family life became too much. Every morning, Mary visited her mother in her bedroom. She would find Clementine, with her hair in curlers, her face covered in moisturiser, reading the morning papers over breakfast in bed. Although the little girl received a warm welcome, Clementine waved rather than cuddled her; being more tactile, when Winston came in to join them he greeted his daughter with a hug before discussing the morning's news with his wife.[13]

Most of Mary's day was spent in the purpose-built nursery wing. As she was an imaginative child, she thought of herself as the princess of her own castle. Her spacious schoolroom and nursery opened out on to the garden. While Sarah had a bed-sitting room on the first floor, the night nursery on the second floor was Mary and Moppet's domain. Reflecting their senior status, Randolph and Diana were given bedrooms in the main part of the house.[14]

Winston wanted Chartwell to be flooded with light, so the architect's design reflected this principle. The arched windows in the dining room opened to allow an easy flow from the house to the garden and the fresh décor of green curtains and white and green arum lilies chintz covering the chairs added to the sense of indoors and outdoors being one. The drawing room also had an airy ambience. With long windows on three sides looking out over the patchwork landscape, Clementine likened the view to being on an aeroplane.[15]

These rooms were the hub of family life. In the dining room, while the adults and teenagers ate at a large circular table, the younger children had their own smaller version beside it. Once the meal was over, in the drawing room, Winston and Clementine played bezique at the card table, while their children chatted on one of the comfortable sofas clustered around the open fire. However, Chartwell was not just an intimate home, it was also Winston's workplace, so there were strict rules that his study was a noise-free area.[16]

For Winston, and particularly Mary, Chartwell was to become a second Eden.[17] It was a place where he could relax, entertain his friends, paint and indulge his great love of animals and although Chartwell had not been her choice, as ever, Clementine threw herself wholeheartedly into helping her husband realise his dreams. Thanks to her, the house ran like clockwork; she paid the bills, planned the menus and drew up the guest lists, smoothing the way so Winston could continue with his politics and writing undisturbed.[18] Her understated good taste provided an elegant setting for Winston to win friends and influence people. She prided herself on always giving her guests the most delicious food, washed down with the finest champagne, port and brandy.

Having lacked a stable childhood home himself, Winston wanted to create happy memories for his family. He built a tree house for his older children which was off limits to the much younger Mary. While they spent hours in their tree-top retreat, confiding secrets, laughing and having fun, Mary was left alone at the bottom, looking up longingly through the branches. She wished that she was part of the gang.[19]

Excluded from her siblings' exciting adventures and lacking friends her own age, Mary enjoyed the company of a vast menagerie of animals. As well as cats, dogs, swans, goats and sheep, she added more exotic creatures to her growing zoo, including orphaned fox cubs and a marmoset.

The animals enabled a strong bond to develop between Winston and his youngest daughter. Influenced by him, Mary grew up treating her pets like people, with their own distinctive personalities. They were part of the family; the cat jumping on to the table to lick from a saucer of cream or a chicken wandering into the dining room just added to the informal atmosphere that made Chartwell such a happy home.[20] The animals' escapades filled Winston and Mary's letters and fired their imagination. When her pug was seriously ill, Winston even found time to write him a poem,[21] and not to be outdone, Mr Cat, the ginger tom, had his portrait painted by a famous artist.[22]

Spending halcyon days together at Chartwell, Winston and Mary became great companions. For example, in order to switch off from work, Winston found he enjoyed constructing walls, and as soon as she was big enough, Mary became his 'bricklayer's mate', handing him the bricks. They spent many industrious hours working together as a team. She later admitted that she did not really enjoy it because she occasionally dropped the bricks on her toes, which hurt a great deal.[23] However, her hard work paid off when Winston built a one-roomed cottage for his daughter to play in. Ceremoniously, Mary laid the foundation stone for her very upmarket Wendy house.[24]

At Chartwell, the Churchills created their own enchanted world and within its welcoming walls the family formed a tight-knit clique. As well as their nicknames, they developed their own idiosyncratic vocabulary. When they greeted each other, rather than say 'hello', they would say 'wow' or 'meow', the noises made by pets. Apparently, 'wow' originated when Winston tried to talk to his swans, answering their greeting as he arrived to feed them.[25]

Chartwell became a base not just for the Churchills but for their extended family. The foibles of their relatives fascinated the Churchill children and caused them much amusement. Nicknamed 'the Jagoons', Goonie and Jack were regular guests with their children, Peregrine, Johnny and Clarissa. However, even though Clarissa was only two years older than Mary, they had little in common. While Clarissa was a cool character, her cousin was exuberant and Mary was rather embarrassed by the 'fulsome affection' her aunt lavished on her icily indifferent only daughter.[26]

Chartwell was also treated as a second home by Clementine's younger sister Nellie with her husband, Bertram Romilly, and their two sons, Esmond and Giles. The Churchill girls mocked Aunt Nellie's indulgence of her badly behaved sons. Inappropriately called 'the lambs' by their doting mother, they were aggressive children, and even when they had become teenage tearaways, she still insisted on calling them 'My darling angelic boys, Gy-gy and Ese-wee'.[27]

It is interesting that both Sarah and Mary focussed on their aunts' relationships with their children. They described them with disdain as being overly maternal and smothering, but one cannot help wondering if they were so uncharacteristically critical because they were slightly jealous. Both Goonie and Nellie overtly displayed their affection in a way Clementine would never do. Winston was the more affectionate parent, who openly expressed his emotions, and the children took their lead from him. Many years later, Mary told an interviewer:

We all tended very much to show our feelings. When we were happy, we laughed and smiled and, when we were sad, we cried. My father used to weep quite easily. We were quite emotional ourselves and showed it. We certainly weren't examples of the stiff upper lip.[28]

Every year, the three branches of the family got together for Christmas at Chartwell. It was always memorable. After months of meticulous planning, Clementine excelled herself and, decked with holly and mistletoe, the house was transformed into a magical winter scene.

Centre stage was a huge Christmas tree decorated with dozens of glowing candles. Unfortunately, one year the tree caught alight. While Clementine and Nellie panicked, Moppet calmly fetched the fire extinguisher and put the blaze out.

When it snowed, the children skated on the frozen lake while Winston built a life-sized snowman. In the evenings they staged very professional amateur dramatics and in one play Clementine's performance was so tragic it made Winston cry.[29]

Although Christmas was the highlight, a constant stream of family and friends visited throughout the Chartwell year and Clementine's relatives, the Mitfords, were regular guests. If the rumours were correct that Clementine's biological father was Bertie Mitford, the second cousins were doubly related. Bertie's son, David, would be Clementine's half-brother as well as her first cousin.

Known to his children as 'Farve', David had one son, Tom, and six daughters, Nancy, Pamela, Diana, Unity, Jessica and Deborah, who became known collectively as the Mitford girls. Tom became Randolph's greatest friend at Eton, while their sisters also became friends.

The cousins slotted easily into each other's lives, spending holidays together at Chartwell and Asthall Manor, then Swinbrook, the Mitfords' Oxfordshire homes. The two clans had much in common since in both households individuality was valued above conventionality. There was no pressure to conform and it was fine to be eccentric but a crime to be a bore.

Although Diana Mitford could be fun, being friends with her was not good for Diana Churchill's self-esteem. Even her own grand-mother preferred her dazzling cousin. They first met at a children's party, where Blanche sat the two little girls on her knees and dubbed them 'The Two Dianas'. Perhaps recognising a kindred spirit, Blanche became much closer to her great-niece than her granddaughter.[30]

The coolest of the Mitford girls grew into a blue-eyed, patrician beauty and, reflecting her goddess-like status, the Churchills dis-tinguished between the two Dianas by nicknaming Diana Mitford 'Artemis' or 'Dinamite'.[31] However, she was never as sweet-natured and kind as Winston's daughter.

Nicknamed 'Chatterbox' because she never stopped talking, Diana Churchill was the odd one out in the foursome that the girls made up with their two brothers.[32] The others would run away and hide from her, leaving her to wander around looking for them, tunelessly singing her favourite song, 'Yes! we have no bananas'.[33]

As the children grew up, youthful romances developed between the cousins. Graduating from assignations in the tree house to games of tennis, swimming in the pool or woodland walks, there was plenty of scope for flirtations. From the age of 15, Randolph was in love with Diana Mitford. Perhaps the attraction was partly because she bore a striking resemblance to his mother.

However, despite the fact that Randolph was the male version of that distinctive blue-eyed beauty, he stood no chance. A photograph of them sitting around the Chartwell dining table suggests why. While Randolph, aged 16, looks like a schoolboy, 'Dinamite' is every inch a woman, and displaying a precocious penchant for powerful politi-cians, she was far more interested in Winston than his son. (She was not the only one to admire an older man: Diana Churchill thought 'Farve' looked 'like God the father'.)[34]

A more reciprocal relationship developed between Sarah and Peregrine. She claimed to have been 'passionately and devotedly in love' with him since the age of 4.[35] By the time Sarah was 14,

Clementine complained to Winston that they seemed more wrapped up in each other than ever[36] and, according to Peregrine, his aunt banned him from Chartwell because she was afraid 'they might marry'.[37] As a marriage between first cousins was highly unlikely and they were very young, it seems that perhaps Clementine was reacting rather hysterically to their youthful flirtation.

Not to be outdone by her elder siblings, Mary had a crush on her rather sadistic cousin, Esmond Romilly. When they developed chickenpox, they were quarantined together. Mary thought Esmond, who was four years older than her, was most dashing as he lay languidly on the bed smoking a cigarette. To fill the time, they began discussing religion and, always a rebel, Esmond told his pious cousin he did not believe in God and it was 'absolute tosh'. When Mary disagreed, he bet he could make her deny Jesus Christ in thirty seconds flat. He then proceeded to get a basin of water and hold her head under till she denounced her faith. She later wrote, 'I never got a kind word, but I adored him despite his tyrannical ways.'[38]

As they became teenagers, Clementine did everything she could to protect her daughters' innocence. When they were away from home, they were strictly chaperoned, and if they travelled on a train the guard was given strict instructions to look after them.[39] Displaying her censorious streak, Clementine warned Winston not to allow 'any low conversation' in front of them.

When the press baron Lord Beaverbrook visited Chartwell with his mistress, Clementine hoped their illicit relationship would not be obvious to Randolph and Diana's 'inquisitive marmoset-like eyes and ears'.[40] Inevitably, of course the teenagers knew far more than their parents intended, and shortly after Winston's friend, the future politician Brendan Bracken appeared on the Chartwell scene, Diana told Dinamite, 'There's a rumour that Mr Bracken is papa's son!' Rather than taking it seriously, this hint of scandal amused Winston's daughter.[41]

Celebrities often visited the Churchills at Chartwell. Lawrence of Arabia would arrive on his motorcycle wearing his air force uniform and Mary was most impressed by the heroic figure with his piercing blue eyes. She never forgot being called down to the drawing room in her dressing gown to see him dressed in his long, flowing Arabian robes. When the comedian Charlie Chaplin came to lunch, Diana was a great hit with the famous film star. His 'pacifist Communist soliloquy' did not go down well but, because Winston admired him, for once he said nothing.[42] Before he left, the comedian redeemed himself by doing an impersonation of Napoleon using a coat and hat grabbed from the coat cupboard.[43]

No matter how charismatic the guests, no one was as scintillating as Winston in his daughters' eyes. Around the dining table at Chartwell he held court and his daughters hung on his every word as the brilliant conversation leapt from literature to politics, history to art. Encouraged to join in the sophisticated discussions, they knew it was vital to be amusing. Favoured by his father, Randolph was treated as an oracle, giving his opinion as though he was an equal to the high-powered politicians around the table.

However, for the girls, it could be a stressful experience. They were taught not to mumble and told, 'Say what you have to say, say it clearly or don't say it at all.' This inhibited Sarah, who became a silent child. She was always worried about whether she would be quick-witted enough to follow her father's train of thought and keep him entertained. Winston made a joke of her silence, saying, 'Sarah is an oyster, she will not tell us her secrets.'[44]

Diana also found it challenging, but she covered up her shyness by chattering away garrulously.

Although Clementine was serene on the surface, she was sometimes seething beneath. As she was also passionate about politics, occasionally her temper would explode in a volcanic outburst. She would then sweep out of the room, leaving her embarrassed children not sure of what to do. After one of these eruptions, Winston described his wife, with amused pride, as attacking her victim 'like a jaguar' pouncing out of a tree.[45]

Although the debate could sometimes become heated, one of Winston's most important lessons to his children was to be tolerant. They were taught to respect their 'enemies'. Many years later, Sarah explained, 'You sort of spoke of them almost with a sneaking affection – of course "they" were wrong. Of course "we" were right – and that was all. Each and every one was respected.' There was 'never, never hating.'[46]

This magnanimity made a great impression on his daughters and they inherited this spirit of generosity from him. It is remarkable how rarely in their letters there is a vindictive comment about anyone – however much they might deserve it.

During the Chartwell years, the Churchill girls began to hero worship as well as love their father.[47] Listening, 'spell-bound', to him telling anecdotes or reciting poems, they realised they were in the presence of greatness. To have such an outstanding parent was a privilege but also a potential problem, because as his children they were also expected to be special. The burden of expectations was even heavier on his son, but it was there for them all. Having such a bright star in their orbit also changed the dynamics of the family. Their mother's world had always centred on Winston, but as they grew up his daughters also treated him as their lodestar.

5

The Chancellor's Daughters

During the twenties, the Churchill girls had the best of both worlds as they enjoyed a town and country life. When they were not at Chartwell they lived in London. In 1924 Winston was made Chancellor of the Exchequer in Stanley Baldwin's Conservative Government, and the family moved into No. 11 Downing Street. Mary's nursery was above the iconic front door.

With her siblings at school, Mary was often the only child at home. As Clementine was away on her frequent holidays, Winston enjoyed having his youngest daughter for company. First thing in the morning she would bounce into her father's bedroom to join him for breakfast in bed. Sharing their passion for animals, when Winston had time, he took her to London Zoo, the aquarium and the circus.

Mary was self-possessed from a young age and took everything in her stride. She treated Mr Baldwin not as prime minister but as an avuncular neighbour. Climbing on to his knee, she talked to him like a little adult until Moppet dragged her away.[1] After another enthusiastic encounter between the premier and the little girl, Winston quipped to Clementine, 'How women admire power!'[2] He noted that his precocious daughter often talked like a woman of 30.[3]

One afternoon Mary was playing in the garden when Mrs Baldwin invited her to see the Cabinet room. Afterwards, Winston asked

Moppet, 'Was she dressed all right?' (meaning Mary), to which his 5-year-old daughter replied, 'Oh yes, she [Mrs Baldwin] was wearing a nice grey frock!'[4]

As a teenager, Sarah was sent to boarding school at North Foreland School, in Broadstairs, Kent. The seaside town was chosen because her parents hoped it would improve her health. Since Lullenden, Sarah had been a sickly child and as well as the usual childhood illnesses she was also accident prone. Whenever there was a loud crash, the rest of the family would look at each other and say, 'That's Sarah.'[5]

A poem written by her suggests that she enjoyed the attention these incidents brought. Entitled 'Casualty', it described 'the joy of cutting one's knee'.[6] Perhaps it was one of the few ways she could make her preoccupied parents focus on her. In later life, this early pattern was repeated as she developed more sophisticated ways of attracting their attention.

Remembering his own unhappy schooldays, when Sarah was going back to school Winston asked her, 'Do a few tears fall on your pillow the first night?', but Sarah experienced no similar pangs.[7] At her new school, she became much healthier and happier, and although at first she was criticised for being 'restless' and lacking self-control, the teachers became very fond of her.[8] She made the most of every opportunity, becoming captain of the cricket team, and playing tennis and lacrosse. She also enjoyed acting and had her first lead role in *Alice in Wonderland*.[9]

Even at school, Sarah could not escape the fact that she was a famous politician's daughter. She found it embarrassing when inquisitive adults asked her questions about Winston. However, there were bonuses to having a father who was Chancellor of the Exchequer, and when she was asked to present a miniature Budget in the school's mock Parliament, Winston took the time to prepare a scaled-down version for her. Sarah thought perhaps her head-mistress had an ulterior motive and hoped to discover Winston's economic thoughts.[10]

It was not just her father who made her stand out from the crowd. She described the embarrassment of her mother coming to present the awards at prize-giving, looking so glamorous that she was totally unlike the other frumpy mothers. Sarah recalled, 'She was not "mum-shaped", and she made what was referred to as a rather racy speech.'[11]

Sarah became closer to Clementine in her teenage years. In trying to get to know her mother better, she wanted to hear about her schooldays. A daughter establishes her own sense of self in relation to her mother, and naturally, as Sarah grew up, she began comparing herself to Clementine. She wrote:

> I too, am very happy at school, only the great difference between your childhood and mine is that I love being at home and always look forward to the holidays and to the time when I have left school and shall be at home with you.[12]

Although Diana also liked her new school in Holland Park, London, her examination results were still dire and she failed everything except French. It was only once she left school that her life began to take off. It was her chance to take centre stage while her younger sisters waited in the wings.

When Diana was 16, Winston wrote to Clementine that he did not know which one of his daughters he loved most:

> But Diana is going to be a great feature in our lives in the next few years. Nature is mysteriously arming her for the ancient conflict. She has a wonderful charm and grace, which grows now percepti-bly from month to month.[13]

To gain the polish required to make her debut in society, Diana was sent to stay with a family in Paris. These were carefree days when she was able to develop her own identity away from her overpowering family. Her letters exuded enthusiasm for everything her new life had to offer. Determined to be fashionable, she wrote to her parents telling them she wanted to have her auburn plaits cut off and shingle her hair. The short, curly hairstyle was all the rage and two her Mitford cousins, Nancy and Diana, had done it. Although girls across the country were shingling, it was considered slightly transgressive in upper-class circles.[14] However, Clementine could not preach because she had already shingled hers. Once Diana had done the deed, she wrote ruefully to Winston, 'I am no longer your Gold Cream Kitten but your Goldless Cream Kitten.'[15]

Enjoying Parisian culture, Diana was stimulated by visits to the theatre, art galleries and museums and, away from her family, she shone. Her host family admired her enquiring mind and thought she was a very intelligent and interesting girl.[16]

Once back in England, Diana continued to have fun. Describing herself to her father as 'a would-be flapper', she whizzed around London in her little car, meeting friends and shopping.[17] When she came out as a debutante in 1928, she was featured on the cover of several society magazines, looking chic in a cloche hat and fur-trimmed coat. She was described as 'picturesque' with hair 'like spun gold with a touch of red in it and skin of exquisite cream and roses' and was likened to her beautiful mother.[18] However, it was noted that she had also inherited her father's 'slightly impish smile'.[19]

Planning a party at Downing Street, Diana was full of anticipation. She wrote to Clementine, 'I am so excited for when you come home and for the season and for everything.'[20] She was determined that every aspect should be perfect for her presentation at court and carefully matched her shell pink dress and shoes, then pirouetted around the drawing room, practising her curtsy in front of an admiring Mary.[21] Believing that she was on the brink of a new life, she seemed more confident than ever before. When Clementine introduced her to the society hostess, Lady Cunard, the old dragon looked Diana up and down and said, 'My, but you are pretty.' Diana coolly replied, 'Aren't I meant to be?' and swept past her.[22]

Unfortunately, her debutante days turned out to be an anticlimax. Clementine was ill so she could not act as her chaperone[23] and, stepping in at the last minute, Winston made the time to accompany Diana to dances. Once Clementine recovered, neither mother nor daughter enjoyed the endless round of balls and country house parties.

Shallow society social life never appealed to Clementine or her girls because they had far more intellectual depth than the average aristocratic butterflies who flitted through the season. Nor were they impressed with the supposedly eligible young men on offer. Clementine wrote to Winston that she knew it was her duty to try to find their eldest daughter a suitable husband but, '[I] cannot do with these inbred effete sprigs of the *ancien regime!*'[24] Understandably, Diana felt uncomfortable in this blatant marriage market which so publicly put to the test a young woman's attractiveness to the opposite sex.

As the season progressed, Diana's delicate ego deflated. After being matchmade at one house party with a young man who was a 'girl hater', naturally she became timid[25] and, on yet another unrewarding encounter, she admitted to her father that it would be 'lovely to be home again where one never feels "genee" [embarrassed]'.[26]

At the end of the season Diana remained single. She had failed in the one goal set for her by society. It did not help that yet again she had been upstaged by her glamorous cousin, Diana Mitford. She was one of the debs of the year and immediately found herself a rich husband.[27]

However, the season had not been a complete failure for Diana because it allowed her to get to know her mother better. Clementine had more in common with her girls as they became adults. She was at least as responsible as Winston for her daughters developing into the cultured, well-read women they became. Diana and Clementine went to the theatre regularly together and discussed the latest books.[28] They both found trips abroad stimulating and, spending time alone together in France and Italy, they had 'the most heavenly time'.[29] While sightseeing and visiting art galleries, Diana discovered her mother was more relaxed when she was away from home. She wrote to her father, 'Mummie is a completely different person, she is so much stronger and more carefree and better in every way [...] If it lasts it will really be too wonderful.'[30]

Clementine also brought her daughters up to have a social conscience and to realise that not everyone was as privileged as themselves. She never forgot the financial hardships she experienced in her youth. While in Venice she taught Diana how to keep her room tidy and darn her own stockings so that she could cope without a maid. She did not want her daughters to expect that they would always be waited on.[31]

Although their relationship improved, mother and daughter never became close. Diana felt that she did not measure up to Clementine's exacting expectations. Often described as 'unusual', she was pretty, but not in the same way as her lithe mother. History was repeating itself and as Clementine had always felt her mother Blanche preferred her more beautiful sister Kitty, Diana was sure Clementine favoured her sister. Sarah had inherited her mother's strong features and was the most physically like her of the Churchill girls. Diana was more curvaceous and shorter than her mother and sister. As a child she had been slightly plump and throughout her life she was always sensitive about her weight.[32] When Diana was at a dress fitting with Clementine and Sarah she was deeply upset when her mother commented that it was always so much easier to dress her younger daughter. Diana never forgot this casual remark.[33]

Her cousin Anita Leslie remembered finding her in tears at the end of her first season. She told Anita, 'I am so unhappy and Mummy is horrid to me because I haven't been a success. I have sandy eyelashes.' Anita claimed that Clementine was 'downright unkind' to her eldest daughter.[34] However, the dynamic between them was far more nuanced than that. It seems unlikely her mother ever intended to hurt her, but Clementine's sharp tongue left lasting scars on Diana's thin skin. Sadly, Clementine was unable to reach out to her daughter and repair the damage. Perhaps she saw uncomfortable echoes of her own vulnerability in her eldest daughter's insecurities.[35] When painful emotions were reignited for Clementine, it seems that she blocked them and the person who triggered them out. The rest of the family could only look on with regret as the two sensitive women misunderstood each other.

Wanting her mother and sister to get on, Sarah often acted as peacemaker between them. As they left the dressmakers after Clementine's thoughtless comment, Sarah squeezed Diana's hand and said, 'Mama didn't mean it unkindly. She was trying to bolster me up.' This sisterly solidarity sealed their close relationship. Recognising each other's insecurities, the two girls developed a mutually supportive relationship which was to survive for the rest of their lives.[36]

There was never any bitchiness between the three Churchill girls – Sarah and Diana's issues were with their mother, not each other. Clementine's tart but often truthful remarks are reminiscent of the dialogue between the Mitford girls. They could be razor sharp to each other, too – to a degree, it was witty, a bit of a tease, but it could also be mortally wounding. None of Clementine's daughters inherited her lacerating tongue; they managed to be amusing without being unkind.[37]

Decades later, when Mary was writing her biography of her mother, she was still wondering what went wrong between Diana and Clementine. Talking to her cousin Peregrine, she asked was their relationship always wrong? Was Clementine always closer to Sarah? Peregrine told her he did not remember any tensions between Diana and her mother when she was growing up.[38] It seems the antagonism developed later, as Diana became a young woman.

Diana was always much closer to her father than her mother. When Clementine was away, Winston's eldest daughter often kept him company. The newspapers described her as his special 'chum' who could always cheer him up.[39] They shared a passion for politics. As a teenager, Diana showed a precocious interest in political ideas. At school she wrote an essay on the complex subject of Tariff Reform versus Free Trade for a competition, and, determined to win, she asked her father for a few hints.[40] Winston later told Clementine that Diana had gained a great deal of information from the newspapers and talked 'quite intelligently about politics'.[41] She also found campaigning exciting. If Clementine was unavailable, Diana attended meetings with her father.[42] She sat proudly beside him on the platform as he gave his speeches.[43]

When Winston presented his first Budget in 1925, she listened attentively in the parliamentary gallery with her mother and brother, and three years later, she was photographed with her father as he stood on the steps of No. 11 Downing Street holding his red box. Followed by press photographers, she walked with him to the House of Commons where he delivered his Budget. Although she was naturally shy, she began to grow in confidence through her political activity and represented her father at Conservative events and even occasionally made speeches herself.[44]

Women's roles in politics were changing. Since 1918 many women had the vote and they began to sit as Members of Parliament. The daughters of two of Winston's Cabinet colleagues, Herbert Asquith and David Lloyd George, were to follow their fathers into Parliament.[45] Diana also had the potential to become a political figure in her own right. She had the connections, the political knowledge and the commitment, but the one thing she lacked was the confidence. It would have taken a woman with a far larger ego than Diana ever had to push herself forward.

Although Clementine had supported votes for women, even when her husband opposed it, the male members of the Churchill family saw politics as a career for men, not women.[46] While he was at Eton, Randolph wrote a derogatory article about women in politics,[47] and decades later, he was still complaining that it had been a great mistake to give women the vote.[48] It was also evident that Winston only thought of his son, not his daughters, following in his footsteps. His view at this time was that women should be attractive adornments to male politicians but not politicians in their own right. Diana's political apprenticeship, it seemed, was to prepare her to marry a rising star, not to be one herself.[49]

In the 1929 election, all three of Winston's daughters joined him on the campaign trail in his Epping constituency. He held on to his seat, but the Conservatives lost the election, so the Churchills had to move out of Downing Street.

Later that year, Winston lost a substantial amount of money in the Wall Street Crash and, financially stretched, the Churchills had to shut up Chartwell temporarily. Winston and Clementine moved into a London flat while Mary and Moppet lived in a cottage on the estate. Once he was out of office, Winston was to spend the next decade in the political wilderness, relying on his writing and lecturing for his income.

6

Diana in the Limelight

Although Diana never sought the limelight, sometimes she was thrust into it. In December 1932 she married John Milner Bailey, a rich bachelor. The wedding reflected her parents' taste more than her own and, reminiscent of their wedding two decades earlier, the congregation at St Margaret's Westminster was packed with politicians. Crowds crammed the streets, but they were more interested in seeing Winston than his daughter.

This should have been Diana's moment of triumph, but it turned into a trial. Rather than appearing a radiant bride, she seemed intimidated, and fragile and fairy-like in a shimmering white satin dress and a tulle veil. As she left home with Winston, the flashbulbs from dozens of cameras went off around them. Looking slightly stunned, she blinked, looked down and fussed with her train.

Although her father was by her side, there was surprisingly little contact between them. Winston was too wrapped up in himself to reassure his nervous daughter. As he acknowledged the crowds, she seemed very alone and unsure of what to do. When they arrived at St Margaret's, all the attention remained on Winston. As flunkeys greeted him and ignored her, Diana scurried towards the church without waiting for her father.

After the ceremony, she still seemed a little lost and as the bride and groom emerged from the church, they went the wrong way and had to double back on themselves. The crowds broke through the cordon and rushed towards them. Only the mounted police stopped the situation getting out of hand.[1] It was an inauspicious start to married life for Winston's eldest daughter.

Diana's wedding marked the end of an unsatisfying few years when she had tried various potential roles but never found her niche. In this era, upper-class women were not expected to have careers; any work they did was merely to fill in the time until they got married and had a family. Diana spent one summer working as a Voluntary Aid Detachment for the Red Cross, looking after hop-pickers' children in Kent. The experience did not make her want to become a nurse; instead, she decided that she would like to be an actress. Unfortunately, when she enrolled at the Royal Academy of Dramatic Art she discovered there was another actress called Diana Churchill in her year. Yet again, as with Diana Mitford, even her name was not exclusively her own. She only lasted nine terms at drama school. Like all her family she was very much an individualist and she disliked being told what to do by a director.[2] Perhaps more crucially, she also showed little acting ability.

Without a career or a husband, in December 1931 Diana accompanied her parents on Winston's lecture tour to America. However, the trip did not go as planned. Shortly after the Churchills arrived in New York, Winston was knocked down by a car as he was crossing Fifth Avenue. He suffered severe shock and concussion, and he was covered in bruises. If he had not been wearing a thick fur-lined coat, he could have been killed. After arriving in hospital, his condition worsened as he developed pleurisy and Diana and Clementine spent a worrying few days by his bedside until his health stabilised.

After convalescing in the Bahamas, Winston continued with his lecture tour and when Clementine returned to England in February, Diana stayed on to keep her father company. They had great fun together. When she was with Winston, all her self-consciousness disappeared. Some evenings she put on a dance routine for him or they would sing songs from the musicals together. When Diana had been on a shopping spree, she would give Winston an impromptu fashion show, sashaying up and down the room in her latest outfits. After scrutinising her from every angle, he would give his verdict, 'I heartily approve.'

Winston rarely put himself out for anyone, but he did for his eldest daughter. Late one night, Diana begged her father to take her dancing because there was a famous band playing at the hotel that she wanted to hear. Even though he was in his dressing gown, sipping a whisky and soda, Winston indulgently agreed to take her. Once they were on the dance floor, he rather awkwardly piloted his daughter through several foxtrots and a waltz before returning to bed.

During the American tour, Diana became friends with Winston's private secretary, Phyllis Moir, who had worked in Hollywood. Diana would dash into her office and chat excitedly to her about clothes, young men and movies – but especially the movies. Diana wanted to hear all about the film stars Phyllis had met. Passionate about the cinema, Diana was 'frantic with excitement' when it looked like she might become a movie star herself.[3] After her photograph appeared in American newspapers, a motion picture executive from Warner Brothers wanted her to do a screen test.[4] Her parents said it was 'only for fun', but there was great anticipation in the Churchill family.[5] When news got out, the *Daily Express* ran an article on Diana under the headline 'Mr Churchill's Daughter a Film Star?'[6] Unfortunately, the results of the screen test were disappointing and, once again, she had reached a dead end.

The pressure on Diana to find a husband was increasing. Soon Sarah was due to come out as a debutante and it would be humiliating for Diana to still be single when her younger sister was joining the marriage market. Just in time, Diana found a fiancé. She became engaged, at the age of 23, to John Milner Bailey, the son of the wealthy

South African diamond tycoon, Abe Bailey, who was a great friend of Winston's. The reports of their engagement lacked the slightest hint of romance, simply recording that the couple had been friends for several years. Diana later told her daughter that she only married John to get away from Chartwell meals – they went on for so long and she was worried that she would get fat.[7]

On paper, the tall, rather gaunt 32-year-old seemed very eligible, but the engagement was so brief there was little time to discover potential pitfalls and 10-year-old Mary was the only member of the family to show much enthusiasm. The young romantic thought John was very good-looking, and she relished all the wedding plans.[8] It seems that Diana's parents were just relieved to see her settled.

The marriage was to be short-lived; the couple separated after less than two years. It is not clear exactly what went wrong and the only clue comes from the romantic novelist Barbara Cartland. Apparently, John had been deeply in love with Barbara, but she had rejected him because he was such a heavy drinker. When sober he was charming, but when he drank he became vile.[9]

Whatever the problems between Diana and John, they must have been serious because divorces were rare in this era. There were only about 5,000 a year and there was still a great stigma attached to divorcing. Incompatible couples usually just struggled on or led their own lives within their marriage. For Diana to get out, the relationship must have been profoundly detrimental to her well-being.

She told her husband she was leaving him at a hotel in Sussex. With her strong moral compass, she had strict views on how people should conduct themselves and, scrupulous to the point of self-denial, she gave back all the jewellery John had given her during their marriage – this was particularly self-sacrificing considering his father was a diamond magnate.[10]

Diana was deeply unhappy about the failure of her marriage and was once again looking for a purpose in her life. Rather than move home to Chartwell, she lived alone in London. In her hour of need, her mother seemed unable to reach out to her and the relationship between them became increasingly strained.[11] As usual, Diana turned to her father instead. He provided the warm, loving support she required during this difficult period in her life. Knowing she needed pampering, he made sure she joined him at the ageing film star Maxine Elliott's luxurious villa in the South of France.

An invitation to the white art deco Château de l'Horizon was one of the most coveted on the Riviera, and guests enjoyed a hedonistic existence. After breakfast on their private balconies overlooking the azure sea, they could drift down in their silk pyjamas to lounge on the terrace or swim in the spectacular swimming pool. Nothing was too much trouble; if your feet ached after dancing all night in Cannes, a bath would be filled from bottles of iced champagne to refresh them. When the real moon was not shining, Maxine turned on a large electric 'false moon', set in the trees, to create the romance of a Mediterranean evening.[12] It was just the sort of unchallenging holiday Diana needed to cheer her up.

Once they were back in England, Winston continued to keep a paternal eye on his vulnerable daughter. When Clementine went away on a long cruise to the Dutch East Indies, Winston and Diana were both at a loose end and they often kept each other company. They spent a harmonious New Year's Eve alone together at Chartwell. They were very compatible as they shared many of the same interests and, reviving her love of politics, Diana helped Winston in his constituency. They watched sentimental films together, providing the escapism she needed.

It was a two-way relationship which was beneficial to them both. With Clementine away for so long, Diana filled the vacuum for Winston. He appreciated the affection she showed him and was full of praise for his thoughtful daughter. He wrote to Clementine saying how 'sweet and demure' she was, and noticing a change in her, he added that she had become very dignified and charming.[13] He thought she had learned a great deal from the last few years.[14]

However, when Diana went to court to get divorced in February 1935, it was Moppet, not her parents, who was by her side. Clementine remained on the other side of the world, while Winston said he would have accompanied her but was worried it would just attract publicity.[15] The usually measured Moppet was furious to see Diana go through this ordeal. She wrote to Clementine, 'Poor little thing, she looked so pathetic in the [witness] box.' A stickler for the truth, Moppet could not stand the unfairness of the whole situation and, describing it as 'the most appalling sordid farce', she complained:

> Poor little Diana was given her divorce not because her husband had treated her in a perfectly beastly way, but on the obviously trumped up evidence of a hotel waiter. All the real bitterness and suffering through which she has gone was hushed up in case she seemed vindictive.[16]

Rather than having the real grounds for divorce exposed in the courts, many couples divorced by mutual consent. The husband would provide evidence of 'adultery' for his wife by a procedure known as 'a hotel bill case'. This involved a young woman being hired to stay in a hotel room with the divorcing husband. She would then be found in bed with him the next morning when breakfast was brought up to them by a member of staff. In Diana's divorce, it was claimed that her husband had stayed with another woman in a Kensington hotel. Conveniently, what really went on behind closed doors in their marriage remained a secret.

Diana's divorce must have felt like another failure to her. It seems she did not want to discuss it with her mother and, playing down her distress, she just wrote that it was a relief to have it settled and joked that she had been bound over to keep the peace for six months.[17] Knowing what her sister had been through, Sarah stayed with her in her London home. She wrote to Clementine that Diana seemed 'a little less strung up', but her heart ached for her because she was afraid that she still loved her ex-husband a bit. Sarah added, 'I do hope she will meet someone soon – she seems to have so little in her life.'[18] Clementine also prayed that she would find some happiness to make up for this unpleasant experience.[19]

In subsequent years, Diana rarely talked about her first marriage. Her daughter Celia only found out her mother had been married before when she discovered an old suitcase in the garage with the initials 'D.B.' embossed on it.[20]

To distract herself from her personal problems, Diana threw herself into politics. Winston wrote to Clementine that her principal occupation was now fighting elections.[21] When Randolph stood in the Wavertree by-election Diana and Sarah rushed up to Liverpool to help him. Winston had strongly disagreed with the Conservative leadership when they supported the granting of Dominion status to India and Randolph took his father's stance a step further by standing against the official Conservative candidate in the by-election. It was a violent campaign with bricks thrown at the Churchills' car and rowdy meetings. However, Diana and Sarah enjoyed the rough and tumble of political life and found it 'thrilling'.[22] As their friends joined them to help, the campaign developed a party atmosphere.

At first Winston disapproved of Randolph's maverick action, believing it would split the Conservative vote and let the Socialists in. However, as the campaign gained momentum, he could not resist speaking for his only son. He began to fantasise about bringing Randolph back to Westminster with him.[23] Characteristically, on the other hand, Clementine was only really concerned about the effect Randolph's behaviour would have on Winston's career.[24]

Adding an air of respectability, Moppet joined the Churchill children on the campaign trail and, interestingly, it was Sarah, rather than Randolph, who made the greatest impression on her. She wrote to Clementine that her daughter had been 'simply magnificent'. She was an excellent canvasser and had 'gained such poise I am quite amazed at her'.[25] Sarah was classless and had the ability to talk to anyone.

Her charm won over people from all walks of life; never being patronising, she was genuinely interested in them. Sarah told Mary that she had met 'interesting people with souls'.[26]

Hearing how good Sarah was at campaigning raises the question, would she have made a good politician? Like Diana, she had the right background, political understanding and intelligence to make an excellent Member of Parliament. Unlike her sister, she also had the charisma to do it, if she had wanted to. However, her vocation lay elsewhere – she intended to make her mark in a different world from her father.

Like so many of the Churchill women, Sarah was happy to be the support act not the star in the political arena. She was very good at handling her volatile brother, and she praised him when praise was due but also did not hesitate to tell him when she thought he was 'lousy'. She could get him to do things when no one else could.[27] During the campaign, she began to see Randolph in a new light. Watching him speak to packed audiences, she believed he had a magnetism which drew people to him. Young men and women hero-worshipped the 'Fat Boy of Wavertree', as he was dubbed by the *Daily Express*.[28]

Randolph did not win, but he made his mark by getting over 10,000 votes. As Winston had predicted, splitting the Conservative vote let the Socialist candidate win and the Conservatives were furious with both father and son.

Later that year, Randolph supported another independent Conservative candidate in the Norwood by-election in Surrey. Even Diana thought this was a mistake, but once again she loyally joined Sarah in campaigning for him. It became a real family affair when 12-year-old Mary was roped in to address envelopes. This time, Winston was even more certain that Randolph was doing the wrong thing. Father and son had furious rows about it, particularly as Winston felt it could rebound unfavourably on his own career. For much of the campaign, they were not talking to each other so Diana had to act as go-between.

When Winston met the Conservative leader Stanley Baldwin, he was understanding. Baldwin told him that his wife had said to him, 'One's children are like a lot of live bombs. One never knows when they will go off, or in what direction.'[29] The comment was certainly true of the Churchill brood and their cousins, and over the next few years a whole bomb disposal squad would have been required to defuse their explosive actions. However, Winston was wise enough to realise that the new generation had to make the world as they chose, not as his generation wanted it.

As everyone expected, Norwood was a fiasco. Randolph's candidate came bottom of the poll and the official Conservative, Duncan Sandys, won. However, not all the repercussions from Norwood were negative. At the election hustings, Diana and Duncan Sandys' eyes had met across a crowded hall. Shortly after the campaign ended, they met again and fell in love.

It was an attraction of opposites: while Diana was gentle and hesitant, Duncan was suave and confident. This time she had found a suitable partner to bring into the Churchill dynasty. Aged 27, Duncan had the perfect Establishment credentials. After being educated at Eton and Oxford, he had been a diplomat before entering politics. Perhaps subconsciously, Diana was trying to emulate her parents' political partnership. Duncan was ambitious and, with Winston's daughter by his side, he seemed to have found the ideal wife to help him reach the top.

At first Winston and Clementine were 'rather staggered' by the speed of the courtship, but they liked their new son-in-law and welcomed him wholeheartedly into the family. They were relieved to see that Diana and Duncan were very much in love.[30] Signalling their approval, they gave the couple £1,000 and a new car as a wedding present.[31]

In September 1935 the couple married in a low-key ceremony at St Ethelburga's Church, Bishopsgate, London. Diana's first wedding had been designed to please her parents while her second one expressed her personality. She requested that it should be as quiet as possible.[32] Wearing an understated stone-coloured dress, a matching hat and sable wrap, she chose Mary and Sarah to be her only bridesmaids. The forty guests were just family and close friends.[33]

A year later, Diana provided her parents with their first grandchild, Julian. After the christening, as Winston proposed the toast to the latest member of the Churchill family it was a proud moment for his eldest daughter. Photographed in *Tatler* holding her bonny baby, Diana looked like a radiant Madonna.[34] She had finally lived up to her parents' expectations.

7

Sarah Takes Centre Stage

As Sarah watched Duncan and Diana go out for a walk in the rain, looking so happy and in love, she wondered what the future held for her. She realised that she was not like her sisters and did not want the same things out of life as them. In a revealing letter to Mary, she wondered whether 'I shall ever be an old lady with memories and grandchildren – or whether I shall always remain so alone, in spirit'. Brought up by her father to believe in destiny, she added that it was in fate's hands. She would play her part in the bargain by working hard but she hoped fate would treat her kindly.[1]

Out of Winston's daughters, Sarah was the one who had inherited his touch of genius. It was a double-edged sword, which meant she had the potential to soar to the summits or descend to the depths. With her luxuriant Titian hair, magnolia skin, large eyes and svelte figure, she was almost a great beauty but, like her temperament, her looks were never static. As Clementine noted, sometimes she looked 'absolutely lovely – but on the other hand she can look like a moping raven'.[2]

Although Sarah could be shy and unsure of herself, it was her personality as much as her looks which made her so attractive. Brimming with energy, she was one of those life-enhancing people who bring that touch of magic and mischief to everyday life. Her great sense of humour combined with her Churchillian charm made her fun to be around.

After leaving school, Sarah attended a finishing school in Paris and, like Diana, she was excited by the sophisticated Parisian life. She studied philosophy, history and literature, but she also learned the art of flirtation and good grooming. Her chic mentor instilled in her the philosophy that a woman must never lose her vanity.[3] Sarah held on to this advice for the rest of her life and wherever she was in the world, she would immediately locate a hairdresser – even when she was at her lowest ebb, she would look immaculate.

Being attracted to older men, she had a flirtation with one of her tutors, a literary professor at the Sorbonne. When he paid her a compliment, she instantly fell in love.[4] It came to nothing but she enjoyed that first frisson of adult sexual attraction.

Once her time in Paris was over, Sarah returned to Chartwell. Mary hero-worshipped her sister because, unlike Randolph and Diana, who were distant figures, Sarah played with her and shared confidences. The nicknames they gave each other in their imaginary games reflected the sisterly dynamics; while Sarah was the *soignée* 'Lady Helen', Mary was the frumpy 'Mrs Podgy'.[5]

Although she humoured her little sister, Sarah had really outgrown the nursery world and, stuck at home with Mary and the animals, she was bored. She mooned around playing romantic records loudly on Diana's gramophone, which annoyed Winston as it disturbed his writing. He soon nicknamed the offending music 'Sarah's Solace'.[6]

Unlike her sisters, Sarah always had a rebellious streak. When she joined her parents at Maxine Elliott's villa, a fellow guest described her as 'a Bolshie Deb', and thrown in among the Riviera set she behaved like a moody teenager. The vacuous comments of Doris, Lady Castlerosse, the 'unrivalled nitwit' with the impossibly long legs, were hardly stimulating,[7] nor did she hide her disdain for her ageing hostess.

Maxine was a dear friend of Winston's and he reprimanded his daughter for her gauche behaviour, saying, 'My dear. I feel that you are still too young to appreciate the rich and mellow vintage.'[8] But it was not about age, it was a matter of taste. Like Clementine, who loathed the louche Riviera lifestyle, Sarah was appalled by the excesses of the super-rich.

Sarah was never a snob, so she found the aristocratic world equally unappealing. When she came out as a debutante in 1933 she was bored stiff by the stuffy social life. She spent most evenings in the loos playing cards with her fellow debutante and cousin Unity Mitford.[9] Always wanting to bite her fingernails but restricted by her long, white gloves, Sarah never felt she fitted in.[10] The 'season' was just not her 'scene'; she found the other girls dull and decided that she was a loner.[11]

Clementine felt equally out of place. She found it so tedious sitting with the 'depressing back-biting tribe' of mothers on the chaperones' bench that she considered taking a cookery book to read, rather than listen to their gossip. She admitted that both she and Sarah were longing for the season to be over.[12]

Clementine was much closer to Sarah than she had ever been to Diana. Mary observed that they had a special rapport. They often breakfasted together in Clementine's bed. In between reading the morning papers, Sarah would amuse her mother with tales of her latest love affairs. Sharing a passion for clothes, they would discuss their outfits in detail. Although Clementine loved being with Sarah, feeling so close to her daughter revived painful long-buried emotions and made her anxious. She told a friend that she was terrified something would happen to her daughter. She thought part of the reason was that she reminded her of her beloved older sister, Kitty.[13]

Sarah attracted a flock of eligible admirers including Harry Llewellyn, who was a keen rider; Dick Sheepshanks, a Reuters journalist; and William Sidney, a local landowner. They met frequently at house parties or on the hunting field, but although Sarah went through the motions expected of a well-bred upper-class English girl, she always seemed slightly half-hearted. When her boyfriends visited

Chartwell, Winston turned a critical eye on them, while Clementine thought none of them were good enough for her daughter. Watching from the sidelines, Mary fell half in love with her sister's beaux if they showed her even the slightest attention.[14]

Sarah was less enamoured. The tweedy, hunting and shooting existence several of them offered never appealed to her; it was too tame and safe, and sequins and greasepaint were more her style. Bored with socialising, Sarah now had a new purpose in life – she wanted to perform.

At first, Clementine underestimated her daughter's potential. She wrote waspishly to a friend, 'It is very strange that both she and Diana should have this passionate wish to go on the stage without the slightest talent or even aptitude.'[15] However, Sarah proved her mother wrong. She had found her vocation and she pursued it with the same single-mindedness her father showed for politics. She attended the De Vos School of Dancing, where she learnt ballet, tap and modern acrobatic stage dancing. She spent four hours a day practising and then went out to balls in the evening. Enjoying pushing herself to her physical limit, she had never been happier.

Sarah was ambitious and wanted to reach the top. To her delight, she got an audition with the impresario C.B. Cochran. After performing for him, she was selected on her own merit as one of his dancing girls. He thought she had real talent, but he asked her father's permission before employing her. Winston and Clementine did not like the idea of their daughter going on the stage – in their generation, debutantes did not become chorus girls – but recognising times had changed, they did not stand in her way.

Cochran warned Winston that Sarah would be living in a very different world from the one she was used to.[16] However, that was part of the appeal; she wanted to break free from her parents. At first, she planned to adopt a stage name, but Cochran advised her it would make no difference – she would always be referred to as Winston's daughter. He added, 'Don't back down – try and live up to it.'[17]

In December 1935, Sarah made her debut as one of 'Mr Cochran's Young Ladies' in the chorus line of the revue 'Follow the Sun'. It was an exciting moment for the young starlet. Cochran's shows were extravaganzas which were known for their glamour. The best in the business were employed to create a visual feast. The sets and costumes were designed by Cecil Beaton and the choreography was by Frederick Ashton.[18] Cochran's young ladies were not your average gaiety girls and many of them were the daughters of famous parents.[19] It was a clever move, which attracted both publicity and a socialite audience.

In the revue, Sarah appeared in a series of sketches in costumes ranging from the risqué to the ridiculous. When not high-kicking across the stage in a very short skirt and frilly knickers, she played a wounded pheasant in a ballet satirising an Edwardian shooting party.[20] It was not quite the same as the dying swan in *Swan Lake*, but it was her first step on the ladder to fame. After seeing the first night, Clementine was very proud of her daughter as she looked 'graceful and distinguished'.[21]

Sarah was totally intoxicated by the theatrical lifestyle. She felt that she belonged to 'a lovely big family'. Although many of the other girls were from very different backgrounds they never showed any resentment towards her. The only thing they teased her about was still being a virgin.[22] However, her love life was soon about to steal the show. While appearing in 'Follow the Sun', she fell passionately in love with the star, the Austrian Jewish comedian Vic Oliver. Tall, blue-eyed and broad-shouldered, he had charisma – he wanted to make Sarah a star and she wanted that too.

When news of the relationship reached her parents, they were horrified. Clementine thought Sarah was not just stage struck, she must have been 'bewitched'. She could not believe that her daughter had such bad taste.[23] Winston was equally critical. He complained about Vic's 'horrible mouth' and 'foul Austro-Yankee drawl'. He thought that her boyfriend was 'common as dirt'.[24] Their criticisms reek of snobbery, which was unusual because Winston was usually attracted to flamboyant self-made men and Clementine despised effete aristocrats. However, it seems that where Sarah's interests were concerned inclusive ideas went out of the window and they reverted to their upper-class prejudices.

Those unpleasant personal comments about Vic raise the question, was there also a hint of anti-Semitism? It seems unlikely. Many of the British upper-class were casually or blatantly anti-Semitic but Winston was not one of them. He had always had many Jewish friends and he considered Zionism to be an 'inspiring movement'.[25] Throughout the 1930s he was among the few British politicians to defend the rights of Jews against persecution. Three years before he met Vic, he sent a message to Hitler: 'Anti-Semitism may be a good starter, but it is a bad sticker.' He genuinely could not understand why the Führer was so violently against Jewish people. He believed that it was senseless to attack a person simply because of their birth.[26]

There were more valid concerns about Sarah's boyfriend: he was eighteen years older than her and had been divorced twice.[27] Born Victor Samek, in Austria, he had moved to America where he changed his name and starred in vaudeville and cabaret shows. Although he had lived there for many years, he had not gained American citizenship. As Winston feared Britain would soon have to go to war with Germany, issues of citizenship mattered. The last thing Winston wanted was a son-in-law who might have to return to an enemy country.

As it became obvious that the relationship was serious, a meeting between Vic and Winston was organised at the Churchills' London flat. It turned into an interrogation with Winston in full bulldog mode, protecting his daughter. The relationship between Sarah and her father was always more complicated than with his other daughters. Some observers believed she was his favourite but that was not necessarily true. It seems that he loved all his daughters deeply but in very different ways, reflecting their different personalities. However, he did appear to be more possessive of Sarah and was often critical of the men she fell in love with.

When Sarah and her boyfriend arrived, Winston did not shake hands with Vic. Such a snub must have been hurtful to the Austrian who had admired Churchill since he was a boy in Vienna.[28] After Sarah and Vic suggested getting engaged, Winston told them bluntly that if they did, he would make an immediate public statement which would be 'painful to them both'. However, he promised that if they would not see each other or communicate for one year, and they were still in love after that time, he would withdraw his opposition. At this point, Vic became emotional but he agreed to Winston's proposal. When he left, Sarah followed him downstairs without returning to see her father.[29]

True to his word, Vic went back to work in America. In the months they were apart Sarah was desperately lonely. She felt estranged from her critical parents and found it hard to hear the man she loved 'insulted and treated as a low adventurer'. She complained that she was made to feel that she had committed an error of taste.[30] Only Mary's kindness and understanding made those difficult days bearable. She understood Sarah's attraction to Vic and was secretly on her side.

During the separation, Sarah's parents did everything in their power to make her move on. Clementine introduced her to eligible young men and even offered to buy her a London flat where she could enjoy 'total freedom'.[31] Sarah was shocked that her mother was willing to abandon her usually rigid moral code in a bid to separate her from Vic.

Winston also put his previous principles aside. He pulled strings to try to get her acting roles. Hectoring her as though he was addressing a public meeting, he told her she would be making a great mistake if she abandoned her career to marry 'an itinerant vagabond'. Diana overheard the interview. Afterwards, Winston said to his eldest daughter, 'I think I have put her off!' Knowing her sister well, Diana replied, 'On the contrary, I think you have chased her away.' She was right, these subversive tactics backfired.[32]

8

Sarah Follows Her Star

The more Sarah's parents opposed her relationship with Vic, the more she found it appealing. Strong-willed and obstinate, she was soon plotting her escape. She was constantly in touch with Vic, and persuaded him to send her a transatlantic ticket. After telling her mother she was going to London to visit her hairdresser, she took the boat train to Southampton. On 14 September 1936 she set off for America to be with her love.

Eloping was a characteristically dramatic gesture, and Sarah played the role of star-crossed lover to perfection. Before leaving she confided her plans to Mary, who thought it was incredibly romantic. She was given the unenviable task of telling their parents that Sarah loved them dearly but felt she had no choice.[1] Before she left, Sarah also sent a letter to Clementine. 'I don't like "backing out" – but I think it is the best solution,' she explained. 'The blessing and "consent" we were going to get in January were going to be very hollow – how could they be otherwise when both your hearts and minds are so set against it.'[2]

Clementine received the letter on Mary's birthday. When she opened it, the birthday girl was summonsed to her bedroom. Dressed in a towelling dressing gown and a turban, with her face covered in moisturiser, Clementine was sobbing uncontrollably. Mary had never seen her mother cry before and seeing her so distraught shook her to the core.[3] Clementine was totally bewildered by Sarah's behaviour. She just could not understand how she could want to marry Vic.[4]

Winston was also very surprised and hurt. He wrote to Sarah saying that he deserved to be treated better and he thought they were close enough for her to talk frankly to him about her emotions and what she had decided to do.[5] Knowing how much he loved his daughter, his friends realised how upset he was. He discussed with his cousin's wife, Alice, how 'tempestuous' this generation of young people was.[6]

In retrospect, Sarah wrote in her memoirs that she had needed to get away from her 'happy home' and her protected upbringing. However, it turned out that she was only exchanging one restrictive environment for another. By choosing a man eighteen years her senior, she realised that she was perhaps looking for a substitute for Winston. She wrote, 'Indeed, I have sometimes thought that I was trying to marry my father.'[7] Vic was happy to play that role. He wanted to control her and enjoyed treating her as a child. He later admitted that part of her attraction was that she was 'so shy and innocent and young'.[8]

In the years to come, Sarah would always be searching for a man who measured up to Winston. The partners she chose were often exceptionally talented in their own fields but, as with Vic, there was usually an element of rebellion in her choice. When she was a child, she enjoyed the attention she got when she hurt herself. As she grew older it seems that she was still trying to shock her parents into noticing her, except her self-destructive streak was expressed emotionally rather than physically.

Winston was not willing to lose his daughter without putting up a fight. Randolph was sent to pursue Sarah across the Atlantic on the ocean liner *Queen Mary*. This dramatic action just inflamed the situation and confirmed the rumours circulating in the press. The newspapers had a field day with headlines such as 'Dash Across the Atlantic' and 'Brother chases Cupid'. As Sarah had left just twenty-four hours earlier in the rival liner to the *Queen Mary*, the *Bremen*, the newspapers speculated whether the British or German cruise ship would arrive first in New York. Would Randolph be in time to stop his sister marrying?

During the five-day transatlantic crossing, press interest in the story gathered momentum. Constantly pursued by journalists, Vic got so angry he raised his fist and shouted, 'If you don't stop, I'll beat you up.' Inevitably, a photograph of him looking like a 'gesturing gorilla' appeared in the newspapers the next day.[9]

Trying to minimise the risk of a full-blown scandal, Vic and Sarah changed their plans. They had intended to marry as soon as she landed, but Vic now denied the rumour, saying, 'No engagement awaits Sarah that I know of except an engagement in my show.'[10]

Despite being delayed by a hurricane, Sarah arrived in New York before her brother. She had only a few minutes with Vic before being besieged by journalists. On the advice of her fellow passenger, Lady Astor, the couple held a press conference.[11] It was to be Sarah's first experience of the uncontrollable publicity her life would unleash, but she gave a virtuoso performance. She was a natural with reporters and instinctively knew just how to handle them. Appearing calm and in control, she told them she had come to America to pursue her professional activities.

The months after her elopement were an exciting time for Sarah. America more than lived up to her expectations. She wrote excitedly to Mary that New York was 'unbelievable it is so thrilling – one is really left gasping – I love it'.[12] Even eating hot dogs seemed so much more glamorous than gourmet dinners at home. Vic was also every-thing she had hoped for in a partner. Kind and considerate, she never felt lonely or depressed with him around.

Overnight, the publicity had turned Sarah into a celebrity. When she joined Vic in his show, 'Follow the Stars', her name appeared in lights alongside his on billboards. At last she experienced the heady taste of fame she had craved all her life. Appearing in front of large audiences, she was finally the centre of attention. As the curtain went up, out of the darkness a spotlight focussed on her as she languidly waltzed across the stage. She earned fees she could only have dreamed of in England.[13] The money was enough to make her financially independent of her parents. However, it was a physically gruelling tour in which she sometimes performed in four shows a day.

Back at Chartwell, Winston was plotting his counter-offensive. Using delaying tactics, he hoped that given enough time the couple would change their minds. He employed a sharp lawyer to try to dig up dirt on Vic's past. However, much of the information the investigation uncovered was positive. Colleagues described the comedian as a hard worker, who earned good money and showed integrity. More problematic was the evidence about his first marriage. The couple had divorced in Illinois, but the divorce was not valid in Austria, where his first wife now lived. Churchill's agents encouraged her to contest the divorce, but she refused.

This was not Winston's finest hour. If he had really understood his daughter's psychology, he would have avoided such underhand tactics. Sarah was aware of exactly what her father was up to. Although she knew he was doing it because he loved her, it only made her more determined.[14] Even Randolph could see that Winston was fighting a losing battle because the couple were very much in love. Their relationship had survived all the obstacles put in their way.

Despite the attempts to vilify Vic's character, he had behaved honourably throughout. Once he gained his American citizenship and his divorce was valid, nothing could stop them. The couple married on Christmas Eve 1936 in a quiet register office ceremony in New York's City Hall.

Ironically, Sarah's marriage took place at the same time as the abdication crisis in Britain. As Edward VIII made the fateful decision to give up his throne for Wallis Simpson, the American divorcee he loved, Winston stood firmly by his monarch. He hoped until the last minute that some solution could be found to keep the king on the throne.

His attitude to unconventional, twice-divorced partners seemed much more lenient when it affected the palace rather than his own home. However, in both cases once the decision was made, Winston believed in making the best of the situation. Aware of the parallels, he wrote, 'Like the ill-starred D of W [Duke of Windsor] she [Sarah] has done what she liked, and has now to like what she has done.'[15]

If they did not want to lose their daughter, Winston and Clementine had no choice but to accept Vic as their son-in-law. They had to face that their little girl had grown up and entered a new phase in her life. Clementine rarely put her pride in her 'beautiful young Sarah' into words, but she did so now in a moving letter which marks this rite of passage. Giving her a precious eagle brooch, she wrote:

When you were a baby and you were round and chubby and [...] all covered with golden down, I used to think of you as a fat luscious bumble bee and now you are grown tall and spare, I think you are the Eagle [...] I think he [the brooch] is particularly suitable for a lovely ambitious young actress.[16]

Neither Winston nor Clementine liked falling out with Sarah. Her elopement had shocked them, but they loved her too much to bear grudges and they now wanted to put the past behind them and move on. Clementine explained:

I think of you a great deal often in pain but always I retain confidence in your character and hope for your happiness. I should grieve if you thought me incapable of understanding the depth of your constant Nature.[17]

Winston expressed similar sentiments and he also hoped that she had found lasting happiness.[18]

When Vic and Sarah returned to England in January 1937, they visited her parents at Chartwell. After quizzing Vic about his earning capacity and shuddering at his use of American slang (apparently the word 'cute' particularly offended him), Winston showed his new son-in law around the grounds. He was greatly amused when one of Mary's more aggressive goats butted Vic in the backside.[19] When it was time to go, Winston shook hands with his new son-in-law and wished him the best of luck. Vic wrote in his memoirs that there was never 'a hint of snobbery or discrimination' towards him, but perhaps this was just wishful thinking. It seems Winston still found it hard to accept this outsider was part of the family. Throughout the visit Winston avoided calling Vic by his name and it was to be a long time before he finally deigned to call him 'Victor'.[20]

Clementine was pleased to find that marriage had not changed Sarah; she was 'as virginal and aloof as ever'.[21] It was an odd description for a young bride in the first flush of married life, but Clementine knew her well. Even now Sarah was one half of a couple, she still stood alone. There was part of her that could not be reached even by those closest to her. It made her a lonely woman who was always searching for that elusive soulmate to complete her. She had seen that type of relationship in her parents' marriage and part of her wanted to recreate it, while the other part rejected it knowing it would threaten her individuality and creativity. She was to spend her life trying to reconcile these irreconcilable desires.

Once they were back in the fold, Vic and Sarah moved into a London flat in the same block as Randolph. As a wedding present, Winston and Clementine helped them furnish their new home. Rebuilding their relationship with her, they tried to make their daughter financially secure. However, they still had their doubts about whether the marriage would last so they tied up the money they gave her in trust funds. They were also concerned that, as actors, neither Vic nor Sarah could guarantee earning a high income in the future. Knowing his daughter would resent these restrictions, Winston reassured her that their only wish was for her permanent welfare.[22]

Although Vic would have liked Sarah to give up her career after their marriage, she refused. Left alone all day, without work, in their luxury flat, she felt like a 'pampered and lonely Persian cat'.[23] It was not long before she returned to the stage. Changing from dancing to acting, she was willing to work her way up from the bottom and took small parts in plays in provincial repertory companies.

Although she could be tremendous fun once she knew someone well, her fellow actors described her as reserved. Many years later, she admitted to an interviewer, 'I am a shy person. I didn't become an actress to find myself. To lose myself was what I wanted.'[24] By the late 1930s she got her first lead role in the theatre and played a small part in a film.[25]

Vic's career was also going well. After appearing on BBC Radio programmes, he was dubbed Britain's 'favourite American comedian'. But juggling two careers was disastrous for their marriage; they were often apart and when they were together their egos clashed. Sarah's fiery temper and burning ambition meant that sparks flew and, like many comedians, Vic was not so much fun off the stage. Although he claimed to be willing to help his wife's career, she felt he did not really want her to succeed.

During blazing rows, he told her she was no good on stage although he claimed that he wanted to make her furious so that she would give her best performance. Apparently, their mutual mentor, C.B. Cochran, had advised him to give her 'a stern and hard school' so that she never felt complacent.[26] It was a counterproductive approach, as Sarah was the last person to be self-satisfied and Vic's cruel comments just played on her insecurities. She was a perfectionist, like her mother, and every night she left the theatre worrying about the quality of her performance. She was also self-critical about her looks. While married to Vic, she had an operation on her nose done by Harold Gillies, who was known as 'the father of modern plastic surgery'. She told her father it was to improve her breathing but admitted that to her 'great delight' it had left her 'beak' quite straight.[27]

Although Vic was totally absorbed in his career, he resented Sarah showing the same dedication. He complained when she invited actors back to their flat and spent hours discussing technique. During weekends, she learnt her scripts curled up on the sofa. She would spend hours in front of the mirror repeating one tiny gesture until she was satisfied with her performance.[28] Vic began to wish that she was less keen on the 'glamour' and 'thrill' of the theatre and would behave more like a traditional wife.[29] There was only room for one star in their marriage, and Vic thought it should be him.

9

Mary Faces the Gathering Storm

Mary described her childhood at Chartwell as like growing up in the Garden of Eden, but as the 1930s progressed the atmosphere changed. Rather than the biblical serpent, the force for evil which shattered the peace of Chartwell was the fascism that swept across Europe. With the rise of Hitler in Germany, Winston became convinced that war was inevitable. He was determined that Britain should be ready for the conflict, and campaigned for rearmament. Frustratingly, most of his political contemporaries were less clear-sighted, and for many years Winston remained a lone voice in the wilderness.

Discussion of the international situation around the dining table at Chartwell was often so gloomy that guests left the table feeling physically ill and depressed.[1] Winston was one of the few British politicians to draw attention to the mounting persecution of the Jews in Germany and Austria.[2] As tensions between Germany and Britain increased, he warned his listeners that the first thing that would happen if there was a war would be a gas attack.[3]

During dinner there were often long periods of silence, when Winston would sit looking straight through his guests, wrapped up in his own thoughts. His nephew, Johnny Churchill, found these occasions difficult to handle. However, one potentially torturous evening was relieved by the presence of Winston's beloved marmalade cat.

As Winston sat at the head of the table with Sarah and Johnny opposite each other, 'Mr Cat' was in pride of place, sitting on a cushion placed on a chair. Treated as an honoured guest, the pampered pet was given pheasant and cream which was presented to him on a plate on the table. As they ate their meals, Winston and the cat appeared to be bowing to each other. When Sarah and Peregrine got the giggles, Winston was not amused. 'What on earth do you think you are doing?' he asked crossly. 'I do not see anything funny at all.'[4]

Although her sisters visited often, Mary was the only daughter still living at home. She missed having Sarah around and found life far more boring without her. She wrote to her sister, 'I don't like staying behind and running messages and telling cooks please will they go to Mrs –, and playing croquet and having my hair brushed and washed out of my head.'[5]

Her life may have seemed mundane compared to the glamorous lifestyle of her old playmate, but she had a very secure routine. She later said that she had no complexes about her parents because she knew that they adored her. She described herself as a spoilt child.[6]

After attending the village school, Mary became a day girl at the Manor House School, in Limpsfield. She was good at tennis and swimming but not popular with the other pupils as she precociously preferred talking to her teachers. Mary later admitted she must have seemed 'a rather odd, prissy little creature'.[7] Like the good girl she was, she focussed on her schoolwork, her religious faith and her growing brood of animals. As she grew older, she became a keen horsewoman, mucking out the stables and doing the pony club round of gymkhanas before graduating to hunting. Clementine had high hopes for her youngest daughter and wrote to a friend, 'I think that if we concentrated on any one accomplishment that she could become a champion rider, lawn tennis player or swimmer!'[8]

During the thirties, Clementine went on several long trips abroad, leaving Winston, Mary and Moppet at Chartwell, sometimes for months on end. Mary missed her mother but there was no real gap in her life as Moppet was there. While Clementine was on her exotic cruise to the Far East, Mary's vivid imagination came into play as she wrote, 'Darling Mummie, I do want you home so much, but don't come home unless your [*sic*] not enjoying yourself. Please don't let yourself get eaten by CANNIBALS!'[9]

Winston and Mary's mutual love of animals continued to be a strong bond between them. Winston's 'Chartwell Bulletins' to Clementine were full of stories about the growing menagerie. Displaying an early entrepreneurial spirit, Mary set up a business called 'The Happy Zoo', selling budgerigars to guests.[10] Her goats butted important visitors, her unhouse-trained dogs ruined the carpets and the swans mated with their close relatives, but animals behaving badly lightened the atmosphere as the storm clouds gathered over Chartwell.

As Mary reached her teens, Clementine suddenly realised that she had failed to build strong relationships with her elder daughters. She was determined not to make the same mistake with her youngest. However, there was competition for Mary's affection and Moppet and Clementine became jealous of each other.[11] Sometimes, when they argued Clementine would become hysterical and Moppet would leave the room in tears.[12] At first Mary's loyalty was to her nanny, but the dynamics began to change. From 1935 Clementine took Mary on a series of skiing holidays which allowed mother and daughter to develop a lasting bond.

For three years they went skiing in Switzerland or Austria in the Christmas holidays. During these trips Mary got to know her mother as a person, not just a parent.[13] In the evenings she would go to Clementine's bedroom and, cocooned in dressing gowns, they would read their favourite poems aloud to each other. In this intimate atmosphere, Clementine opened up to her daughter about her childhood and her sister, Kitty, played a central role in many of the stories.

Developing a close mother–daughter relationship did not always go smoothly. Mary sometimes found Clementine's behaviour hard to understand and she dreaded her emotional outbursts.[14] However, unlike with Diana, their temperaments were more compatible and Mary's confidence and stability calmed her mother's nerves.

In 1936, while Mary and Clementine were skiing, Winston spent Christmas at the Hotel Mamounia in Marrakech with Duncan and Diana. The luxurious hotel had been built in 1922 and mixed art deco design with Moroccan architecture.[15] Surrounded by orange trees and olive groves, it looked out over the snow-capped Atlas Mountains. The clear air and bright sunshine lifted everyone's spirits, and it was to become a favourite destination for the whole Churchill family.

Unlike Vic Oliver, Duncan had always been treated as a welcome addition to the family and during the trip, Winston and Duncan painted side by side. Churchill was impressed with his new son-in-law and commented on how in love the couple seemed. Diana and Duncan read political books to each other under the palm trees. Duncan looked back on it as a very happy, sunny, carefree time. He also relished the opportunity of getting to know his father-in-law better.[16]

The following year, Duncan and Diana joined Mary and Clementine on their skiing holiday. Away from England, Duncan was not so preoccupied with his political career and the couple had fun together tobogganing every day. Clementine said that she was growing to like Duncan better because he showed Diana more attention while they were on holiday. She wrote that on their 'renewed honeymoon', Duncan had time to talk or play with Diana, who 'is a lovely fragile little flower which droops when neglected'.[17]

In the early years of their marriage Diana was a very supportive political wife and she often travelled with her husband. She went with him on his speaking tour of Northern Ireland and joined him in Italy where they met Mussolini's son-in-law, Count Ciano. Following in her mother's footsteps, she enjoyed being involved in her husband's career and her letters are enthusiastic about her new role. However, Winston firmly put his foot down when Duncan suggested that

Diana should go with him to Barcelona during the Spanish Civil War. He feared the scenes of devastation would be too much for her and that they might not get back safely.[18]

Throughout the thirties, Winston entertained guests who kept him informed about what was really happening in Germany. Mary was an observer over the lunch table of many of these meetings. As a teenager she became increasingly politically aware, but it was the Czechoslovakian crisis which first fired her Churchillian spirit.

In 1938, Hitler demanded the incorporation into the Reich of those parts of Czechoslovakia where the German population were in the majority and the potential for war became very real. In September 1938, Chamberlain flew to Germany to meet Hitler and Mussolini. After signing the Munich Agreement, which sacrificed the interests of Czechoslovakia, he returned to Britain claiming he had averted war and achieved 'peace with honour'. Winston saw this pact as an act of betrayal.[19] He was right, and in March 1939 Hitler's troops invaded Czechoslovakia.

Influenced by her father's views, in Mary's eyes there were 'goodies and baddies'.[20] As an appeaser, Neville Chamberlain was one of the 'baddies', while a definite 'goodie' was one of Clementine's distant cousins, Sheila Grant Duff. She was a dynamic young foreign correspondent, who was deeply involved with the leaders of Czechoslovakia and championed their cause at Chartwell. She brought several of them to lunch with the Churchills. Inspired by her cousin, Mary became a devoted supporter of Czechoslovakia and, like her father, she was furious about Chamberlain's Munich Agreement. As the issue divided the nation, Mary fought Winston's corner at school. She was outraged when her headmistress prayed for Mr Chamberlain during morning prayers, saying it would have been more appropriate to pray for the Czechs who had been betrayed.[21]

Although Mary modestly described herself as 'a plodder' academically, she did very well in her school certificate, passing with credit in seven subjects.[22] Her parents were so pleased with her that they bought her a horse. Making up for lost time, her mother spent as much time as possible with her youngest daughter and Clementine joined Mary out hunting and took her for a cultural trip to Paris. She wrote delightedly to a friend that Mary was 'my comfort and my glory'.[23]

The same could not be said about other members of the family. Many of the cousins who had been regular visitors to Chartwell were now adults and leading controversial lives. They personified the polarised politics of the thirties. Diana Mitford claimed that anyone who was intelligent thought about politics in these years. They believed their parents' generation had 'made' the First World War and by 'will plus cleverness' the world could be changed.[24] However, one cannot help thinking it was not all down to such high-mindedness. The cousins were bored by a stultifying aristocratic existence and wanted an adventure. They were also competitive and once one rebelled the others were soon to follow.[25]

Diana and her sister Unity were flirting with Fascism. In the early thirties, Diana caused a scandal by divorcing her first husband and becoming the mistress of Oswald Mosley, the leader of the British Union of Fascists. The two Mitford girls often visited Germany and became ardent admirers of Hitler. The Führer welcomed them into his inner circle. When Diana married Mosley in Joseph Goebbels' drawing room, the dictator was guest of honour.

Diana Mitford was one of the only people to know both Hitler and Winston Churchill personally and, interested to hear what she thought, the Churchills invited her to dinner. According to Sarah, they all questioned her about the Führer and found what she said fascinating. However, when she suggested that Winston should meet the German leader, he replied firmly, 'No!'[26]

Esmond Romilly had gone in the opposite direction. Referred to as 'Winston's Red Nephew' in the press, after running away from school he became a Communist. During the Spanish Civil War, he fought in the International Brigade against Fascism. On a trip back to England in 1937, he eloped with Diana Mitford's younger sister, Jessica (Decca). She was a fellow rebel who, in reaction to Diana and Unity's Fascism, had become a Communist. The Mitford family were devastated by her defection and the divisions within the clan never completely healed.

The Churchill children's private lives had also been tumultuous but at least they were politically united. The extremes of Fascism and Communism had no appeal for them. They shared Winston's political views and stood loyally by his side throughout the wilderness years. Although Randolph had not fulfilled Winston's dream of sitting with him in the House of Commons, he championed his father's political causes as a journalist. He exposed in the newspapers what Hitler was doing in Germany.

By the late 1930s Winston could only count on a handful of Members of Parliament in the Commons. Duncan was one of them and he became a loyal supporter of his father-in-law. In 1938 Duncan threatened to expose the deficiencies of British military equipment in Parliament. A complaint was made, and he was summoned to answer for the source of his allegedly secret information. When he refused to disclose his informant, he was threatened with prosecution under the Official Secrets Act. There was widespread press coverage of 'The Sandys Affair'. Winston backed him and the bond between the two men became even stronger. Duncan was taking on the role Randolph had hoped to play as Winston's second-in-command.

In January 1939, shortly after Diana had prematurely given birth to a daughter, Edwina, Duncan joined Randolph to launch a short-lived new party which opposed Chamberlain's policies. Loyally, Mary immediately became a member, but not many other people joined and it soon fizzled out. Winston joked that the new baby was thriving more than the party.[27]

With war on the horizon, Vic Oliver wanted to become natural-ised as a British subject, so when he was going with Sarah to New York Winston wrote to the Home Office supporting his application because he wanted to ensure that his son-in-law's travel documents made it impossible for the Germans to have some claim on him as a Jew.[28] Winston explained to the senior official at the Home Office that although he had originally opposed the marriage he had come to like and esteem Vic.[29] However, even Winston could not pull strings to get the five-year residency for naturalisation changed and Vic was also dependent on a labour permit to work in Britain. Eventually, the Home Office made him a special case so that he could continue to stay and work in the country indefinitely.

As international events were reflected in the turbulent life of the Churchill family, the cosy world of Chartwell was shattered for ever. The final summer before the war, Mary watched as Winston built a cottage on the estate that could also be used as a bomb shelter.[30] Diana had already signed up to become an air-raid warden. The whole family was aware that it was only a matter of time before such precautions would be needed.

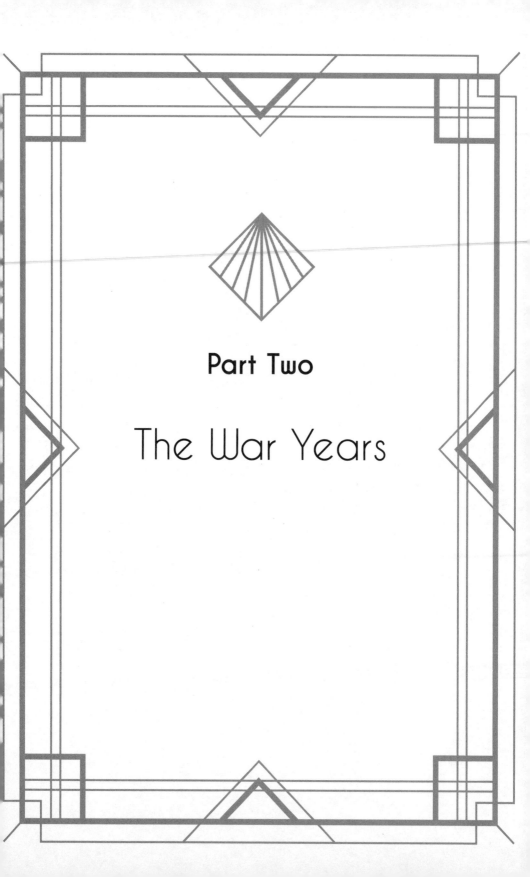

Part Two

The War Years

10

The Churchill Girls at War

The Second World War changed everything for the Churchill family. Finally, Winston's time had come. He was the man of destiny in Britain's darkest hour. He led the country with courage and certainty of purpose, but to do that he needed the support of his wife and daughters, both at home and abroad, and throughout the war they unstintingly provided that security.

On 3 September 1939, the day war was declared, Neville Chamberlain invited Winston to join his War Cabinet as First Lord of the Admiralty. Winston and Clementine celebrated the end of his wilderness years at lunch with their children at Vic and Sarah's Westminster flat. They opened a bottle of champagne and Winston proposed the toast to 'Victory'. According to Vic, his eyes glistened as he said, 'No one would listen to my warnings but now war is here, we shall have to forget the past. Britain shall never yield to her enemies.' When asked exactly what he intended to do, he replied that he was going to sleep and promptly went off for his afternoon nap, after which, refreshed, he rushed off to the first meeting of the War Cabinet.[1]

The Churchill girls were determined to do their bit for the war effort. Diana was the first to join up and at the end of September she began doing welfare work at the Women's Royal Naval Service's headquarters. Mary noted that Diana 'looked ravishing in her tricorn hat and black stockings!'[2] Diana was also an air-raid warden and Sarah commented on the glamour her elder sister brought to that role, too. She described her as 'an unlikely sight' in her trousers and high heels.[3] As the threat of bombing increased and Diana was so busy, her children, Julian and Edwina, were moved to a cottage on the Chartwell estate to be looked after by Moppet.[4]

However, the war provided Sarah with a dilemma – would she continue with her acting or do war work? It was not an easy decision, since now she was in her mid-twenties this was potentially the peak period in her career. When war was declared she was appearing at the Coliseum but due to the threat of bombing the London theatres temporarily closed. The provincial theatres remained open, so Sarah travelled around the country starring in the psychological thriller *Gaslight*. With a conviction in her performance which was perhaps partly due to her personal experience, she played Mrs Manningham, a wife who is manipulated into thinking she is going mad by her sinister husband. It was to be a breakthrough role for her and one which gained her widespread critical acclaim. Critics compared her to Katharine Hepburn and Joan Crawford.[5]

Wherever Sarah performed, she was instantly recognised as Winston's daughter. People rushed up to her and shook her by the hand, congratulating her because of him. When he appeared on a newsreel, a buzz of excitement spread through the theatre which made her feel 'so inordinately proud' that she was his daughter. Trying to justify continuing with her career, she told him that she hoped to make her acting worthy of his name one day.[6]

Mary was also keen to make her father proud. Living with her parents at Admiralty House, she was totally exhilarated by her new London life. When she was not studying at college, she helped in a forces' canteen at Victoria Station. Bubbling over with enthusiasm, she chatted so much to the servicemen that her supervisor complained and put her behind the tea urn out of the way.[7] Even more exciting was helping her mother entertain political and naval visitors at the Admiralty. When an officer arrived with information, Winston would leave in the middle of a meal and go through the locked door to where the war at sea was being conducted. Mary felt a 'secret thrill' at hearing the news as it happened. Inevitably, she became emotionally involved with some of the young sailors who visited and was devastated if they were killed.[8]

Casting aside her pony-club jodhpurs and 'Mrs Podgy' persona, Mary had become a very attractive young woman. Men liked her and she liked men. The newspaper owner Cecil King described her as 'a real winner'.[9] She was plumper than her sisters, with large eyes, a dazzling smile and glowing skin, and there was a wholesome sexiness about her. She was flirtatious and exuded warmth, but she could still sometimes be prim and take herself too seriously.[10] Jock Colville, who became Winston's youthful junior private secretary, wrote that she had Sarah's 'emphatic way of talking and is better looking, but she seemed to me to have a much less sympathetic personality'.[11] However, Jock's attitude to her soon changed and, like many men, he seems to have fallen slightly in love with her.

Although Mary was denied an official debutante season because there were no courts during the war, the annual Queen Charlotte's Ball at the Grosvenor House still went ahead. Mary spent hours getting ready for her debut. Everything had to be just right. After putting on her white taffeta dress, she carefully placed camelias in her hair.[12] As she entered the ballroom, there was a heightened atmosphere of anticipation.

Many of the young men were in uniform and about to go off to fight and none of them knew if they would return, but they laughed in the face of danger. Showing their indestructible sense of humour, as the ball was held on Leap Year night all the unmarried young men wore reversible badges with 'Stop: I am engaged' on the red side and 'Go ahead, you may propose' on the green side.[13]

Understandably, Mary wanted her father to be there for her big night. Although he was too busy to come for the whole evening, he unexpectedly arrived at the end of dinner. It was a moment of intense mutual pride when the partygoers enthusiastically applauded him as he crossed the dance floor to be with his daughter. Mary wrote ecstatically in her diary, 'I can only say the evening was a dream of glamour and happiness.'[14]

Over the next few months, events took place which would sweep Winston to power. As the Germans invaded Denmark and Norway forcing the British troops to evacuate, his hour finally came.

Mary witnessed the key moments in the fast-moving situation. On 7 and 8 May, she went with her mother to hear Winston wind up the parliamentary debate which had become a vote of censure on the government. As Prime Minister Neville Chamberlain left the Chamber there were shouts of 'Go! Go! Go!' Mary wrote in her diary that she was 'gripped and excited' by what was happening.[15]

On 10 May 1940, Winston became prime minister of a national government and when Clementine and Winston moved into Downing Street, Mary came with them. She was delighted with her suite of rooms, which she described as 'most Hollywood!'[16] Weekends were often spent at the prime minister's country residence, Chequers, in Buckinghamshire. Set in acres of rolling Chilterns countryside, the red-brick mansion, which had been remodelled in the sixteenth century, provided both grandeur and comfort for its guests. With panelled rooms, elaborately plastered ceilings and a Great Hall, it was a quintessentially English country house. However, when 'the moon was high', the house was considered a target for enemy bombing, so the Churchills decamped to Ditchley Park in Oxfordshire, the elegant house of the wealthy Anglo-Americans Ronnie and Nancy Tree.

Although these were working weekends, they were also family affairs. Winston and Clementine liked to have their daughters around them at this crucial time and, while Winston worked with officials, Clementine and the girls would go for a walk or play croquet on the lawn with their guests. Winston would appear in time for dinner in one of his siren suits, called by the family his 'rompers'.[17]

Despite wartime rationing, the food was excellent thanks to Clementine and her indefatigable cook, Georgina Landemare.[18] The conversation around the dinner table was often top secret, but the family always understood that information was not to be repeated. As Cabinet colleagues, service chiefs and foreign leaders visited, only close family and the most trusted friends were included on the guest list. The Churchills had always been a close-knit clan, but they now became such a tightly bound unit that they described themselves as being 'padlock'.[19]

Throughout the war Winston confided in his wife.[20] Clementine would not have wanted it to be any other way, but it was a tremendous pressure on her. She had never had many friends but during the war she became even more isolated and, terrified that she might inadvertently let slip information, it was easier to avoid socialising than take the risk. Instead, she relied on Sarah and Mary as confidantes.[21]

It was this family chain that kept Winston's show on the road. He depended on his wife, and in turn she relied on her daughters for emotional support. It was incredibly flattering for them to be so trusted and needed, but occasionally Mary found keeping so many secrets suffocating.[22] Staying strong for each other was no longer a purely family matter, it was of national importance.

Diana's role was different from her sisters'. As Clementine was never as close to her eldest daughter, she did not rely on her in the same way. However, Winston particularly liked to see Diana because her sense of humour cheered him up. She would sometimes act as hostess at Chequers when Clementine was unavailable.

Diana and Duncan were there on the fateful night in June 1940 when Winston learned that the situation in France was deteriorating fast.[23] Depressed by the news, they sat silently over dinner because any of their efforts to make conversation were rebuffed by him. Winston spoke gravely about the war becoming 'a bloody one for us now', but he hoped the British would stand up to the bombing.

Champagne, brandy and cigars cheered him and after dinner he recited poetry and discussed the drama of the present situation. He said that he and Hitler had only one thing in common – a hatred of whistling. He murmured to himself the popular song, 'Bang, bang, bang goes the farmer's gun; run rabbit, run rabbit run, run, run'. Then, unusually for him, he told a few 'dirty stories' before saying, 'Good night, my children' and going to bed.[24]

Duncan was delighted to be so close to the centre of power but not everyone appreciated having him around. Jock Colville considered Winston's son-in-law a probable opportunist.[25] He resented the way Duncan showed no shame in sitting in on informal meetings after dinner, 'drinking in' the most secret information.[26] Jock much preferred Diana, who he considered an astute observer of people and politics.[27]

During the war the family circle shrank because Clementine's cousins were once again causing controversy. The Mitfords were at the centre of an anti-Fascist furore. When England declared war on Germany, Unity Mitford shot herself. Unable to bear the two countries she loved fighting each other, she wanted to die. She survived, but the bullet went through her brain and she was never the same again.[28]

The public had no sympathy for Hitler's special friend, nor her equally notorious sister. In June 1940, Diana Mitford and her husband, the British Union of Fascist Leader, Oswald Mosley were interned under Emergency Regulation 18B (1A), which permitted the arrest and internment of 'enemy aliens and suspect persons' without trial. Diana was sent to Holloway Prison.

When Winston asked the Home Secretary for the list of prominent people arrested, she was near the top. This news caused his eldest daughters 'much merriment'.[29] Perhaps the fact that 'Dinamite' was considered one of the most dangerous women in Britain piqued their sense of humour. Clementine was even less sympathetic than her daughters. She had no time for Fascist sympathisers and did not want her husband's reputation sullied by any connection with her undesirable relatives. Only Winston showed any concern for his former favourite.[30]

In September 1940 the Blitz began, with heavy bombing raids on London. During these, Mary would join Cabinet ministers in the shelter.[31] After a bomb narrowly missed No. 10, killing four people nearby, the prime minister's residence was considered unsafe[32] and so the Churchills and their staff moved into the No. 10 Annexe flat over the Cabinet War Rooms at Storey's Gate.

Instead of her 'Hollywood' suite, Mary moved into one of the 'emergency' bedrooms. Her clothes were kept in a suitcase in a bathroom and, to her embarrassment, she had to pass a sentry in her dressing gown and tin hat to reach it.[33] However, any minor hardships she faced were put into perspective when she witnessed the devastating effects of bombing on people's lives.

During the week, she stayed at Chequers and worked for the Women's Voluntary Service at Aylesbury. Her job was to arrange accommodation for families who had been made homeless by the Blitz. The people she met made a deep impression on her as she had never seen such suffering and poverty before.[34] She also accompanied her parents when they visited recently bombed cities. The courage and resilience of the British people moved her deeply as they ran out of the still-smoking ruins of their houses to cheer her father.[35]

The news was increasingly grim. Hitler's armies had invaded Poland, overrun the Low Countries and even France had fallen to the Nazis. The British armed forces were on the defensive everywhere, but they lacked adequate arms and ammunition. With German submarines operating in the Atlantic, sinking merchant shipping and gradually cutting off British supply lines, there was a distinct possibility that the civilian population might face starvation.[36] As Britain stood alone, with the threat of invasion hanging over the country, Mary described this period as the most anxious time in the war. She wrote, 'One could scarcely breathe.' Everyone lived from one news bulletin to another, dreading what the news might be.[37]

11

Transatlantic Alliances

To win the war it was essential that the United States supported Britain. At first, President Roosevelt was wary of committing himself as going to war was unpopular in America. The outgoing US Ambassador Joseph Kennedy opposed fighting and told the president that Britain would soon be defeated. However, the new representatives Roosevelt sent to London were far more sympathetic.

In February 1941, the US House of Representatives had passed the Lend-Lease Bill which allowed Britain to buy £3 billion worth of arms from America and make repayments over many years.[1] Roosevelt sent a wealthy businessman, Averell Harriman, to Britain as his special envoy to implement the scheme. Harriman was joined by the United States' new ambassador to Britain, John Gilbert (known as Gil) Winant. Realising how important these two men were, Winston and Clementine launched a charm offensive to win them over to their side. The Churchill girls helped in wooing these influential Americans in more ways than could have at first been imagined. They went far beyond the call of duty — and thoroughly enjoyed it!

One of Winston's most powerful secret weapons turned out to be his daughter-in-law, Pamela. After a whirlwind romance in October 1939, Randolph had married the fresh-faced 19-year-old aristocrat Pamela Digby. Curvaceous and sexy, with a knowing smile, Pamela became a great favourite of Winston's. She knew just how to win him over, playing bezique, laughing at his jokes and listening to his anecdotes.[2] She was soon treated as an additional daughter and called Winston 'Papa'. What his real daughters thought of her flattery of *their* 'Papa' can only be imagined. She was always more of a man's woman and it seems that she did not waste much time cultivating her sisters-in-law. She knew where the power lay in the Churchill family and focussed her laser-like attention there.

Soon Clementine was also getting on better with her daughter-in-law than her son. On 10 October 1940 Pamela delighted the family by providing the essential heir. Her baby was immediately christened Winston in honour of his illustrious grandfather. However, her marriage was virtually over. It did not take long for Pamela to discover that her husband was totally unreliable. While posted abroad, Randolph was gambling and drinking heavily, so rather than stay at home and mope, she left her son with his nanny at Lord Beaverbrook's house and went to London.

It was now that her own transatlantic alliance began. In April 1941, she went to a glitzy dinner at the Dorchester Hotel and was placed next to Roosevelt's envoy, Averell Harriman. The spark between the nubile girl and the sophisticated womaniser was instant and electrifying. Square-jawed and raven-haired, Harriman was 'the most beautiful man' Pamela had ever met.[3] At the age of 49, he was more than twice her age – and married – but his urbanity just added to his appeal. He was the son of the Union Pacific railway king and he had been one of America's top polo players.[4] After dinner, the president's special envoy invited Churchill's daughter-in-law back to his suite. As the bombs rained down on London, she never left.[5]

The affair was soon known about in Churchill circles. The next morning, after a devastating air raid, Jock Colville saw Pamela and Averell walking arm in arm through Horse Guards Parade examining the debris.[6] At a Churchill family party shortly afterwards, Duncan

Sandys 'intercepted glances and felt vibrations' between the two.[7] Diana and Sarah knew about the affair first and then Sarah told Mary.

The Churchill girls were indignant and felt loyal to Randolph rather than Pamela. No doubt they had seen through her feminine wiles which had been honed on the Churchill men and were now targeted with an Exocet's focus on the wealthy American.

Whether Clementine and Winston knew about the affair remains the subject of debate, but it seems that, at the least, they turned a blind eye. Certainly, Pamela believed that her parents-in-law were well aware of what was going on.[8] They regularly invited both Pamela and Averell to Chequers. The Churchills may have condoned the affair, partly because it was in the national interest but also because they realised how difficult it was to be married to their son.[9]

Randolph never forgave his parents for their betrayal. Over the next few years there were some stormy rows which divided the family and, although the Churchill girls were no fans of Pamela's, they were always protective of their father. When one violent argument with his son nearly made Winston ill, Clementine banned Randolph from their home for the rest of the war. Never having been close to her older brother, Mary was furious with him for upsetting the whole family.[10]

In the early years of the war, the Churchill girls had enough problems of their own to deal with. In April 1941 Duncan had a serious car accident. He had been working as liaison officer between the Defence Secretariat and Anti-Aircraft Command. One night, while driving back from an experimental rocket station in Wales, his driver fell asleep and the car hit a bridge.

Sandys' feet were crushed and he suffered injuries to his back, and it was feared that he would have to have both feet amputated. Fortunately, Diana arrived just in time to stop the surgeons amputating. After the accident, Duncan spent a long time in hospital. As a naturally nurturing person, Diana gave up her role in the WRNS (Women's Royal Naval Service) and dedicated herself to looking after her husband and children.[11]

Duncan was unable to continue his military career, and instead rose through the political ranks with Diana standing loyally by his side. He was made Financial Secretary to the War Office, although his promotion was to lead to charges of nepotism.

When Winston considered appointing Duncan as Undersecretary for Foreign Affairs, the Foreign Secretary, Anthony Eden, wrote to Winston advising him against it. He warned the prime minister that a direct leap into such a high-powered position would create jealousy and not give Duncan the best start.[12] A joke went around in political circles suggesting that Winston should make his other son-in-law, Vic Oliver, Minister of Information.[13] Apparently, on the day Duncan became a minister, Vic came on the stage during his show and said, 'Ladies and gentlemen, I am sorry, but I may not be able to finish my programme. I am expecting a call to Downing Street at any moment. You will understand.' Winston was not amused.[14]

The jokes could not have been further from the truth and Vic was soon to lose even his position as son-in-law to the prime minister. To outward appearances everything was going well for the celebrity couple and, providing the public with the escapism needed in wartime, Vic and Sarah performed together in revues, a comedy film and radio programmes.[15] Their solo careers were also flourishing.

Vic was soon at the height of his fame, starring in a new weekly BBC comedy series called *Hi Gang!* Within four weeks of its first airing, the show became the most popular programme on BBC Radio.[16] Sarah was also on the cusp of fame. She appeared in several plays in London and a comedy film with Margaret Rutherford. Jock Colville wrote that she had a reputation for being 'a thoroughly bad actress', but having seen her perform he revised his opinion.[17] Just a few more successful appearances and she would be an established actress.

However, beneath the glittering surface there were serious problems in the Olivers' marriage. As an American citizen, Vic was expected to return home because the US Government would not take responsibility for the safety of American citizens in Britain. Vic was particularly at risk if the Nazis invaded Britain because he was of Jewish descent and the prime minister's son-in-law.

Sarah faced a dilemma: should she go to America with Vic or stay in Britain with Winston? For the daddy's girl, her decision was non-negotiable; she refused to leave her father. She wrote to Clementine, 'I have fought and fought against going back to America with every reason, every heart-beat – every instinct I possess. So passionately do I feel about it.'[18] Vic felt they should leave, but he agreed to stay because she asked him to.

Vic's self-sacrifice did not resolve their marital problems, however. The dynamic between the couple no longer worked because Sarah had grown up. In a revealing letter to her, Vic admitted that he had constantly undermined her mental and physical abilities, and he now realised it had been 'a cruel mistake' as it made her lose her own personality and sense of balance.

Although he admitted their marriage might have worked better if he had been kinder, he still believed that much of what she had accomplished was because of his tough, critical approach. He conceded that she had the potential to become one of the finest actresses in the country, but only 'if someone takes a firm hand and interest in you'.[19] This sort of backhanded compliment was typical of the mind games Vic played on Sarah. He would build her up one minute only to knock her down the next. No wonder she played Mrs Manningham so well: she was experiencing her own form of 'gaslighting'.

Needing to play the role of Svengali, Vic found himself a new protégée. Since early 1939 he had appeared in several shows with a young actress called Phyllis Luckett. As with Sarah a few years earlier, he wanted to make Phyllis a star. Apparently, Vic and the starlet were not having an affair, but in a way, his focus on another woman's career was more hurtful to Sarah than if they had committed adultery. Her career mattered more to her than anything, other than her family.

Showing an unbelievable lack of sensitivity, Vic suggested to Sarah that as they were childless and Phyllis had no father, she should treat their home as her own. Although Vic did not legally adopt her, she changed her name by deed poll to Oliver.[20] Whether not having children together was by choice or circumstance, we do not know, but Vic's bizarre behaviour was another cruel blow to Sarah's self-esteem.[21]

After much self-examination, Sarah decided to leave Vic. It was not an easy decision, and she kept asking herself, 'Why do I have to leave this delightful man?'[22] Years later, she was still pondering the question, writing, 'Perhaps if I had been older when we met, our happiness might have survived. His was a mature love, a caring love, and sadly, I just wasn't ready for it.'[23] However, to an outside observer the reasons she had to leave were clear. The fact that she blamed herself rather than him reveals her self-destructive psychology.

In 1941, the couple separated but did not divorce as this would have caused embarrassing publicity. Once she was apart from Vic, Sarah wrote that she felt able 'to breathe again'.[24] However, the separation came as a complete shock to her family as she had kept her marital problems to herself.

Predictably, Mary was the most upset. She had been genuinely fond of Vic and she wept about the news.[25] She admitted that she was too inexperienced to really understand so, inspired by the recent film *Gone With the Wind*, she suggested Sarah should just be like Scarlett O'Hara and think, 'Tomorrow is another day.'[26]

Although Clementine had developed a good relationship with Vic, Winston had never liked him.[27] When the prime minister heard the news he said, 'I hope he is going to be a gentleman and give you a divorce.'

Sarah answered, 'Of course not. I am leaving him.'

Her father then replied, 'You cheeky bitch – I wouldn't let you leave me!'[28] This robust repartee reflected their relationship. Winston would never have used such strong language with his other daughters – Diana was too sensitive and Mary too innocent. He knew Sarah was strong enough to take it and both father and daughter turned everything into a joke.[29] They brought out the showbusiness streak in each other and often their banter had the humour and rhythm of a music hall act.

Behind the brave face, Sarah was very hurt by the break-up of her marriage. She told her parents that it was vital for her new start in life that there should be as little bitterness as possible.[30] It hurt her less if people thought kindly about Vic. Whatever had gone wrong, he had meant a great deal in her life and it had been 'a big adventure'.[31] After their separation, Vic and Sarah remained on amicable terms. She could never stand abrupt endings and preferred any failed relationship to just gradually fade out of her life.

While her sister's marriage was coming to an end, Mary's love life was just beginning. Enjoying the 'zest' flirtations added to life, the dangers of wartime added an extra intensity to her brief encounters.[32] Decades later, she told an interviewer, 'When you are young you are determined to have a good time come what may. It wasn't the same as we would have had before but being young and healthy and in high spirits, we did [enjoy ourselves].'

She went to dinners and dances at the Savoy, the Dorchester and the Café de Paris with young men who would soon be off to fight. Looking back at her old diaries, she was shocked to read that the night the Café de Paris received a direct hit, killing many people, when her gang of friends arrived to find ambulances outside, they just carried on and found somewhere else to dance.[33] It was an example of the resilience of youth rather than callousness.

Strictly supervised by Clementine, Mary was not supposed to go out alone with a man or go to nightclubs. Unlike Sarah she was no rebel, and she usually obeyed her mother. When her gang of friends walked home through the blacked-out London streets she was often the first to be dropped off.[34]

Although Clementine was not ready for it, Mary was ripe for romance and during a weekend at Lord and Lady Bessboroughs' house, Stansted Park, near Chichester in Sussex, Mary fell in love with their son and heir, Eric Duncannon.

A 28-year-old officer in the Coldstream Guards, Eric was cultured, intelligent and a keen amateur actor.[35] Mary described him as 'good-looking in a rather lyrical way', and playing up to his poetic image Eric 'elegantly' courted her with John Donne's poetry.[36]

In May 1941, Eric was invited to Chequers. He knew just how to play it with his inexperienced girlfriend and, perhaps trying to make Mary jealous, after lunch he left her behind and went for a long walk with her coolly attractive cousin, Clarissa Churchill. He arrived back late for tea and made a dramatic entrance into the Long Gallery, where Mary and the other guests were waiting.[37] During the same weekend, Eric proposed to Mary in the White Parlour. She was taken by surprise and said, 'Yes.'

It came as a shock to everyone, not least Mary, that she had agreed. Unlike when Sarah eloped with Vic, Winston was too busy with the war to give the engagement much attention,[38] but Clementine was totally focussed on persuading her daughter to call it off. She thought Mary was far too inexperienced and had just been swept off her feet with excitement.[39] She begged her to wait six months.

Mary swung between having doubts when she talked to her mother and feeling confident about her decision when she was with her fiancé. Worldly-wise Pamela gave her the best advice – she told

Mary, 'Don't marry someone because <u>they</u> want to marry <u>you</u> – but because YOU want to marry them.'[40]

Reflecting the extent to which the key Americans had become honorary members of the family, Clementine turned to Averell Harriman for help. She appealed to him as the father of two daughters who knew what young women were like.[41] (As his affair with Pamela showed, he certainly did, but perhaps not in the paternal way Clementine had envisaged.) Averell was flattered to be asked and took Mary for a walk in the garden, where they discussed her engagement. He managed to persuade her it was a mistake to make such a hasty decision.

When Mary called off the engagement, Eric was angry with Clementine, but nonetheless behaved well. Always sensitive to other people's feelings, Mary was sorry to have hurt him and she felt deeply embarrassed, but she knew that she had done the right thing.[42] Over the next few years, there were to be many flirtations which added to the excitement of Mary's wartime life.

Sarah was also not to be on her own for long. After separating from Vic, she fell deeply in love with the new American Ambassador, Gil Winant. He was an idealist, a man of great integrity, who had campaigned for social justice all his life,[43] and as a close friend of the Roosevelts, who called him 'Utopian John', he had been tipped as a potential president.[44]

As an ardent Anglophile, Gil did everything within his power to encourage his country to enter the war.[45] The British people took him to their hearts as he stood by them in their hour of need.[46] In the heaviest raids of the Blitz, he walked through the streets of London, asking the injured or homeless what he could do to help.[47] Within a short time, he became a friend of the whole Churchill family.

He was unhappily married, and his socialite wife spent most of her time in America. As Gil was on his own in London, Clementine took him under her wing. There was a real rapport between them, and they enjoyed a gentle flirtation.[48] He often sent her flowers and carefully thought-out gifts.[49] Clementine had become isolated from many of her friends and began to confide in the ambassador.[50] Mary wrote that Gil 'understood intuitively' her mother's complex nature and the challenges she faced.[51]

Although Clementine had found a kindred spirit, there was an even greater attraction between Gil and Sarah. A photograph of them together at an Independence Day lunch in July 1941 suggests there was an immediate rapport. As they shake hands, he is looking at her intently while she looks slightly uncomfortable, perhaps because his wife is in the background.[52] When their friendship turned into something deeper is not clear, but in her diary, written many years later, Sarah recalled seeing him in the formal atmosphere of her parents' world and falling 'madly in love with him' before she really knew him.[53] The 'daddy's girl' had fallen for another older man – Gil was twenty-five years her senior.

The appeal of the powerful but sensitive man who managed to be both saintly and subtly sexy is easy to understand. Tall, dark and brooding, Gil looked like Abraham Lincoln. Although he was shy, unassuming and sometimes tongue tied, his intensity was attractive. The diarist 'Chips' Channon described how Gil's 'farouche charm [...] and inarticulate sincerity, completely seduced us all'.[54] The ambassador's unkempt ebony locks would fall over his deep-set, piercing grey eyes as he focussed all his attention on a woman.[55] He would then make her feel that she was the most important person on earth.[56] Apparently, at one lunch party at Chequers, Princess Marina, the chic Duchess of Kent, sat next to Gil and 'quite lost her heart' to him.[57]

A man with Gil's finely tuned moral compass would not have committed adultery lightly. It seems his feelings for Sarah went far beyond pure physical attraction and were based on a profound psychological bond. Although they were often surrounded by people, they were both fundamentally lonely characters; a friend of Gil described him as 'one of the loneliest men I've ever known'.[58] As someone who gained a sense of belonging when he was included in the Churchill family, Sarah's complicated combination of vulnerability and glamour must have proved irresistible. In the more liberated wartime atmosphere, conventional morality was moribund. Instead, spurred on by the attitude 'Live today, for tomorrow we die', people who would have been more cautious in peacetime seized the moment.[59]

Gil and Sarah conducted their affair with great discretion. In a private letter written about the relationship years later, Mary explained that she did not know when it became serious. Although she was very close to Sarah, she never talked to her about it because she was 'still very much the little sister'. Possibly Sarah confided in Diana, as she was 'her great confidante'. As for Clementine, Mary thought her mother must have known, or at least guessed.[60]

It seems that, as with Pamela and Averell's liaison, Winston turned a blind eye to his daughter's affair. Later, Sarah described it as a 'love affair which my father suspected but about which we did not speak'.[61] If the story had become public the scandal would have ruined both Sarah and Gil's reputations and damaged her father. It might also have harmed relationships between Britain and America at a crucial time in the war. It remained so private that Sarah did not include it in her otherwise candid autobiography.

Although their affair was secret, Sarah and Gil often spent weekends together at Chequers, and Gil was staying at the prime minister's country house at a vital turning point in the war. On the evening of 7 December 1941, Averell Harriman and Gil were dining with Winston. His valet, Frank Sawyers, brought in a portable radio so that they could hear the nine o' clock news. After a few insignificant domestic stories, there was a short news item stating that the Japanese had attacked Pearl Harbor, the American naval base in Hawaii.

There was a dead silence around the dining table until Winston burst out, 'What did he say? Pearl Harbor attacked?' At that moment, Sawyers returned and was asked if he had heard anything about Pearl Harbor. He confirmed that he had. An electric atmosphere passed around the room as it became clear that America would now enter the war.[62] Winston and his American allies called Roosevelt. At last the prime minister heard the words he had waited so long to hear – Britain and America were now 'in the same boat'.[63] Overcome with relief, Churchill and Winant did a little dance together around the room.[64]

12

Doing Their Duty on the Home Front

Recognising the great threat Britain was facing, the Churchill girls were determined to serve their country. They knew that, as Winston's daughters, the eyes of the world would be on them. By entering the forces, they acted as role models for other young women. Their exemplary war records were to win their father's respect and help to change his attitude to women.

While working hard, they grew tremendously as people. The war years were to be one of the happiest, most fulfilling times of their lives. After her separation from Vic, Sarah was keen to start a new chapter in her life. In autumn 1941, she asked her father to do her a favour and get her a wartime job as soon as possible. She gave up two lucrative film roles, worth £4,000, to join up.[1] It was a big sacrifice, but she had made up her mind to put her country first. She had always wanted to make her parents proud and acting did not seem the most worthwhile use of her talents at this moment of national crisis. One friend said, 'I feel she had to prove herself again, in her father's eyes.'[2]

Mary's motivation was similar. There was the personal reason of wanting to put her broken engagement behind her, but there was also the overpowering belief in public service that had been instilled in the Churchill girls from their birth. In May 1941, the first mixed (men and women) anti-aircraft batteries had been set up as the principal defence of Britain's cities and ports.[3] Mary overheard Winston discussing with the chief of the anti-aircraft services the acute shortage of men who were available to man their guns. It was agreed that women would be recruited to do the work of the displaced men. After hearing this conversation, Mary had a flash of inspiration and immediately volunteered.[4]

In September 1941 she took up a position as 'a gunner girl' in the Auxiliary Territorial Service with her best friend, Judy Montagu.[5] They were sent first to Aldermaston then to Oswestry for their initial training. Living in barracks with other girls from all walks of life was a culture shock for the two sheltered young women. Mary wanted to be treated just like any other 'gunner' so she willingly scrubbed floors and did her share of the chores.

Inevitably, the press were interested in anything Winston's daughters did. Photographers came to her camp to take pictures of her parading, drinking tea and emptying dustbins. She felt mortified, describing it as 'one of the BLOODIEST days of my life'. She regarded such publicity as 'persecution', but her senior officers persuaded her that it would be good for recruitment. They were right, as there was an upward trend in recruiting figures after the story appeared.[6]

Not all the publicity Mary received was so positive. She learned the hard way that once the press was let into her life she could not control what was printed in the newspapers – like a modern celebrity, she had become public property. *The New York Times* ran a story under the salacious headline 'US Soldier Spanks Mary Churchill'. Apparently, at a party of international servicemen, Mary was talking to truck driver Bill Adams when he suddenly got the idea of bending her over his knee and spanking her 'for a practical application of democracy'. After thirty whacks from the soldier, Mary managed to escape his clutches.

Bill's friend told the press, 'Miss Churchill seemed embarrassed. I guess it was the first time anything like that had happened to her.'[7]

It certainly was. In the 'Me Too' era, Bill would have probably been charged with assault, but eighty years ago, Mary had to just put up with this boorish behaviour and treat it as a laddish prank. It was treated as one of the occupational hazards of being both Winston's daughter and a very attractive young woman. When she was picked on, she had to just keep calm and carry on.

Once her training was finished, Mary was posted to a gun site near Enfield on the outskirts of London. As the prime minister's daughter, she found it hard to work out what tone to take with her comrades. It was a no-win situation: if she was 'quiet and unassuming' they would say she was 'smug and stuck up', while if she was 'noisy and matey' she would be accused of drawing attention to herself.[8]

Although on the surface she seemed very confident and mature, it was a real challenge for a 19-year-old girl who had been protected all her life. When she was put in charge of a barrack room of thirty-two girls, the responsibility weighed her down and she found herself with no time to do anything 'civilised' such as reading or writing.[9] However, although sometimes Mary felt exhausted, she made a real success of her position. Like Sarah, she had the ability to get on with people from different backgrounds. By just being her open, eager self, she became well respected by the officers and girls alike.

Mary was soon progressing up the ranks, but she wanted to do so on her own merit. Any suggestion of special treatment mortified her. When she was posted to 481 Battery in Hyde Park, which kept her in London close to her parents, she was embarrassed people might think she had pulled strings. In fact, she had not requested it, but it seems that the people in charge had decided it would be a solace for her father.[10]

Winston liked having her nearby and he often visited her unannounced. He wrote proudly to Randolph, 'Sometimes I go to Maria's [Mary's] battery and hear the child ordering the guns to fire.'[11] Day or night, she took a regular turn on duty on the battery site, standing with her girls in an open pit during some of the heaviest barrages.

Her hands were as red raw as the other girls', and she was considered as just 'one of the gang' by her comrades.[12]

Sarah joined the Women's Auxiliary Air Force (WAAF) in October 1941 and she also wanted to be treated like everyone else. However, she could not avoid being noticed, partly because of her father but also because she had a glamour that made her stand out from the crowd.

When she was interviewed by the WAAFs, she arrived in 'a very lively mood' after lunch at the Savoy. Her interviewer went through the usual questions on the application form, although she skipped over 'Father's Name and Address' and ignored the question of references. She then looked at Sarah's abundant red hair and suggested that she should have it restyled because she 'shuddered at the thought of what the camp barber would do to it'.[13]

Sarah's initial training at Morecambe, in Lancashire, was tough. She described to her mother how 'a straggling bunch of nervous civilians change in about 48 hours into fairly passable looking WAAFs'.[14] As she was used to theatrical digs, she easily adapted to living in billets, and although it was bitterly cold and she developed chilblains on her feet, she thoroughly enjoyed her fortnight's training. The biggest bonus was that it gave her no time to brood on her complicated personal life.

In November 1941 Sarah finished her initial training and was sent to Nuneham Park in Oxfordshire to be trained as a photographic interpreter. Sharing a room with five other women, the only thing she minded was being rationed to one bath a week. On the two-week course there were men and women from all three services, and Canadians and Americans mixed with British trainees.[15] They learnt to identify objects seen from the air and calculate their dimensions and they were taught to be 'curious in the unusual', as this might signify enemy activity.[16]

At the end of the course everyone had to take a test. Sarah's room-mate, Hazel Furney, felt that the prime minister's daughter had 'an awful inferiority complex' and was terrified of letting her family down. When they did a test report on an aerial photograph Sarah got the scale wrong and, later that day, Hazel found Sarah 'sobbing her heart out' on her bed, convinced that she had failed. In fact, she had passed and was able to go on to the next stage.[17]

Once she had completed her training, Sarah was posted to RAF Medmenham in Buckinghamshire. As an intelligence operation, it had much in common with Bletchley Park, home of the codebreakers. It was based at Danesfield House, a large crenellated mansion at Medmenham, between Marlow and Henley in Buckinghamshire, which boasted spectacular views over the Thames. However, few remnants of its elegant past remained; the formal gardens were soon filled with Nissen huts and the ground-breaking work began.[18]

At Medmenham, a substantial proportion of the skilled specialists were women, who ranked absolutely equally with their male colleagues.[19] Women made up about one-quarter of the photographic interpreters.[20] The young WAAF officers in their smart blue uniforms became noted throughout the services for their style.[21] Always vain, Sarah admitted, half-joking, that the colour of the uniform had attracted her to join. However, what she genuinely relished was doing a 'real job'.[22] She told her parents that she felt 'ridiculously proud' of her uniform and all it stood for.[23]

She was involved in top-secret work of vital importance in winning the war. It involved monitoring aerial photographs of targets for bombing raids. Each day, survey pilots risked their lives flying over occupied Europe to photograph enemy sites.[24] When they returned, their photographs were processed, plotted on a map and interpreted. The information was immediately sent to the Air Ministry and once a site was identified, Allied bombers would attack it. Photographic interpretation provided one of the largest sources of intelligence and was used to plan virtually every Allied operation. At Medmenham they worked for months on producing precise information for the landings in North Africa, Italy and Normandy.[25]

Over the next four years, Sarah worked with at least six different teams. It was precise work which demanded excellent eyesight and intense concentration. She still lacked confidence in her mathematical skills so when she had to set a slide rule, she slipped off downstairs and asked a friend to do it for her.[26] The pressure was relentless: interpreters worked twelve hours on and thirty-six hours off. They would come off duty both mentally and physically exhausted, feeling that life in the outside world did not really exist because they were still so involved in the scenes captured in the photographs.[27]

It was an intense atmosphere because many of the reconnaissance pilots they watched leave failed to return.[28] Sarah wrote a poem about her feelings for the young airmen who risked their lives for their country. She imagined a boy who had just left school, facing the challenge before him with 'courage cool' and, as the planes flew overhead, she felt an emotion which was 'deeper than grief, greater than pride'. She prayed the young men would return, but she knew many would not, so she steeled her heart by saying, 'Thy will be done'.[29]

As with her dancing, Sarah pushed herself to the limit. One colleague recalled that she could be 'almost hyperactive and I've seen her too exhausted when she went to bed to take her face off'.[30] Although it was challenging, she loved it. She said it was the first time she was treated as an ordinary person. The opposite of deferential, people pushed her to the back of the queue just to show they were not impressed with who her father was.[31] Like Mary, she did not want any special favours and when Winston tried to persuade her to transfer to Bomber Command under Air Marshal Harris she refused. She found fulfilment in her role as a photographic interpreter and believed she was useful.[32]

Medmenham was the perfect place for someone as individualistic as Sarah. It felt more like an academic institution than a military base. There was an ill-assorted collection of dons, artists, ballet designers, dilettantes and writers in the unit.[33] Locals referred to them as 'the Mad Men of Ham'. Although her acting career was on hold, during her time at Medmenham, Sarah helped stage very professional amateur performances. Among members of the unit were the future movie star Dirk Bogarde and the choreographer Frederick Ashton. However, although she appeared in some serious plays, her sensual performance of an Egyptian dance in the mess won her the most fans.

Sarah made some good friends at Medmenham. The aesthete and painter Villiers David was to become Sarah's life-long confidant. Wearing bright red braces under his blue RAF uniform, he rowed across the river every day to get to work.[34] Sarah and her friend Jan Magee socialised in the local pubs with American officers. London was close enough for Sarah and her gang to go up for the evening and see a West End show or to party at her new London flat at 55 Park Lane.

At weekends Sarah often went to Chequers. Although it was not far away, it often took all her ingenuity to get there. Sometimes she borrowed a motorcycle, and occasionally she hitchhiked. On one occasion, she asked a photographic interpreter, who had a Hillman sports car, to give her a lift. He said he would love to, but he had no petrol. Sarah took him to a nearby garage that was used by the prime minister's driver and told the garage owner, 'Give him two of Papa's!' Everyone was happy: her driver got his petrol and Sarah got her lift.[35]

Sarah and Mary were the perfect role models for other young women. As one friend said, Mary was 'extraordinarily wholesome, and always so beautifully turned out in her uniform' that she would have been ideal for an ATS (Auxiliary Territorial Service) recruitment poster.[36] By the middle of 1941, manpower shortages were becoming critical. Later that year, the War Cabinet introduced the conscription of women. All unmarried and childless widows were liable for compulsory service. At first, only women between the ages of 20 and 25 were called up but the limit was later dropped to 19 and could be extended to 30 if necessary.[37]

The Churchill girls were in the vanguard of this movement and set a fine example for their contemporaries. Both Winston and Clementine were very proud of their daughters. The prime minister wrote to Randolph, saying that his sisters had taken on the toughest challenges possible and he thought they were very heroic.[38]

Their positive contribution to the war effort helped to change their father's attitude to women. As a man born in the Victorian era, he was brought up to believe the abilities of men and women were different and neither sex should seek to usurp the other's role. However, as he saw his daughters' war work, he realised they were not just attractive accessories to men but competent people who could perform as effectively as the opposite sex. Although she was never a vocal feminist, Clementine had always believed in women's rights. She was annoyed by any displays of masculine complacency or implied superiority. Winston began to share her view that women's rights were compatible with their maternal and domestic duties.[39]

Although it was more a personal crusade than a political creed, Sarah was always the most feminist of the three sisters. Both Diana and Mary chose the more conventional route. Even during the war, when she was proving herself to be any man's equal, Mary's attitudes were not as feminist as her actions. In an interview with an American journalist, she complained that it was difficult to stay feminine in the army and that it was a real 'tonic' to wear a dress again. She believed that after the war there would be a complete swing back to women wanting homes and babies. She explained, 'Women know now that is what they want – that and all the fine little comforts and luxuries that we think of as American – efficient and home-like little flats with electric toasters and mechanical refrigerators and automatic washing machines.'[40] Whether Mary really imagined herself in a cosy flat crammed with labour-saving gadgets remains to be seen, but the desire for a traditional home and family life was her lasting aspiration.

Although they were such different characters, Mary and Sarah's shared experiences in the services gave them much in common. During their leave in summer 1942 they had 'tremendous fun' together and, briefly reverting to their pre-war lifestyle, the two girls went to parties and Clementine took Mary on a shopping spree.[41]

However, it was not all light relief. During this leave, the girls supported their parents through a particularly stressful period. On 21 June, the German Afrika Korps commanded by Rommel recaptured Tobruk, Libya, forcing the British to retreat to Egypt. Tobruk's fall undermined British morale and Winston described it as 'one of the heaviest blows' he could recall. A few days later, a motion was tabled in the House of Commons that 'this House [...] has no confidence in the central direction of the war'. Opposition members tried to place the blame for British reverses in North Africa on Winston.

Mary was passionate about defending her loved ones, and was indignant that her father should have to face a political crisis at home when he should be concentrating on winning the war. She saw that he was 'terribly worried and perplexed and harassed'. Mary and Sarah joined Gil Winant and Clementine to watch the debate in the House of Commons. Noticing 'the unhappy set of Papa's shoulders', his youngest daughter could scarcely control her rage. However, the atmosphere changed as Winston spoke with 'determination and sober hopefulness'. He won the vote 475 to 25. Delighted with the result, his wife and daughters rushed off to his room to congratulate him.[42]

Without her father knowing, Sarah was involved in the preparations for the Anglo-American landings in North Africa, known as Operation Torch. Security at Medmenham was tight and no one could discuss the work they were doing. Sarah kept her activities secret even from her father. One Sunday in November 1942, she arrived at Chequers in the early evening. Her father was keen to see her, so she was immediately ushered upstairs to his bathroom.

When she arrived, he had just got out of his bath and was wrapped in a large fluffy towel. As he dressed for dinner, he reflected that Operation Torch was about to begin. To his surprise, Sarah corrected him on a detail and then explained that she had been working on the operation for three months. When he asked why she had not told him, she replied, 'I believe there is such a thing as security.'

Winston was very impressed. Afterwards, he repeated the story to Eleanor Roosevelt, the American First Lady. She used the story in a speech about women's war work in Britain. When the speech was reported, Sarah was reprimanded by her superiors for a breach of security; however, once they knew it was her father who had passed the story on no further action was taken.[43]

The pressure on the Churchill girls was immense. Not only were they juggling their own demanding lives, they also shared the roller coaster of emotions experienced by their parents. Mary's daughter Emma explained what it was like for her mother:

> She was deeply proud and passionately almost in love with her father. She felt agony on his behalf when things were tough, or the war was going badly, or he was having a difficult time. She really lived every minute with him.[44]

Sometimes it all became too much. After their summer leave together, Mary wrote to Sarah apologising for sometimes being 'awful'. She explained that it was because of the struggle she was having inside herself. In the army, her responsibilities meant she had to behave like an adult and be cool and collected; once at home, suddenly her sophisticated veneer would crack, and she behaved 'like an idiotic baby'. Afterwards, she felt 'miserable and futile'. Looking up to her sister, she added, 'I wish I was more like you because you're always just right and perfect.'[45]

Since their childhood, Sarah had been the person Mary turned to for advice. As she grew older, her sister became like a relationship counsellor to her. With her own chequered romantic history, perhaps Sarah was not the ideal person to turn to for advice, but she was a good listener and she seems to have been better at analysing other people's relationships than her own.

Flirtatious and warm-hearted, Mary had got herself into another romantic scrape, when 'a very good-looking, very nice and excruciatingly dull' American officer called Ed Conklin asked Mary to marry him. She invited him to meet her parents at Chequers before making her decision. Although Winston had more serious matters on his mind, he listened patiently to Ed's tedious, long-winded stories, which even Mary found irritating. However, when Mary saw her father alone, he said, 'Now don't you go marrying that young man – he's very nice but you wouldn't like American life.' Although Mary valued her father's opinion, it was Sarah's advice which sealed Ed's fate. Later that weekend, the two sisters had a 'heart-to-heart' chat. After discussing her emotions with Sarah, Mary knew her feelings for Ed were just a crush and she decided to turn down his proposal.[46] For the moment, Mary's focus was on her war work rather than marriage.

During these years, Diana was too busy with her husband and growing family to take as high-profile a role in the war as her sisters. However, as well as being an air-raid warden, she took various part-time jobs: helping in a hospital, working for St John's ambulance, and in a munitions factory.[47] Duncan said that by the end of the war she would have tried almost everything.[48]

It seems to have been a fulfilling time in her life. Even the premature, high-speed birth of her third child, Celia, in May 1943 did not faze her. She was 'over the moon with joy'.[49] She wrote to her father, 'We have such a lovely new little daughter and I am so longing to show her to you.'[50] When Mary visited her sister she found Diana sitting up in bed 'looking beautiful, happy and peach-like'.[51]

13

Travels with Their Father

As well as doing their own rewarding war work, Sarah and Mary were by their father's side at many of the most historic meetings of the war. They travelled with him across the world to meet Roosevelt, Stalin and de Gaulle. Getting an insider's view of history was a wonderful experience for them, but it was also a tremendous responsibility because Winston was not a healthy man and their role was to look after him. The pressure on them was enormous because they knew that their father's survival was essential, not only for them but for the future of the world.

During a visit to the White House in December 1941, Winston suffered what appeared to be a mild heart attack. His doctor, Lord Moran, told Clementine that her husband's heart was weak and that the flying required in his position could be fatal.[1] This caused a major dilemma because Winston's journeys were an essential part of his diplomacy. By meeting other world leaders and getting to know them, he achieved far more than if he stayed at home.[2]

Faced with a difficult decision, the person Clementine turned to was Mary. During a walk at Chequers, she confided her concerns. Rather than tell her husband about Moran's assessment and add to his worries, Clementine decided to keep it secret from him and, to minimise risks to his health, she made sure that Winston was always well cared for when he travelled abroad. As she found overseas visits stress-ful, Mary and Sarah often stepped into her elegant shoes. Over the next few years, they acted as his aides-de-camp on many foreign trips.

Not everyone approved, and some critics saw it as another example of Churchill's nepotism.[3] However, it was not just a self-indulgent whim; Winston was happier with people around him he could trust. After Clementine, his daughters came next on the list of the faith-ful few, and their calming presence made events run more smoothly. General Lord Ismay said Mary was 'worth her weight in gold' as no other member of staff could march into Winston's bedroom and make him get up in time for his appointments.[4]

In August 1943, Mary and her parents crossed the Atlantic for the Quadrant Conference in Quebec. Churchill, Roosevelt and the Canadian Prime Minister Mackenzie King were meeting to begin planning Operation Overlord, the code name for the Allied invasion of north-west Europe.

When they arrived in Quebec, the Churchills stayed in the Citadel, the historic fortress dominating the clifftop overlooking the St Lawrence River. Before the conference began, Clementine was suffering from exhaustion and did not feel well enough to travel, so Mary went with her father to visit President Roosevelt at his home, Hyde Park, on the Hudson River.

After a long train journey, Winston and Mary were met at the sta-tion by President Roosevelt in his Jeep. Even though she had met statesmen since she was a little girl, at first, Mary felt 'a bit terrified'. However, the Roosevelts soon put her at ease.[5] After drinking a very intoxicating cocktail mixed by the president, she soon forgot to be shy. At dinner she was placed next to Roosevelt, who she found very charming.

The president and first lady did everything they could to give Mary an all-American experience. The next day, she went riding with a 'charming Corporal' in a rodeo hat who started each remark with, 'Yes indeed'.[6] After her ride, Eleanor Roosevelt took her to her cottage, Val-Kill, for a swim, then they joined the rest of the party for a picnic. Mary always liked her food, and starved of many culinary delights by British rationing, she was excited by the novelty of eating hot dogs, hamburgers and chowder.

The next day, after more outdoor activities and a picnic at the president's pavilion, Mary and her father visited the Secretary to the Treasury, Henry Morgenthau. It was like being transported into one of her favourite films, *Gone With the Wind*. While her father discussed world affairs, Mary sipped mint juleps on the terrace of Morgenthau's colonial-style white wood house, complete with its pillared porticoes and green shutters.[7]

This once-in-a-lifetime trip was all too quickly over and after dinner, Winston and Mary left on the train back to Canada. It had been a productive meeting and the president and prime minister had agreed that Britain and America would exchange nuclear information with each other but with no other power. They would not use nuclear weapons without the other's approval.[8]

On her return to Canada, Mary became a celebrity in her own right. Showing herself to be her father's daughter, she rose to the challenge of making unscheduled speeches, talking to the press and meeting hundreds of people. She flew 900 miles to Kitchener, Ontario, to see the Canadian Women's Army Basic Training Camp.[9] She was most impressed by the West Indian girls who were being trained there. After sitting on the grass talking to her, they sang her calypsos.[10]

To celebrate the third birthday of the Canadian Women's Army, she gave a broadcast in both English and French. Speaking with Churchillian eloquence, she told her listeners that a massive change had occurred during the last few years as now women in the services were treated as a matter of course. Demonstrating that she was no threatening feminist, she added that it was not in the spirit of competition that women were going into the forces, instead it came from their desire to 'serve to the utmost the cause of freedom'. After making the second part of her broadcast in fluent French, she signed off 'Goodnight and *Au revoir*'.[11]

It was an accomplished performance, which demonstrated that Mary could have become a politician in her own right. Of the three Churchill girls, she was the one most suited to following in her father's footsteps. Diana was the most passionate about politics and Sarah was the most charismatic, but Mary had the greatest overall political potential. She had charm, political experience and a desire for public service, which would have made her an asset in Parliament. Unlike her sisters, she seriously thought about a career in politics. When her father's old friend, the newspaper baron Max Beaverbrook, suggested that she ought to stand for Parliament at the next election Mary wrote, 'I got enthused and visualised myself in distinguished black (with a soupcon of white) making a speech about drains.'[12] However, her traditional view of women's roles made her more likely to follow in her mother and sister's footsteps and marry a politician rather than become one.

Once the Quebec conference had finished, after a brief break, the Churchills visited Washington. Staying with the president in the White House provided Mary with the opportunity to get to know Roosevelt better. She became devoted to him, and Clementine described them as 'thick as thieves'.[13] Mary admired the president's courage and found him 'magnetic', but she admitted his anecdotes could become 'tedious' and at times he rather bored her.[14]

Roosevelt was less compatible with Clementine. His informal manner jarred and she resented him taking the liberty of calling her 'Clemmie'. She was even more outraged when, over dinner, Roosevelt whispered to her that it would be 'wonderful' if something happened between his son Elliott and Sarah. Furious, Clementine replied, 'I have to point out to you that they are both married to other people!'[15]

During her Washington visit, Mary's innocent charm won her many admirers. She came across as fun but not frivolous, worthy but not dull. Her father's principal private secretary, John Martin, wrote in his diary that she was 'wonderfully unspoilt, ready to be excited and interested in everything'.[16] When Mary wanted to see American women's war work, the Secretary for Labour, Frances Perkins, arranged for her to visit the Bendix Radio Towson plant. To her horror, Mary was expected to make an impromptu speech to the 2,000 men and women at the factory. Although she felt sick with nerves, she carried it off with verve. Afterwards, Frances Perkins wrote to her opposite number in Britain, Ernest Bevin, that Mary was 'intelligent, modest, dignified [...]. She treated the girls like any other girl and made a great hit.'[17]

On the journey home on HMS *Renown*, Mary celebrated her 21st birthday, but her time in America had marked her real coming of age. She had handled every challenging situation with great maturity and been a credit to her parents. However, her triumphant trip nearly ended in tragedy. One stormy evening, while walking with an officer on the quarter-deck, a huge wave washed over the ship nearly sweeping Mary overboard. She only saved herself by grabbing the anchor cables.[18] It had always been feared that Winston would not have been able to carry on if Randolph had been killed in action, but he would have been equally bereft if anything had happened to Mary. After all the excitement of the past weeks, it reflects her priorities that watching the sunset alone with her father on the quarter-deck that night was one of the moments of her life she most cherished.[19] On the American trip she had given her all, and she had done it out of love for her father and her country.

Sarah had an equally unforgettable adventure with Winston when she accompanied him to the Tehran Conference in November–December 1943. It was the first meeting of all three leaders – Churchill, Roosevelt and Stalin. However, there was a private reason that made it even more memorable for Sarah: Gil Winant also attended the conference. It seems that away from their normal routine, their relationship moved on to a new level.

Before the main meeting, the Churchills and the American Ambassador travelled on HMS *Renown* to Malta where they stayed in the San Anton Palace. It was a magical place for Gil and Sarah to spend time together. With five walled gardens full of flowers, fruit and herbs, there were plenty of places for secret assignations.[20]

A highlight of the stay was when Sarah and Gil flew side by side in two Mosquitoes. Flying over Sicily in one of the fastest aircraft in the RAF, Sarah saw places she recognised from examining photos at Medmenham. It was an exhilarating experience; the only downside was that as the plane twisted above Mount Etna, she felt violently sick. It was only by an act of willpower that she managed to stop herself vomiting.[21]

From Malta, the British contingent sailed on to Egypt. They stayed in a villa in Mena, which was so luxurious Sarah thought it surpassed a Hollywood set. The only disappointment was that Gil was no longer staying with them. As President Roosevelt and the Chinese leader, Chiang Kai-shek, and his wife were also in Egypt there was strict security. Sarah wrote, 'I spend my time trying not to be overheard by lurking sentries beneath the windows.'[22] No doubt, scheming how to meet her lover without being detected added to the thrill.

When Sarah and her father paid the president a visit, Gil was with him. It must have been strange for the couple having to switch back to a formal footing and conceal their forbidden love. It was the first time Sarah had met Roosevelt, but as Winston had so much to discuss with him she only got to say a brief hello. The following evening Sarah and her father dined with the Chinese leader and his wife. Winston was very impressed with the vivacious Madame Chiang, but Sarah was not so sure. She described her as 'exotic – sinister, smooth, a trifle phoney? Perish the thought!'[23] When Madame Chiang attended meetings at the conference with her husband, she wore a clinging black satin dress, slit to her hip and exposing a shapely pair of legs. Her entrance caused quite a stir among the male delegates.[24]

During the conference, Roosevelt, Churchill and Chiang Kai-shek outlined the Allied position against Japan during the Second World War and made decisions about post-war Asia, but while her father worked, Sarah enjoyed an active social life. Most precious were the moments spent alone with Gil.

One afternoon they drove around Cairo in a shabby carriage and, like a scene from the film Brief Encounter, they ate chocolate cake and drank tea together in a café. In the evening, they were both guests at President Roosevelt's Thanksgiving party. Bringing the spirit of America to Egypt, the president carved a huge turkey for twenty people while an American services band played in the background. After the meal, Roosevelt and Winston made short speeches. Knowing how essential the transatlantic alliance was, tears poured down the prime minister's cheeks. Once the formalities were over, everyone sang 'Home on the Range', then there was dancing to gramophone records.[25] As Sarah was the only woman present, she was much in demand.[26] She told her mother that she was 'having the time of my life'.[27]

It seems that Sarah and Gil's relationship became more intense in Egypt. She later sent him cufflinks and a little animal ornament as a memento of their fleeting moments together. Sarah was infatuated, not just with her ambassador but with everything American. She told Clementine that Roosevelt was 'awfully charming I have fallen completely'. Her father was equally devoted to the president.[28] There was a special chemistry between the two leaders, which was transformative. Sarah told her mother that she believed when Roosevelt was with her father, he forgot that he could not walk. One day after lunch, Winston decided that he wanted to show the president the pyramids. When the prime minister got up from the table to organise the tour, Roosevelt lent forward in his chair as if he was about to get up too.[29]

Although they were enjoying themselves, neither Sarah nor her father forgot the seriousness of their mission. During the trip,

Winston shared his innermost feelings with his daughter. He was keen she understood that beneath the bonhomie there remained a steely resolve. Before they left for Tehran, Winston said to her:

> War is a game played with a smiling face, but do you think there is laughter in my heart? We travel in style and round us there is great luxury and seeming security, but I never forget the man at the front, the bitter struggles, and the fact that men are dying in the air, on the land, and at sea.[30]

Their time in Egypt over, Roosevelt and Churchill moved on to Tehran with their entourages to meet Stalin and plan the invasion of Europe in Operation Overlord. When they arrived, Winston was suffering from laryngitis, but he wanted to start talking to Stalin immediately. It was at moments like this that Sarah's ability to cajole her father into doing what he should was indispensable. Backed by his doctor, Lord Moran, she persuaded him not to meet the Russian leader until he was better. Instead, Winston had dinner in bed 'like a sulky little boy'. Knowing her father's psychology well, Sarah thought he was 'nervous and apprehensive' about the conference because he was not feeling well. She had made the right decision because after a good night's sleep, his voice returned.

The highlight of the conference for Sarah was the celebration dinner for Winston's 69th birthday. She was delighted to see that her father got on really well with Roosevelt and Stalin. She felt there was a genuine desire for friendship. Sarah believed that her father was responsible for creating this positive atmosphere as his 'buoyant vitality' infused the meetings. Evidently the Communist dictator was on his best behaviour as Sarah wrote to her mother that he was 'a great man', with a sense of humour 'as darting and swift as Papa's'. The joke of the evening came when Winston commented that Britain was 'getting pinker', referring to the growth of socialism. Without missing a beat, Stalin replied, 'It is the sign of good health.'

The world leaders knew just how to flatter an impressionable young woman, while pleasing her doting father. To Sarah's delight, one of the first toasts drunk at dinner was to her, and with a choreography worthy of her beloved Hollywood movies, President Roosevelt proposed the toast and then Stalin walked around the table to touch glasses with her. When Sarah went to the president to thank him, he said, 'I'd come to you my dear, but I can't.' After Roosevelt's gallant gesture, Sarah wrote emphatically to her mother, 'I love him.' Intoxicated by the whole evening, when a toast was drunk to Winston calling him a great man and prime minister, Sarah wanted to get up and tell them that he was a nice father too, but she was too shy.[31]

On 2 December, the Churchills flew back to Egypt, drinking champagne and supping turtle soup over Baghdad.[32] While she was having fun, Sarah knew that her purpose for being on the trip was to look after her father, and her nurturing skills were soon to be tested to the limit when Winston suddenly became seriously ill. While visiting General Eisenhower at Tunis, he went down with pneumonia. There was a patch on his lung and his pulse became irregular. At one point, it seemed as though he might not survive.[33] When Winston opened his eyes, seeing how anxious Sarah looked, he said to her, 'Don't worry, it doesn't matter if I die now, the plans of victory have been laid, it is only a matter of time.'[34]

Clementine, who was in England, decided to fly out to be with her husband. Throughout those tense days, Sarah stayed by her father's bedside reading him Jane Austen's *Pride and Prejudice*,[35] and by the time Clementine arrived, Winston was getting better. She found him sitting up in bed with a large cigar and whisky and soda in his hand.[36] Clementine appreciated what Sarah had done, writing to Mary that her sister had been a 'pillar of strength' and a 'great joy' to Winston.[37]

Once the prime minister was on the mend, he convalesced for most of January in Marrakech. His party stayed in Villa Taylor, 'a millionaire's pleasure dome' with orange trees and fountains outside.[38] These were golden days which Sarah would look back on nostalgically for the rest of her life. Particularly memorable were the 'dream picnics'. At noon they would drive over the red plain in clouds of dust to the valleys at the foot of the Atlas Mountains. In this magical place, Sarah felt, 'life seemed suspended and the heart could beat lightly'.[39]

The picnics were elaborate affairs with hampers of delicious food. After lunch, hunched up in a deckchair and wearing a huge sombrero, Winston chatted about the past or read Jane Austen's *Emma*. He enjoyed these picnics so much that when it was time to go back, he became 'quite petulant'.[40]

Unlike many in his entourage, Sarah knew just how to handle him. When Winston was in a bad temper, she just said, 'Let's have a bad day and make a fresh start tomorrow.'[41] She was skilled at smoothing over any tensions. According to Winston's shorthand typist, Patrick Kinna, all the secretarial staff adored her because she realised 'we were poor slaves and didn't have much of a let up'. After dinner, she would visit them looking 'terribly beautiful' in her uniform. Sitting on the desk and gossiping, she was always 'very, very friendly and no side at all'. [42]

Although her parents loved having her, Sarah wrote to Gil that she would like to come home to normal life. While she was away, she asked him to write to her to let her know he was well but, aware that they had to be discreet, she told him to post the letters to Downing Street so that they could come direct to her in the diplomatic pouch.[43]

It is likely that Clementine knew what was going on between her daughter and the ambassador. Although the affair could not be openly acknowledged, Clementine was close to both lovers and it seems that she could read between the lines. On his return to London from the Tehran Conference, Gil had visited Clementine. She wrote to Sarah telling her, 'Your Sweet Mr Winant' came to lunch. In between awkward silences, Gil told her the news about Sarah and Winston, 'but chiefly how wonderful you are'. Unlike when Sarah was in love with

Vic, she totally understood her daughter's feelings for Gil. Clementine described him as a really 'divine man'.[44]

'Divine' as he was, it was not an ideal relationship for Sarah to be in. The fact that he was still married was not the only problem and, described by one friend as a 'self-tortured soul', Gil was not an easy man to be involved with.[45] Under tremendous pressure in both his public and private life, his friends noticed his weakened mental and physical state, and they were concerned he would have a breakdown.[46] Capturing his mood at this time, the diarist 'Chips' Channon described him as sitting alone 'brooding like Rodin's Penseur'.[47]

14

Onwards to Victory

The year 1944 was to be a crucial turning point in the war. As Allied troops prepared for the D-Day landings in France, information about the operation was top secret. However, knowing she could trust her daughter, Clementine confided in Mary that the invasion was due to take place on 5 June. As the fateful date approached, Mary was attending a course at Aldershot. When the landings were delayed for twenty-four hours, due to unsuitable weather, her trepidation increased.

In the middle of the night, she awoke to hear the roar of aircraft overhead. Realising the long-awaited day had arrived, she rushed out into the garden and watched as the aircraft thundered overhead. She recalled, 'I fell to my knees and prayed as I had never prayed before.'[1]

In the final phase of the war, Mary was at the centre of the action, both at home and abroad. After D-Day, Hitler launched his V1 flying bombs, known as 'doodlebugs' or 'buzz bombs', on the capital in an eighty-day ordeal which became known as 'The Battle of London'.[2] Mary's battery was involved in defending the capital from these devastating weapons.[3]

Feeling a mixture of excitement and anxiety, her greatest fear was that she would not live up to what was expected of Winston Churchill's daughter.[4] She was fully stretched, only eating and resting at snatched moments. She wrote, 'At night the firing has been unbelievable – the whole sky a mass of lights and tracer tracks and the noise is like hell let loose.'[5]

It was decided that shooting the V1s down over London was counter-productive, so Mary's unit moved to Kent. Working in 'Flying Bomb Alley', which was the highway for flying bombs heading to London, they were in constant action. Her unit was then moved to the coast to play its role in what Mary dubbed 'The Battle of Hastings'.[6]

She loved her work, writing to Clementine, 'Egotistically, I am convinced that 1944 and all this – is quite as exciting and almost as significant as 1066 and all that.'[7] Winston was delighted with his youngest daughter, writing to tell her that her success gave him great pleasure.[8]

Diana and Duncan were also involved in the defence of the capital. While she served as an air-raid warden, he chaired the Cabinet Committee which planned the protection of the city. Known as one of the 'V1 Victors', Duncan won widespread praise for his hands-on role. When in September he announced that the battle was over, Diana proudly sent her father the newspaper cuttings praising her husband as 'one of the big political figures of the future'.[9]

A few months later, Winston promoted his son-in-law to become Minister of Works. It was a challenging role which involved providing much-needed housing. Clementine had doubts about the appointment, fearing that Winston would, once again, be charged with nepotism.[10] However, Sarah told her not to fret because Duncan had real ability.[11]

Following the D-Day invasion, Paris was liberated, and in November Mary travelled with her parents to the French capital for the Great War's Armistice Day. It was the first formal military ceremony in France for more than four years. The Churchills were treated as honoured guests of the French Government. Deeply moved, Mary watched from the reviewing stand with Clementine and Madame de Gaulle as General de Gaulle and Churchill drove in an open car down the Champs-Élysées and laid wreaths at the Tomb of the Unknown Soldier. Tears streamed down Winston's face as he received a rapturous reception from the thousands of people crowding the streets.[12]

After the ceremony, Mary went with her father and General de Gaulle in the presidential train, through a blizzard, to the Jura Mountains to see the French troops.[13] At lunch she sat on General de Gaulle's right. Recognising how lucky she was to be there, she felt very proud as she enthusiastically drank a toast to a resurgent France. On the train journey back, de Gaulle sent Mary a *Croix de Lorraine* to wear on her uniform. It was a small but touching gesture, which made a lasting impression on the young girl.

The sentimental journey continued when she travelled to Rheims with Winston to meet General Eisenhower. She wrote, 'To me every step seemed significant – I cannot get over being in France again.'[14]

Mary's next trip abroad came early in the new year when she was posted to Brussels. The Battle of the Bulge, which was the last major German offensive campaign on the Western Front, had just come to an end in the area. In the immediate aftermath of the battle, Mary was sent to Belgium with her unit to defend Brussels, which was still vulnerable to aerial attack from Germany. It was a great responsibility – aged just 22, she was now a junior commander in charge of 230 women.

Being dependent on her youngest daughter, Clementine was reluctant to let her go, but although Mary did not like being away from her parents for months, she was determined to be with her girls. She wrote to her mother:

Much, and devotedly as I love you – yet I do want to go – I feel jealous of the honour – and somehow with all one's friends fighting – and so many delightful people who have been killed [...] it would give out some little peace of mind to be able to share even one thousand millionth part of the burden.[15]

During her time in Belgium, Mary worked and played hard. On one occasion, she went wild boar hunting with a 'lively captain' she had met at an American dance. Although she was dubious about the outing, she decided to go as, she joked, 'The reputation of imperial womanhood itself was at stake'. Mary did not shoot any animals herself but at the end of the day she was given a live baby boar as a gift. Back at camp, her major was shocked when the creature appeared out of a milk box. Mary then had a disturbed night as the animal screamed and banged to get out. In the morning 'the boarlet' was taken away to the gamekeeper's cottage where Mary feared suckling pig would soon be on the menu.[16]

Sarah was slightly envious of Mary's adventures. The last few months had been difficult for her. In October, she had celebrated her 30th birthday, which she admitted was quite a landmark. This is an age when a woman assesses what she has achieved so far and what the future may hold. The war had derailed her plans. Her acting career was on hold, she was separated, childless and involved with a married man,[17] and as a natural non-conformist, she was also fed up with the strict RAF discipline. However, she got a much-needed change of scene when she accompanied her father to the Yalta Conference in February 1945.

The trip to get there was exhausting. On the flight to Malta, the plane was cold, so the heating was turned on. Sitting huddled in his greatcoat, Winston began to get too warm and looked like 'a poor hot pink baby about to cry'. His temperature went up to 102 degrees Fahrenheit and Sarah thought he was about to be ill again. However, rather than alarm her dejected father, she reassured him that he would feel better soon. To everyone's relief, after a good sleep, the prime minister was fine.[18]

On 2 February, President Roosevelt sailed in aboard USS *Quincy*. It was a memorable sight and Churchill and his entourage turned out on deck and everyone sang 'God Save the King' and 'The Star-Spangled Banner'. Later that day, Sarah and Winston visited Roosevelt and his daughter, Anna Boettiger.

The two women immediately got on well, particularly when Anna admitted that she was also nervous about the trip. Sarah wrote to Clementine that she thought Anna was very like her mother, Eleanor Roosevelt, but much better looking. Showing her ongoing tendency to compare herself unfavourably to her mother, Sarah joked that she supposed strangers thought she and Diana looked like Clementine, only not as good-looking. However, Sarah was shocked at how much the president had changed since they had last met; she realised that he was a very sick man.[19]

From Malta they flew to Crimea, and Winston and his team then had a six-hour drive to their destination. Travelling in convoy, the cars drove slowly on roads that had been ravaged by the war. After an hour, Winston asked how long they had been travelling. When Sarah said just one hour, he replied, 'Christ, five more of this' and 'gloom and muttered bad language set in'.[20]

Once they reached the mountains, the countryside improved and for 100 miles the road was lined every 200 yards with Red Army men and women who sprang to salute as they passed. In need of a break, they stopped at a rest house.[21] After eating Russian delicacies, they took to the road again for another two hours. Winston passed the journey by reciting Byron's *Don Juan*.

At last they arrived at Yalta. Situated on the Black Sea, Winston described it as 'The Riviera of Hades', while Sarah found it 'oppressive and ominous'.[22] The British contingent were staying in the Vorontzov villa. Like a Scottish baronial hall crossed with a Moorish palace, its gardens fell in terraces to the Black Sea.

It was grand, but sadly faded. The shortage of bathrooms meant that three field marshals had to queue to use one bucket in the mornings. Fortunately for Sarah, Winston generously agreed to share his bathroom with her.[23] However, hygiene left a lot to be desired. There were bluebottles in the library and bed bugs in the bedrooms. After Winston was bitten on the feet, Lord Moran went around all the beds squirting the insecticide DDT. However, the Russian hospitality was lavish – caviar was served at breakfast, lunch and dinner. When Sarah mentioned that caviar was improved by lemon juice, a large lemon tree was brought by sea and installed in the orangery.[24]

At Yalta, Churchill, Stalin and Roosevelt discussed the future of post-war Europe. Roosevelt conciliated the Russians on almost every point, which left Winston isolated. However, Sarah felt the conference was less physically tiring for her father than Tehran had been.[25] She enjoyed looking after him, making sure he ate regularly and did not get over-tired. The meetings were emotionally demanding and the momentous decisions they were making weighed heavily on Churchill. One evening, he said to Sarah, 'I do not suppose that at any moment in history has the agony of the world been so great or widespread. Tonight the sun goes down on more suffering than ever before in the world.'[26]

During the conference Sarah spent time with Anna Boettiger and Averell Harriman's daughter, Kathy. They got on so well they became known as 'the Little Three'. Visiting Russian towns and cities together, they were shocked by the level of deprivation.[27] They wanted to help, but when Anna gave a crowd of hungry children some chocolate, a Russian sailor with a gun and bayonet appeared and ordered the children away.[28]

The depressing poverty they witnessed was in stark contrast to the excitement of the conference. The three daughters were invited to a banquet at the Russian villa, where Stalin was 'in terrific form'. It was a friendly, fun evening.[29] A toast was drunk to 'the Little Three', and Kathy surpassed herself by responding in Russian. Only able to say five sentences in Russian, Sarah could not compete, and when she tried one of her stock phrases out on the Russian next to her, asking, 'Can I have a hot water bottle please?', he replied flirtatiously, 'I cannot believe that you need one! Surely there is enough fire in you!!'[30]

Unlike at Tehran, Gil Winant was not invited to the Yalta Conference. He felt frozen out by the close relationship between Harriman and Churchill and the prime minister's direct contact with the president.[31] When he heard he would not be accompanying Roosevelt to Yalta, Gil was distraught. He wired his old friend in despair about the decision.[32] Sensitive to his feelings, Sarah wrote to her lover that she had been thinking of him often and that he had been greatly missed.[33]

While Sarah and her father were away, Gil visited Clementine. In banter between Sarah and her mother, she asked, 'Are you flirting with my Ambassador? If so — desist for one moment and give him my love will you?'[34] In fact, Gil was having a far more serious conversation with Clementine. Evidently, he was planning a future with Sarah. He took Clementine to see a farm near Beaconsfield in Buckinghamshire that he hoped to buy. He told her that he cared very much for her daughter. When Clementine asked him about his 'private affairs', he told her 'that it will be all right'.

Although Sarah did not know Gil had told her mother about his feelings, Clementine immediately confided the news to Mary. She wrote, 'I feel it will happen. Except for the big difference in age they are absolutely suited.'[35]

The Churchill women were so intertwined that even though they tried to be discreet, nothing remained secret for long. It is interesting to see how supportive Clementine was of Gil and Sarah's relationship. Despite the many obstacles in their way, it seems that she believed they could make each other happy.

The Yalta Conference ended on 11 February. Although the prime minister was disappointed at the failure to settle satisfactorily the issue of the future of Poland, everyone was in a good mood and said affectionate goodbyes.[36] When Winston suddenly decided that he wanted to leave, his party had to pack up at top speed and make the long journey to Sevastopol. Once they were aboard the liner *Franconia*, Sarah revelled in the comfort, but she found all the luxury 'a little unreal' so close to the grim reality outside.[37] During the voyage, Winston talked to his daughter with complete frankness. With her, he was able to let down his guard. When she asked him if he was tired, he replied, 'Strangely enough, no. Yet I have felt the weight of responsibility more than ever before and in my heart there is anxiety.'[38]

The next stop for the Churchills was Athens. They only had a short time, but the grateful Greeks were determined to thank Winston for the support he had given them during their civil war.[39] He was treated as a returning hero, and a crowd of about 40,000 excited Athenians had packed into Constitution Square to greet them. Sarah wrote that she could not enjoy it because such vast crowds made her feel nervous, but her father was thrilled and addressed the masses. That night, in Winston's honour the Acropolis was floodlit for the first time since the German occupation.[40]

After Athens, Sarah and Winston travelled to Alexandria where they had lunch with President Roosevelt aboard his ship. To Sarah's delight, Gil was there, but they did not have long together before their paths separated. He did not have time to tell her about his discussion with her mother. He just said he had taken Clementine for a walk and got her into mud up to her ankles. Sarah wrote to her mother, 'Serve you right!!'[41] By keeping the tone light, it seems Sarah wanted to keep her relationship private and not discuss it in depth with her mother.

After lunch Sarah and Winston said farewell to Anna and President Roosevelt. It was to be the last time they would see the president as he was to die shortly afterwards.

Yalta was the last of the international conferences Sarah attended with her father. She knew how privileged she had been to meet the most powerful men in the war. However, like Mary, even more important to her was the time she spent with her father. She wrote that the months of living very closely with him had enriched her life 'immeasurably'; she would never forget them.[42]

During the final phase of the war, Mary continued to serve abroad with her unit. When Allied Forces crossed the Rhine in March, she rushed out and waved as a huge armada of planes and gliders flew overhead towards the heart of Germany.[43]

Although she always mucked in with her girls and demanded no special privileges, when she was off duty, Mary was let into an exclusive world open only to a Churchill girl or a princess. When Winston and Clementine visited Brussels, Mary stayed with them in the British Embassy. She was invited to lunch at the Palais de Laeken by Queen Elisabeth, the mother of King Leopold III of Belgium, who was in exile following accusations of collaboration with the Germans.

During her visit, Mary met Prince Charles, the bachelor regent, who had stepped in until a decision was made about whether his brother would return. The atmosphere at the palace was 'very royal', but she liked the prince, describing him as 'a very well preserved 40? Rather good-looking – and very shy.' Her warmth melted his reserve and, suddenly, he challenged her to a game of ping-pong. During the table tennis he became 'far less shy and quite gay'.[44] Evidently, there was a mutual attraction as Mary was invited to come and play again. She admitted to finding him 'rather fascinating'.[45] Perhaps it was at this moment that the idea of the regal Mary becoming a real princess first crossed her mind.

As Mary's marriage prospects looked increasingly promising, Sarah was in a very different position. Her divorce from Vic had finally gone through and she was pleased that there was minimal press coverage. When Winston heard the news, he whispered in Sarah's ear, 'Free!'[46] She admitted to her mother that her marriage had been 'an unconscionable time "dying"' but now it was over she hoped to be 'free as air'.[47]

However, the Churchill girls could never be totally free to live their own lives. Following their mother's example, they were expected to put their father first. In March 1945, Clementine left for a tour of Russia for her Red Cross Aid to Russia Fund, which had raised money to help with the deprivations caused by Hitler's advance into the country. Anxious before she left, Clementine wrote to Mary asking her to look after Winston if something happened to her.[48] It is telling that Clementine trusted her youngest daughter most to care for her father.

However, in the short term, with both Mary and Clementine abroad, Sarah was left in charge of Winston. She felt torn between the competing claims on her time as she was doing important work at Medmenham.[49] In a letter apologising for not being able to dine with him, Sarah told Winston that she could not walk out on her colleagues. However, at weekends she was released to act as Winston's hostess at Chequers and, as soon as her work was finished, she rushed off to join him.[50]

Even though it was exhausting, Sarah enjoyed both aspects of her life. She wrote to Clementine that she was 'well-established in your lovely basket' and lived 'like a queen for two lovely days at the weekend'.[51]

On VE (Victory in Europe) Day on 8 May 1945, as millions of people rejoiced at the news that the Germans had surrendered, Clementine was still in Russia and Mary in Belgium. On two days' leave in Brussels, Winston's youngest daughter spent the evening at a party in an apartment. However, her thoughts were focussed on what was happening at home and she went out on the balcony to listen to the BBC's broadcast of the King's Speech without interruption. After dinner with friends, she joined the enthusiastic crowds in the city's streets. As the enormity of the news sank in, she tried to get her head around the realisation that 'the day of deliverance' had finally come.[52]

Winston wanted all his daughters with him to celebrate the victory, so the next morning he arranged for Mary to be flown home from Brussels.[53] When she arrived back, Winston, clad in his dressing gown, welcomed her with open arms. After nearly six long years of war, it was rather an anti-climax to find the great war leader with just his cat, Smokey, for company. Mary wrote, 'It seems a little sad that at this hour of triumph my father was virtually alone.'[54]

Mary and Winston had lunch together on trays in his bedroom and he talked to her about the Germans. Showing characteristic magnanimity, he said, 'Retribution and justice must be done, but in the words of Edmund Burke, "I cannot frame an indictment against a whole people".'[55] After lunch, Mary went with her father to pay diplomatic calls on the French, American and Russian Embassies. As they drove through London in an open car, Mary was bursting with pride as jubilant crowds greeted Winston wherever he went.

That evening, Winston dined with Mary, Diana and Duncan, and afterwards they joined a huge crowd that had gathered in Whitehall to cheer him. The prime minister finished his impromptu speech with a verse from 'Rule, Britannia!', then the crowd roared in reply that 'Britons never shall be slaves'. Exhilarated by the atmosphere, Diana and Duncan rushed off to Buckingham Palace while Mary waited for Sarah to arrive. Eventually, at 12.15 a.m., she appeared with Gil and the trio set off to the palace, making it just in time to see the king and queen appear on the balcony. After joining the ecstatic crowds in cheering the royal couple, they went back to the American Embassy for eggs and bacon.[56]

Although this was Winston's moment of victory, Mary noted that he suddenly looked 'old and deflated with emotion, fatigue and a heart-breaking realisation of the struggles yet to come'.[57]

Once the war was over, the coalition government came to an end and Winston faced a general election. Although he had won the war, it was uncertain whether he would be the peacetime premier. The fighting had finished but there was still much work to be done.

Having supported her father, Mary returned to her unit. They arrived in Germany on 1 June, as part of the occupying force.[58] Conditions were primitive; they slept in tents and as they were living alongside a hostile people, girls were not allowed out without an armed escort.[59] Mary told her mother that they were all very spy conscious, thinking they saw 'Hitler in every moustache'.[60]

Mary was no longer the naïve young girl she had been at the beginning of the war, but the level of devastation in Germany shocked her. Many families were living in cellars under the debris of their shattered homes.[61] She was even more appalled when she visited the hospital at Belsen concentration camp. When the camp was liberated in April, the liberators found 10,000 dead in the camp and mass graves containing 40,000 bodies. Mary had never seen so much human suffering. Visiting the camp hospital, she was horrified by the sight of the starving mothers and 'shrivelled' babies. One survivor said to Mary in broken French, 'We are so happy to receive here today the daughter of the great man who has made our deliverance possible.' Mary nearly wept, she wrote, 'I have never seen such an ardour for life – such a victorious manifestation of the human spirit'.[62]

A month later, in July, Mary accompanied her father to the Potsdam Conference. Churchill, Stalin and the new American President, Harry S. Truman, were meeting to discuss how to administer a defeated Germany and establish a post-war order. Winston and Mary stayed at 23 Ringstrasse, a rose-pink stone villa looking out on to a lawn which sloped down to a 'romantic-looking but unhygienic lake'.[63]

Winston met President Truman for the first time at the Americans' villa, known as the 'Little White House'. On the walk home, Winston told Mary that he liked Truman 'immensely'. He felt that they talked the same language and could work together. Mary wrote, 'I nearly wept for joy and thankfulness, it seemed like divine providence [...] I can see Papa is relieved and confident.'[64]

Later that day, in 'sweltering heat', Mary went with her father to inspect the ruins of Berlin and visit Hitler's bunker. She was shocked by the 'utter squalor and dilapidation of the place – the stunned look on the faces of the people are not easily forgotten'. The press swarmed around, recording the historic moment when Churchill inspected the place where Hitler died.[65]

As before on previous trips, Mary's role was to look after her father and deal with any domestic matters. It was a far cry from her usual war work. She wrote to her mother, 'I'm trying to beat my sword into a feather duster.'[66] Most of her time was taken up with dealing with the chef and the gardener. When President Truman was coming to lunch, Mary had to sort out the menus and rearrange the house to make it look presentable.[67]

Fortunately, everything went smoothly. The Scots Guards formed a guard of honour as Winston met Truman at the garden gate and iced cocktails were served on the terrace, before the prime minister took the president into his study for lunch alone together. A few days later, Winston dined with Truman and Stalin. A fleet of cars drove up to the house and 'Uncle Joe' 'skipped' out in 'the most fetching white cloth mess jacket'.

Mary did not eat with the leaders, but her father invited her to join them later. Sitting on a stool behind Winston's chair, she watched as Stalin went around the room autograph hunting. The evening had gone very well and there was 'a general atmosphere of whoopee and goodwill'.[68]

The Churchills were only at Potsdam for half the conference. They had to leave early to return to England for the general election result.

As their wartime roles were now completed, it was the end of an era for the family. It was not just Winston who had fulfilled his destiny during the war, the Churchill girls had also found a new sense of purpose. It had been a chance for them to make their parents proud – a desire that was always foremost in their priorities. When Mary's war work was recognised with the MBE (Member of the Order of the British Empire) for distinguished and gallant conduct, she wrote to her father that, during 'these glittering years', she had seen, felt and learned a great deal. She added:

> In a strange way they have been happy years – and at all events memorable and exciting. And because of you and Mummie – and your love and tenderness and understanding to me any success or pleasure has seemed enhanced in my eyes because I feel <u>you</u> would be pleased.[69]

Although the war years had tested the Churchills to their limits, their experiences had bonded them even more closely together. Sarah felt that she had become much closer to her parents. She wrote to Clementine, 'I have always loved you, but not always known you and this sudden discovery of you both – is like stumbling on a gold mine.'[70]

Winston knew how much he owed his family. At his 70th birthday party, shortly before the end of the war, after a toast was drunk to him, he replied that his family were the 'dearest there are'. He told them that he had been 'comforted and supported' by their love. He then solemnly clinked glasses with each of them in turn. This acknowledgement of their role in his life made Mary cry.[71]

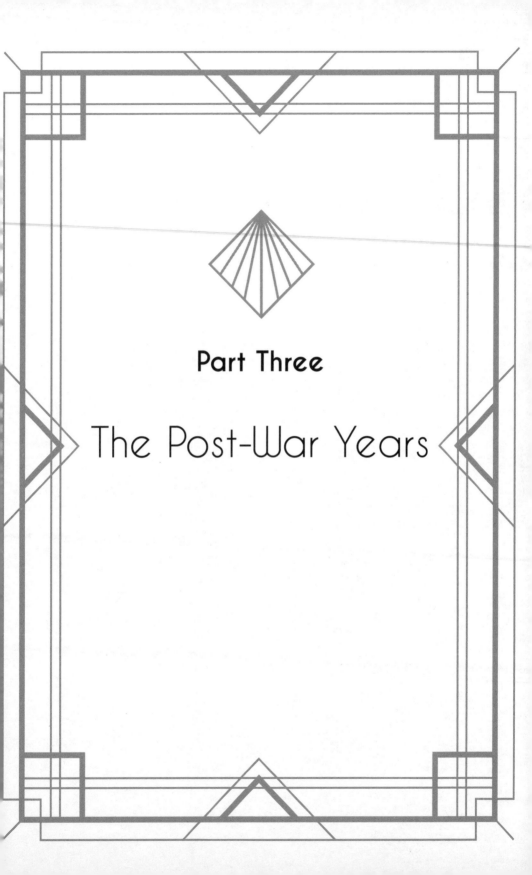

Part Three

The Post-War Years

15

The Aftermath

Once the war was over the shared aims that had united the Churchill family for six years came to an end. They now had a different type of battle on their hands – the 1945 General Election. The demands of peace were very different from the type of leadership needed to win the war and the Churchill girls were not complacent that their father would remain prime minister. However, as usual, they did everything they could to support him.

Sarah brought a touch of glamour to the election campaign, travelling around the country with Winston in an open car. She had been so bewildered by the vehemence of the personal attacks on him that she wanted to see for herself what voters thought. On the campaign trail, she was delighted to discover that he was as loved as ever by ordinary people.[1] Everywhere he went, he was greeted with smiles as the crowds shouted, 'There he is, there he is!'[2]

However, his daughters knew that this election was not just about personality; it was also about policies. They realised that the electorate trusted Labour, rather than the Conservatives, to rebuild the post-war world. While she was still in Germany, Mary subtly sounded out her army colleagues about which way they were going to vote. She found that many of them were Socialists.

After one Conservative broadcast, Sarah analysed why people were going to vote Labour. Showing her political shrewdness, she told her father they believed that it would curb inequalities of opportunity and the privileges of money and class. The Beveridge Report, which promised a welfare state, held 'the limelight'. Recognising that housing was a vital issue, she urged her father to begin a house-building programme with the same level of organisation and imagination he had used to win the war.[3]

Clementine wrote to Sarah, saying that her letter made a great impression on Winston and she considered it very wise.[4] Her advice influenced her father's campaign and in a broadcast on 13 June, at Sarah's suggestion, he elaborated on the coalition government's Four-Year Plan, prepared by Beveridge. He ended the broadcast by referring to a housing programme that would use 'war-time expedients' to ensure that homes were built for all. His commitment to this project was shown when he sent a memorandum to his Cabinet colleagues on 3 July stating that house building should be treated with the same energy that they had put into fighting battles.[5]

The political climate had certainly changed when even one of the Churchill girls was considering not voting Conservative. For once, Diana was the rebel. Shortly before the end of the war, she briefly showed an interest in the Common Wealth Party, which advocated Common Ownership, Morality in Politics and 'Vital Democracy'.[6] Clementine even worried that her eldest daughter would join the Communists, but that was never Diana's intention. She did, however, agree with some left-wing policies and thought the government was doing badly and should be defeated. When she voiced her opinions over dinner with her parents and her husband, Duncan turned pale and, to hide his bewilderment, concentrated on eating his pheasant.[7] For the first time, Diana was showing signs that she would not just conform and be the acquiescent political wife and daughter. Always interested in political ideas, she was thinking for herself and not just passively taking the same line as the men in her family. Evidently, thousands of other people across the country were doing the same.

In July 1945, Winston was voted out of office when Labour won a landslide victory. As he sat in his siren suit in the Map Room at the Annexe watching the results come in, Winston realised a political tidal wave had swept the country.[8] It was a devastating moment, which he handled with good grace.

After the result, Mary, Sarah and Diana joined their parents to commiserate. According to his daughters, his sense of humour never left him. When Clementine said, 'Winston, this may be a blessing in disguise,' Winston looked at her quizzically and replied, 'Huh, it's certainly very well disguised.'[9] Afterwards, Sarah wrote to him:

Darling you were never more wonderful than last night [...] You know your saying: 'In war resolution – In peace goodwill – in Victory magnanimity, in defeat defiance' – Well you taught me a great thing last night – In defeat – humour![10]

When the family spent one final weekend at Chequers, Winston's daughters found it harder to put on a brave face than their father did. In defeat, as in his triumphs, they rallied around. When Winston and Clementine had to move quickly out of No. 10 Downing Street, Diana immediately offered them her family home in Westminster to live in until they had found a place of their own. Reverting to childhood, Sarah dreamed of a Chartwell colony where all the siblings could once again live close to their parents. In her fantasy, they would each have a little cottage, milk cows and feed the chickens, and when their father rang an enormous bell, they would cross the lake and join him for the evening.[11]

Winston went on holiday to Lake Como, Italy, in September. Clementine did not want to go, so Sarah took her place and they stayed in a villa which was like 'a Hollywood palace'. Sarah's apricot and cream marble bathroom had so many mirrors that it made her giggle every time she got out of the bath as a 'chorus' line of six images of herself bowed at her.

With few other guests staying, Sarah was worried she would not be able to keep Winston entertained. As she looked at her father across the huge green glass dining table with four white-coated officers waiting on them, she felt like a 'goldfish in a bowl'. Knowing that a great deal depended on whether the chef could make consommé, it was a relief when the food turned out to be excellent.[12]

Away from the world, Winston and Sarah had an idyllic time together. Travelling in a motorboat, they went sightseeing and had picnics.[13] As Winston took up painting again, he remembered his hin- terland outside politics and regained his equilibrium. He told Sarah, 'I realise more and more that it very likely is a blessing in disguise – The war is over. It is won – and they have lifted the hideous aftermath from my shoulders.'[14]

Father and daughter had fun together. One evening, they played 'The Blue Danube' on the gramophone, then, with a twinkle in his eyes and a half-suppressed smile, he waltzed Sarah around the room.[15] They were partners in crime, and encouraged each other's mischie- vous side. On one occasion, Winston was fed up with the 'perfectly frightful' pictures in the villa, and removed one offending landscape from the wall and painted over it in vivid colours. As they sat back admiring his work, he said to Sarah, 'The most valuable piece of experience I can hand on to you is to know how to "command the moment to remain".[16] Sarah followed his advice and held on to these precious moments forever.

While Sarah looked after Winston, Mary took care of Clementine. Once again, their mother's role was to make a home for her husband. She organised the move into their new London townhouse, 28 Hyde Park Gate, and reopened Chartwell. She was finding a defeated Winston difficult to deal with and the stress of setting up two homes in austerity Britain was exhausting. Although Mary was having 'a glorious time' in Germany, she gave up her post to take a new role back in London because her mother needed her.[17]

Clementine's bond with Mary was so close that she immediately felt 'warmed and comforted' by her daughter's presence.[18] Sarah also understood what her mother was going through and wrote her a sympathetic letter:

> I expect you will feel a little low and tired and oppressed by the million domesticities that will now sink down upon you, for a bit. Six years is a long time to live at such a high tempo, knowing as fully as you did all the moments of anxiety and worry and decisions. You are bound to feel a reaction – as he does, and will for some time.[19]

Once their parents had begun to settle into their post-war lives, their daughters were free to focus on their own lives again. It was not easy; what they needed to do during the war had been clear, now they had to make decisions. Mary found it difficult to adapt to her desk job after the excitement of her wartime experiences, and the London social scene seemed trivial. Now aged 23, she decided that she wanted to find 'Mr Right' and 'live happily ever after'.[20]

As the daughter of Winston Churchill and an attractive young woman, she was extremely eligible. Her name was linked in the press with various suitable men, including royalty, and it seems the initial attraction between Prince Charles of Belgium and Mary developed into a more serious relationship.

Clementine described him in letters as 'your Prince Regent',[21] and when he visited Britain in January 1946, Mary was asked to host a dinner party for him at the Churchills' home. Helped by her sisters, she planned every detail to perfection.

Recalling Mary's first encounter with the prince, they dubbed it 'operation ping-pong'.[22] After a trip to the theatre, organised by Sarah, Mary held a dinner party for eight, which included her sisters for moral support. Once dinner was over, other guests, including Gil, Randolph and Duncan, arrived for dancing in the dining room. Perhaps rather disappointingly, the prince did not dance, preferring to sit on a sofa and talk to Gil. After more champagne and refreshments, the last guests departed, leaving Mary 'exhausted and happy amid the guttering candles'.

The next evening, Mary was invited to dine with the prince at the Belgian Embassy. She wrote to her mother that she found him 'extremely agreeable and rather subtle and a little sad'.[23]

When Mary and Winston stayed with Prince Charles and his mother on a visit to Brussels in September 1946, the press speculated that an engagement was imminent. The family were expecting it, too. It seems her parents would have liked their dignified daughter to become a princess, but nothing happened and, embarrassed by the rumours, Mary felt ill at ease when she sat next to the prince at a farewell lunch at the palace.[24] Clementine wrote to Sarah that the 'Belgian Affair' was 'a mystery not to say an enigma. Nothing definite has been said, but much hinted.'[25]

Sarah's aspirations were very different. Once she was demobbed, she returned to her acting career. In autumn 1946 she went to Italy, in the hope of becoming a film star, but also to escape from her tangled love life. She wanted to be out of the country when Vic Oliver remarried. She also needed space to think about her relationship with Gil Winant. He was still very much in love with her but, unfortunately, she no longer felt the same.

In Italy, Sarah starred as Elena in the historical drama *Daniele Cortis*, directed by Mario Soldati. He thought she was perfect to play the tortured, tragic heroine. After the destruction of the war, the Italian film industry was beginning to take off again. Now that it was full of film stars, Rome was soon dubbed 'Hollywood on the Tiber'.[26] After meeting up with London filmmakers, Sarah described it as a 'reunion of Park Lane, Soho and the Ivy'.[27] Sitting out in pavement cafés in the coral and amber city, she felt far away from grey London with its rain and rationing.

As well as socialising, though, she was working hard. After long days on the set, she became ill with a serious kidney infection. Deputising for her parents, Mary agreed to travel out to Italy to look after her. However, she was in the middle of a life-changing adventure of her own. On the way back from visiting Prince Charles, she met the tall, imposing army officer Christopher Soames at the British Embassy in Paris. Soames was educated at Eton and Sandhurst, and had fought bravely in the war. He was witty, a good mimic and a real party animal who loved being with people.[28]

The 26-year-old assistant military attaché only saw Mary for five minutes but it was love at first sight. He realised that she was the person with whom he had to spend the rest of his life. He pursued her to London and then, when he heard she was going to Rome, he impetuously jumped on the train she was travelling on and joined her on her journey. As the train emerged from the Simplon Tunnel in Switzerland, Christopher asked Mary to marry him. Taken by surprise, she refused.[29]

Mary arrived in Rome looking flushed and excited. She was faced with a dilemma – should she follow her heart and marry the dashing young army officer, or her head, and perhaps become a princess? She wrote to Sarah, 'I keep on feeling I am coming to a dangerous crossroads. I often meditate on how much one ever really controls our destiny. On how much events take charge, and one is swept along.'[30]

When Mary left England, she was sure that if Prince Charles proposed she would accept, even though she was not under any illusions about the 'strange, unnatural life' she would have to lead. At this point, she admitted to being 'swayed by ambition and vain-glorious aspirations'. She knew she could be a perfectly poised princess who could bring 'companionship and gaiety' into the lonely prince's life. However, when it came to the crunch, the romantic in her could not make that compromise. Although she felt devotion, respect and sympathy for Prince Charles and thought he was a 'noble figure', she could not imagine ever being in love with him. She realised that if they married, she would require 'so much courage and control and philosophy to truly accept and make myself happy'.[31]

Christopher's ebullient certainty solved her dilemma. Tall and 'joli-laid', she found him 'enormously attractive'.[32] He wrote to her that his love for her was 'immense, all-encompassing, fathomless. I love you with everything that I have, with my heart, my soul, my body.'[33] This was the type of relationship she had always wanted. She told her parents, 'He offers me his heart – I am sure of that – and a life – an English life – with roots and branches in England.' This combination was what Mary needed to be happy. She required someone totally devoted to her, who did not take her away from her parents. However, most crucially, they were completely in love with each other.

When Christopher proposed to Mary for the second time, on the steps of St Peter's, she accepted. After the emotional turmoil of the past, once she had made her decision, 'a feeling of certainty and peace' descended on her.[34] Although Mary had such a brilliant career in the war, she had always intended to revert to a traditional female role afterwards. With Christopher, she told her mother, 'the old junior commander in me has quite resigned!'[35]

Like Winston, both Mary and Christopher believed in destiny. They shared a strong religious faith which made them certain that the hand of God had brought them together – just in time. If Mary had accepted the prince, she would never have gone back on her promise to him.[36] On the evening that she got engaged she read the marriage service and knew in her heart that she could sincerely say those vows to Christopher.[37]

Like her mother before her, Mary was signing up to be part of a powerful political partnership. Her fiancé told her not to talk of just his career, from now on it would be 'OUR life – OUR career'. Christopher had already decided that he eventually wanted to go into politics. He wrote:

We have not been given all this blissful happiness for nothing. We would not be content were we to sit back and revel in that happiness without giving. We will give all. We know our aim, our object. Alone I would never have achieved it. God willing, together we will.[38]

Understanding her sister more than anyone, Sarah knew Mary had found the right man. She felt Mary had never been really at ease with any of her other boyfriends, but she was completely herself with Christopher. The relationship had developed so rapidly that Winston and Clementine had not met him yet, but Sarah immediately wrote to reassure them. She told them, 'He loves her the way we love her, and for the truly lovable and unique qualities we know her to possess.'[39]

Sarah was at a crossroads in her love life, too. While Mary and Christopher were in Rome, Gil paid her a flying visit. Inevitably, she must have compared the two very different relationships. She told her parents that she was more concerned about her younger sister's happiness than her own. She believed Mary deserved 'real happiness' because she could 'surrender her heart and life to one man'. Sarah knew she could never do that. This defining moment highlighted how close, but different, the two sisters were. Sarah wrote, 'It is an enormous joy for us to be together – for we love each other dearly – and across a difference of age and temperament, as sharply defined as sunlight and shadow, we understand each other.'[40]

In November, Christopher finally met Winston and Clementine for the first time. He described his impressions in a heartfelt thank-you letter to his future father-in-law:

> Lunch at Chartwell was for me, such a great awakening. Please believe me when I say that I had the impression of living for an all-too-short period of time in another world – a world of greatness such as I never believed existed.[41]

Unlike with Sarah's boyfriends, the Churchills were very welcoming. Although Clementine at first had some reservations about this stranger who had burst into their lives, Winston immediately liked him.[42] At his 72nd birthday party, he said, 'We are the past, and that is done with, Mary is the future.'

His daughter replied, saying that she hoped 'to found another English home' with Christopher but her childhood home would always be the greatest influence on her life.[43] She could not wait to settle down, writing to Sarah that she would never want to go back to her 'free' state. She explained, 'It is so wonderful feeling pledged and secure – and that you can claim someone's thoughts and love and care without reservations or inhibitions.'[44]

Mary was blissfully happy, planning every detail of her wedding with her increasingly stressed mother. It was not easy for Clementine to let go of her youngest daughter. Sarah knew what her mother would be going through. She wrote to her, 'Darling Mummie, You don't have to tell me – I know what a heart-aching wrench it will be for you to lose your Baby.'[45] Mary was also aware that her marriage would change her relationship with her parents. She knew it would leave Clementine 'rather alone'. She wished her happiness did not grieve her mother, but she was certain that she was doing the right thing.[46]

Even when the wedding had to be briefly postponed because Clementine was finding it too stressful to get everything arranged in such a short time, Mary and Christopher remained calm. In the run-up to the big day, Mary's 'Pale Prince' sent her a box of priceless orchids, which briefly made her think of the 'what-might-have-beens' – but she soon returned to 'the wide vistas of natural, fulfilled love of ordinary life, of children [...] – and above all I think of Christopher – And like St Paul I thank my God, on every remembrance of him.'[47]

16

Love and Marriage

On a bitterly cold day on 11 February 1947, Mary and Christopher Soames were married at St Margaret's, Westminster. As Londoners struggled through the harshest winter in decades, the Churchill wedding brought some much-needed warmth into the atmosphere. It was like a royal wedding.[1] Thousands of well-wishers lined the streets showing their political allegiance by booing the Labour Prime Minister Clement Attlee, who was one of the guests, and cheering Winston.[2]

Inside, a congregation of 800 waited to watch Mary make her vows. As Winston entered the candlelit church with his youngest daughter on his arm there was no heating due to the shortage of coal causing power cuts. Unlike Diana at her first wedding, Mary looked completely composed in a white satin princess-line dress. It was a poignant event for the whole family, Sarah wrote to her father describing 'how beautifully you both walked up the aisle so proud of each other'.[3]

Reflecting the close relationship between the royal family and the Churchills, there were wedding presents from the king and queen, the Princess Royal and Queen Mary. The reception was held in the ballroom at the Dorchester which was lit partly by candles and partly by electricity run by a small emergency generator.

After the wedding, the couple honeymooned in Switzerland. It was not the most romantic start to married life because Christopher suffered a duodenal ulcer and Clementine rushed out to support her daughter. The arrival of his mother-in-law on the honeymoon caused much amusement among the hotel guests.

Although the newlyweds had intended to live in Paris, Christopher's ill health meant their plans changed. It was agreed that he would leave the army and they would move to Chartwell and run the estate farms. Christopher admitted that his knowledge of farming was negligible, and his long-term aim was to go into politics, but the arrangement suited everyone. It was a great relief to Winston and Clementine to have their reliable daughter so close at hand.

Sarah had flown back from filming in Italy to be at her sister's wedding. Seeing Mary happily married made her reflect on how different her love life was. While filming *Daniele Cortis*, her director, Mario Soldati, had fallen in love with her. He was married with a baby, but this did not prevent them having an intense affair. In a letter to Mario, she admitted that 'to me love has been tears or ecstasy'.

Perhaps influenced by Mary's example, she now wanted a relationship which brought her fulfilment instead of yearning. She fantasised about living a simple, peaceful life with a compatible companion. Knowing they were both 'proud and possessive' of their work, she hoped that they could make films together and she could learn to direct as well as act, then they would 'retire to separate desks and solitude' to write.[4]

Sarah was always looking for a mentor/father figure, and she hoped Mario would teach her about the film industry. After her disillusioning experience with Vic, who had promised so much but delivered so little for her professionally, she did not want to make the same mistake again. She knew that she needed intimacy but also space and it was essential for her to keep her separate identity. She told Mario her career was non-negotiable, writing:

All my life I have searched for a companion who could understand this and with whom I could work – All my life is in the
theatre – I must work somewhere or somehow at it – it is not a
whim, it is not an escape from a social routine life – it is a desperate
urge – not desperate for success but desperate in the necessity I feel
for expression.[5]

Once again, this creative idyll eluded her. By spring 1947 both married men in her life, Gil and Mario, were making demands on her.
Neither could offer her what she desired and her father remained the
most important man in her life. She wrote a revealing letter to him
in which she explored her feelings in depth. Usually reticent about
discussing her private life with her family, she did not find it easy to
write but she needed him to understand her.

She explained that although she respected marriage and loved
children, that sort of secure life had never been right for her. She
feared that level of commitment and believed that her acting career
was incompatible with a 'true marriage'. She felt imprisoned by 'a
cage of circumstances, even affection' and had 'as powerful instinct to
be alone and free as Mary has to find a true mate and family'.

At times, she had tried to compromise and suppress her need to
please other people, but she had to be true to herself. Nicknaming
herself 'The Mule', because she was obstinate and did not breed, she
knew that she did not conform to Winston's idea of what women
should be. She joked, 'I suppose every now and then something goes
wrong, and a mule is born!!'[6]

Once filming had finished, Sarah returned to England and took a
month off to spend time with Gil. Once he had resigned his ambassa-
dorship, instead of returning to America he rented a house in Mayfair
to wait for Sarah.[7] She wrote to her mother that he needed her 'terribly' and was 'ill and despairing'. He was unhappy about both his
public and private life. Disillusioned with the post-war world, he

believed his political career was over. He was not as close to President Truman as he had been to his old friend Roosevelt, and so his dreams of creating a better society after the sacrifices of the war were shattered. Looking back to an era when he was happier, he found writing his memoirs torturous.

When she realised how desperate he was, Sarah felt guilty for going away to Italy 'chasing my windmills'.[8] She hoped to sort out their relationship and help him finish his book.[9] However, unable to resolve their problems, in August Gil returned to his home in Concord, New Hampshire, in America. He shut himself away from his friends and seemed unable to face the future. He was bankrupt, unwell and, most distressingly, he had lost his faith in humanity. On 3 November, he shot himself.

When they heard the tragic news, Sarah and Clementine were numbed with grief. Sarah believed that he died because he was 'spent'. He had given his all to other people, so when he needed strength for himself there was none left. She tried to remember the good times when they had experienced 'all that is possible of human happiness' before the 'despair and confusion of the last two years'. She told her parents, 'When the thought of his agony and the part I played in it gets too much – I try to remember he is at peace now.'[10]

As their affair was secret, Sarah could not grieve openly. She was not even sure it would be appropriate for her to attend Gil's memorial service at St Paul's Cathedral in London. In the end, she did go with her parents and, as the heavily underlined order of service shows, she found solace in the Christian words of comfort.

Although there were many reasons for Gil's suicide, inevitably Sarah felt guilty. She wrote to her father, 'It seems I must always hurt the person who loves me.'[11] Gil's tragic death was to haunt her future relationships. He was a great love of her life and in her diary, written eight years after his suicide, she confessed, 'I was so agonisingly in love with G [Gil] [...] All came to pass with G [Gil] – heaven and hell and death and hell.'[12]

Perhaps to help her grief, Winston invited Sarah to join him over Christmas for his painting and writing holiday at the Hotel Mamounia in Marrakech. It must have been a bittersweet return for Sarah because when she was last there, she had been at the height of her love affair with Gil.

Unfortunately, rather than being a restful break, the holiday added to the strains on her when, while they were away, Winston developed bronchitis. As Clementine was in England celebrating Christmas with Mary and Christopher, once again Sarah had the responsibility of looking after her father. By the time Clementine joined them, Winston was better, but Sarah was worn out with worry. Her mother felt guilty, writing to Diana and Mary, 'I feel rather ashamed because for three weeks she has been doing my job and much better than I do it myself […] What we need is a relay of "Mules". It's too much for one animal.'[13]

When Sarah returned from her holiday, she was still unwell. So, as supportive as ever, Diana went with her to Champneys health spa for some rest and relaxation.

The stability of Mary's life provided a striking contrast to Sarah's chaotic love life. Mary was very happy – not only did she have her husband, family and home but she was also able to live close to her parents. She wrote to her father, 'All this and heaven too!'[14]

Over the next eleven years, the Soames' five children, Nicholas, Emma, Jeremy, Charlotte and Rupert, were born. When she gave birth to her first baby, Nicholas, in 1948, Sarah wrote to her sister, 'Congratulations on achieving with such nonchalance, what is undoubtedly the greatest success of a woman's life.'[15] It was a poignant comment from a woman who was childless. It suggests that there were moments when she questioned whether her career was as fulfilling as motherhood.

As Sarah's remarks reveal, Mary shared none of their mother's issues about having children. Perhaps seeing her like a brood mare compared to Sarah, the mule, Winston told one friend who expressed admiration for his youngest daughter, 'She's a very serviceable animal too.'[16]

Unlike her mother, Mary made sure she did not miss out on her children growing up. She did not like spending much time away from her clan and she told Clementine that they made up such a large part of her daily life that she felt rather lost without them.[17]

Mary wanted to improve on her childhood for her children.[18] She recreated the best parts of it for them while being a more present parent than her mother. She took her family on holiday to the same places she had loved as a child and filled their lives with animals and healthy country pursuits. She told Winston that she hoped to show her family 'the same largeness of heart and steadfastness of love which you have always shown to yours'. She added, 'It is hardly in the nature of things that your descendants should inherit your genius – but I earnestly hope they may share in some way the qualities of your heart.'[19]

Clementine found it much easier being a grandmother than a mother. Both Winston and Clementine relished time spent with their grandchildren. At Chartwell, the Soames family lived at the bottom of the garden and Diana's children often came to stay. During the summer, it became a ritual for the children to invite their grandparents to watch them splash around in the swimming pool. Winston would observe from the sidelines, sitting in a comfortable chair with a whisky and soda in his hand. Mary had inherited her father's love of a good cigar. Her daughter, Emma, remembers watching her mother and grandfather sitting at the table after lunch having a competition to see who could grow the longest tail of ash on their cigar. Emma recalled, 'One day my mother got a longer tail of ash than he did, and he was terribly cross.'[20] Having his family so close made Winston feel like a patriarch. He wrote, 'It is a lovely home circle and has lighted my evening years.'[21]

Mary made sure she juggled her time carefully with all the people who needed her. When she had a romantic break with her husband, Clementine and Winston kept an eye on the children. When her mother was recuperating from an operation, she accompanied her on holiday.

By marrying Mary, Christopher gained not only the perfect wife but the ideal family. As his parents had acrimoniously divorced when he was a child, this stability was very important to him. He was nicknamed 'The Chimp' by the Churchills, and he immediately fitted in.

He became very close to Winston, taking on a role Randolph had proved himself incapable of fulfilling. Christopher's own father had always undermined him, so his relationship with his father-in-law was very precious. In 1949 Christopher introduced Winston to a new passion that filled the gap left by vacating the premiership – horse-racing. Together, they were very successful on the racecourse, most notably with the thoroughbred 'Colonist II', who won thirteen races.

During these years Diana, like Mary, was deeply involved in her own family life. After losing his Norwood seat in the 1945 election, Duncan had become a leader of the European Movement which was working for a united Europe. He encouraged his father-in-law to support the European Movement too.

In 1946 Diana and Duncan had stayed with Winston in Switzerland before his Zurich Speech, in which he outlined his vision for European unity, although he did not intend Britain to join united Europe herself.[22] Over the next few years, Duncan often lobbied Winston, pushing him to go further on the subject.

Duncan organised the international campaign which led to the creation of the Council of Europe. In his new role, he frequently travelled abroad and, when family commitments allowed, Diana went with him. Members of the European Movement admired her 'debonair spirit and smart clothes', but their respect went much deeper than superficial qualities. At one conference, when a delegate had a severe mental health crisis, Diana dealt with the situation with discretion. Woken in the middle of the night by the hotel manager, she calmed the man down and got him the medical help he required. Once he had recovered, she collected him from hospital and took him home to his wife as if nothing had happened.[23] Her common sense and compassion made a great impression on everyone who witnessed it.

17

Sarah Goes to Hollywood

A photograph was to change the course of Sarah's life in 1949.

The society photographer Antony Beauchamp had tried many times to photograph her, but failed dismally. Although he could capture the essence of the most beautiful women in the world, from Vivien Leigh to Audrey Hepburn, Sarah's 'quicksilver expressions' eluded him.[1] She became his ultimate challenge and, determined not to be defeated, he asked her if she would be his guinea pig for an experimental system of strobe lighting. Fascinated by this new technique, she agreed.

Forgetting the camera, she flung her head back excitedly to say something, and as her hair flew out behind her, Antony released the shutter. When he saw the result, he realised that it was one of the best pictures he had ever taken. Exuding *joie de vivre*, the image of Sarah leapt off the page. When it appeared on the cover of *Life* magazine in May 1949, it launched both Antony and Sarah's careers in America and led to them marrying.[2]

Even though she was deeply wounded by the death of Gil, Sarah was never a woman to be on her own for long. In many ways, Antony was just what she needed. A portrait photographer who could portray her as she wanted to be seen was the perfect partner for an aspiring actress who was so keen on her image.

A few years younger than Sarah, Antony's real surname was 'Entwistle', but he changed his name to the more aristocratic 'Beauchamp' when he became a photographer. During the war, he became the Official War Artist with the army in Burma. When he returned to London, with his film-star dark good looks and devastating charm, he was pursued by many glamorous women.

However, Sarah stood out from the crowd and his most difficult subject intrigued him. When they first had drinks together at the Dorchester Hotel away from a photoshoot, she became a completely different person. Antony described her as 'witty, vivacious [...] her beautiful features sparkled with happiness'. After that fateful drink, they both confessed to friends that they had met the person they were going to marry.[3]

With hindsight, it seems Sarah was on the rebound after the tragedy of Gil but, at the time, she believed Antony was just the light relief she needed. She later wrote that he brought 'gaiety and life' back when she was at a low ebb. She added, 'after G [Gil] I could have just faded away.' She needed Antony's 'forceful vital uncomplicated approach to life to challenge me back into the fight'.[4]

By the spring of 1948, Sarah was serious enough about Antony to introduce him to her parents at Chartwell. Naturally, he was apprehensive about the meeting, particularly as he had been warned that Winston did not like having his daughters taken away from him. He also realised that 'no less "suitable" prospective husband for his daughter could exist'.[5] Although Antony was at the heart of trendy London life, in the class-ridden British society of the 1950s, photographers were still considered as little better than 'tradesmen'.[6]

The lunch went better than Antony expected and Clementine put him at ease with her charm. After lunch, Winston showed him around the grounds and introduced him to his herd of cows. Like other visitors, he was immediately aware of what a happy and united family the Churchills were.

However, all did not go so well when Sarah invited Antony to join a family holiday in Monte Carlo. By this time, Antony realised Sarah was more inextricably linked to her family than he had at first imagined and their world of politics was very different to his. During the holiday, it became clear that it was not going to be 'smooth sailing' with Winston. At times, he would be a charming host, but at others, everything Antony did or said was wrong.[7] Whether it was snobbery, or he just did not like Sarah's boyfriends, Winston treated him with the same disdain he showed Vic Oliver.

After her father had been rude to her lover, Sarah wrote an angry letter to Winston, saying that she had been right to build a separate life for herself as 'the slings and arrows of family life are sharp indeed'.[8]

Although she was in love, Sarah wanted to go slowly. She told Antony that it was not her parents' opinion that deterred her but how she felt about herself. Showing her low self-esteem, she believed that he deserved someone better than her. So, rather than making a commitment to him, she decided to put her career first.

After making the film *All Over the Town* in England, she went to Canada and America to promote it. Her publicity tour coincided with the stunning photograph of her by Antony appearing on the cover of *Life* magazine. Overnight she became a celebrity in the United States and Gertrude Lawrence's husband, Richard Aldrich, cast her as Tracy Lord in *The Philadelphia Story*, a role made famous by Katharine Hepburn. Touring 'the straw-hat circuit' for ten weeks, she appeared in converted barns, rural playhouses and village halls across America.[9] Travelling around the country, she inevitably thought about Gil but, to distract herself, she focussed on her acting. As she stood in the wings on balmy evenings, listening to the crickets singing, she felt more at peace. She told her mother that the theatre gave her 'the only serenity I have ever known'.[10]

Finally, Sarah experienced the success she had worked for all her life. Critics said she was as good as Katharine Hepburn in the role of Tracy Lord, but Sarah was 'more soft and appealing'.[11] President

Truman came to see the play in Maryland and afterwards he wrote to her father, praising his talented daughter and sending a photograph and signed programme.[12] Winston replied that he would keep it among his most treasured possessions.[13]

However, Sarah paid a price for her professional success. While they were apart, her relationship with Antony was tempestuous and, communicating by telephone and letters, there were many misunderstandings. Once again, the man in her life found it hard to accept her dedication to her career. He accused her of 'heartlessness' and 'egomania'. Calling him 'Darling Beast', she complained that his constant scolding prevented her from enjoying to the full 'the biggest thing' in her life.[14] Warning bells should have been ringing after her experience with Vic, but once again she chose to ignore them.

Before deciding whether they could have a future together, Sarah needed to sort out her true feelings. The last few years had been chaotic emotionally and financially. Although she had been earning good money from her films, she forgot that she would have to pay a substantial amount of income tax. When a final demand came in for £450, she did not have enough money set aside to pay it.

At first, she was so embarrassed she refused to tell her parents. For the sake of her self-respect, she did not want to be dependent on them. However, eventually Antony wrote to her parents asking for help.[15] Diana lent her sister some money and Clementine paid the income tax out of the trust Winston had set up at the end of the war for his children and grandchildren. If she had been taken to court for failing to pay her taxes, it would have caused a scandal.

Sarah was ashamed of the mess she had made of her affairs. She wrote apologetically to Clementine that she was 'depressed and deflated at my utter incompetence'.[16] However, rather than chastising her, Winston sent a reassuring telegram telling her that he loved her very much and not to worry about finances as they would sort it out.[17]

In autumn 1949, Antony joined Sarah in America. She wrote to her parents telling them that she was likely to marry him, but she would make a final decision when they met again.[18] Before Antony left, he was summoned to an interview with Winston at Chartwell. As they sat by the pond, watching the golden carp, he grilled Antony on his prospects. He was concerned that Sarah's second marriage should be a success. The photographer realised it was not going to be an easy matter to win him over. Antony was in awe of his future father-in-law, but he wrote in his memoirs that he would have wanted to marry Sarah whoever she was. He was madly in love with her and he thought she was 'the most delightful and intriguing piece of red-headed mischief I had ever met'.[19]

Sarah still had doubts about their relationship, but on the spur of the moment she decided to marry Antony while they were on holiday in Sea Island, Georgia, in October 1949. When they arrived, they were both exhausted and stressed, but after a week of relaxation she awoke one morning feeling ready to 'take the plunge'. Sarah knew that Diana would understand her impetuous decision. She confided in her that suddenly she was able to stop thinking about the past and although 'nothing is – or ever will be forgotten – it is not a ton weight on my heart – that made it possible to even contemplate a future'.[20]

Relying on the kindness of strangers, in just a few days Sarah arranged a simple wedding. It could not have been more different from Mary's conventional marriage service. The hotel owner invited them to hold the ceremony in his drawing room, one of Sarah's cocktail dresses was quickly remodelled as a wedding dress, and a hat was created out of a pink veil and matching roses. The couple made their vows to each other, surrounded by flowering azaleas and palm trees. Then, as they watched the sun sink slowly over the Atlantic, they drank champagne with their new friends.

Unfortunately, the telegram telling her parents of her decision failed to reach them and they read about the wedding in the newspapers. Clementine was very upset and there was a temporary breach between mother and daughter. Except for a few telegrams, Clementine did not write for several months and she signed one telegram to Sarah about her business affairs very formally, 'Clementine Churchill'. Only Antony writing to his new mother-in-law and telling her how much her behaviour had upset Sarah ended the estrangement. It was like a repeat of Sarah's elopement with Vic and once again Clementine had made her daughter feel her love was conditional on her behaving in a certain way. Eventually she wrote a letter apologising:

> I am so sorry my darling Child – Now about not having written
> – I confess I felt numb and felt able only to telegraph from time
> to time. [...] Again I am sorry. Please forgive me and believe in
> my love and care for you [...] You are having an exciting arduous
> and nerve-racking life and I grieve that I should unwittingly have
> caused a shadow to fall over it.[21]

During the spring and summer of 1950, Sarah and Antony enjoyed a delayed honeymoon in Hollywood. They rented a palatial house by the ocean in Santa Monica and, driving around in a convertible, they felt 'very Hollywood'.

Living out a teenage dream, Sarah appeared as Fred Astaire's love interest in the film *Royal Wedding*. Sadly, the reality did not quite live up to the fantasy because Fred was 'a little gnome, a sprite, a spirit, and very, very shy'.[22] Although conversation was limited, once Sarah danced for him he was impressed; he applauded her saying, 'You can dance – you dance very well.'[23]

When they first performed together, it was rather awkward because Sarah was quite tall and Fred so short. He apologised for not having his toupee on as it would have made him two inches taller.[24] In the final cut, Sarah's part was minimal; she sat and sighed on a park bench with Fred, danced a few steps with him and, most importantly, she got him in the end.[25]

Combining glamour and the Churchill name, Antony and Sarah were very popular in Hollywood. Antony was soon photographing some of the most beautiful film stars, including Elizabeth Taylor, Greta Garbo and Marilyn Monroe. His photographs of Marilyn, looking her most sensuous on the beach at Santa Monica in a revealing yellow bikini, became iconic. The picture of the elusive Garbo also caused a sensation.

When they were not working, Antony and Sarah socialised with the Hollywood elite. At one of their parties, Zsa Zsa Gabor stormed out of the room when she spotted Marilyn Monroe. Gabor's husband George Sanders had just appeared in *All About Eve,* with the 'deliciously pneumatic' Monroe as his girlfriend. Apparently, her performance had been all too convincing. Sarah spent most of the party trying to pacify Zsa Zsa, who refused to leave the bedroom until it was time to go home.[26]

Unlike Ms Gabor, Sarah claimed she was never jealous of the women Antony worked with. She explained it would have been as ridiculous as her husband resenting her many handsome leading men.[27]

Sarah had never been fulfilled by socialising and became bored with the parties, so she left Antony in Hollywood to continue her career in New York. In 1951, she appeared in a comedy *Gramercy Ghost*. It was her first starring role on Broadway and she nervously stayed up late to read the first-night reviews. She told journalists, 'Now I know how father feels while waiting for election results.'[28] Asked by one interviewer if it was difficult being Winston Churchill's daughter, she replied with a laugh, 'There's no problem having him as a father. I wonder if he hasn't found it a problem having me as a daughter.'[29]

Diana flew out to New York to support Sarah and the two sisters had a great time together. Afterwards, Diana wrote to her father saying what a wonderful year it had been.[30]

Although her first love was the stage, Sarah also began to appear on television. She was a pioneer for the new medium. When Joyce Hall, the owner of the greeting cards manufacturer Hallmark Cards, decided to sponsor a television programme, he invited Sarah to appear in *The Hallmark Hall of Fame*. She readily agreed to be a narrator, actress and hostess on the show.

With her British reserve and husky mid-Atlantic accent, critics described her as bringing taste and intelligence to American television. Her father's legacy made some big names, including Eleanor Roosevelt, agree to be interviewed by her on the programme. Unfortunately, the interview with Eleanor did not live up to expectations: trained in discretion from her childhood, Sarah failed to ask the former first lady any probing questions, so there were no sensational revelations.[31]

Antony worked as photographic director of the shows, but it was not a harmonious partnership. There were echoes of Vic in the relationship. Sarah wrote, 'The Svengali traits in his nature came to the fore and he made me very uptight and, what was professionally very dangerous, he made me photographically nervous.'[32]

Sarah's televised acting was more ground-breaking than her interviews. She appeared in some of the first live ninety-minute programmes shown by the National Broadcasting Corporation coast to coast. When she played Ophelia opposite Maurice Evans in the first televised version of *Hamlet*, 50 million Americans watched – more people than had seen the Shakespearean play on stage during the 350 years since it was written. Foreshadowing the future, in the final mad scene she was forcibly restrained by a doctor and nurse. The *New York Herald Tribune*'s critic praised Sarah's 'poignant and sweet Ophelia', adding that her portrayal of madness was 'an infinitely more piteous and plausible spectacle than having her wander around the castle strewing flowers'.[33]

Thanks to television, Sarah became much more famous in America than she had ever been in Britain. In 1953, she was nominated for the Best Television Actress Award. However, despite her success, Sarah was homesick and missed her family. She wrote, 'Although I had left the "protecting wings", I was never far away in mind and spirit from my parents.'[34] Every night, in her mind's eye, she imagined the view of the Chartwell landscape from Mary's lawn.[35]

Once Sarah's marriage was a fait accompli, like Vic before him, Antony was accepted as a member of the family. As a wedding present that also doubled as peace offering, Clementine used money from the family trust fund to buy a house and studio for Sarah and Antony in Ebury Street, Pimlico, London. She was unable to always express her feelings, so she showed her love for Sarah by thoughtfully decorating and furnishing her new London home.

Winston hoped Sarah would one day live on the Chartwell estate and start a family, but it was an unlikely scenario for 'the Mule'. Although, at times, Sarah yearned for a settled home and children, she was not willing to sacrifice her career.

Left: Firstborn: Clementine with Diana as a baby 1909. (Alamy)

Below left: The Bumblebee: Sarah, aged 3. (National Trust Chartwell Collection)

Below: The Duckadilly: Clementine with Marigold as a baby, 1920. (Mary Evans Picture Library)

New beginnings: Chartwell. (Mary Evans Picture Library)

The
TATLER

Vol. XCVI. No. 1252   London, June 24, 1925   POSTAGE: Inland 2d.; Canada and Newfoundland, 1½d.; Foreign, 1½d.   Price One Shilling

Vandyk, Victoria Street, S.W.

MR. AND MRS. WINSTON CHURCHILL'S DAUGHTERS

DIANA, SARAH, AND MARY

Mr. and Mrs. Winston Churchill were married in 1908, and she is a daughter of the late Colonel Sir Henry Montague Hozier, K.C.B., who was a kinsman of the late Lord Airlie. The eldest daughter, Diana, was born in 1909, the second in 1914, and the youngest in 1922. Mr. Winston Churchill's brilliant political career hardly needs recapitulation. He has probably held more important offices of State than any other living Cabinet Minister

Diana, Sarah and Mary on the cover of *The Tatler.* (Mary Evans Picture Library)

Flower Fairies: The controversial Charles Sims painting of Diana and Sarah. (Alamy)

The Sketch

No. 1829.—Vol. CXLI.   WEDNESDAY, FEBRUARY 15, 1928.   ONE SHILLING.

REGISTERED AS A NEWSPAPER FOR TRANSMISSION IN THE UNITED KINGDOM AND TO CANADA AND NEWFOUNDLAND BY MAGAZINE POST.

THE DÉBUTANTE DAUGHTER OF THE CHANCELLOR OF THE EXCHEQUER:
MISS DIANA CHURCHILL.

Miss Diana Churchill, eldest daughter of the Chancellor of the Exchequer and Mrs. Winston Churchill, is one of the most important débutantes of the year. She was born in 1909, and is thus in her nineteenth year. Miss Churchill closely resembles her beautiful mother, who was formerly Miss Clementine Hozier, and is a daughter of the late Sir Henry Hozier, and of the late Lady Blanche Hozier.
PHOTOGRAPH BY SPEAIGHT, EXCLUSIVE TO "THE SKETCH."

The fashionable debutante: Diana on the cover of *The Sketch*. (Mary Evans Picture Library)

Winston's 'special chum': Diana walking behind Winston as he goes to the House of Commons to present his budget, 1928. (Alamy)

Diana with Winston, Clementine, Randolph and Charlie Chaplin at Chartwell. (Mary Evans Picture Library)

Winston with Mary and her pets at Chartwell. (Mary Evans Picture Library)

Diana, Winston and Clementine arrive in New York for his lecture tour, 1931. (Mary Evans Picture Library)

Diana with Winston on her first wedding day, 1932. (Mary Evans Picture Library)

Diana with her father going to her second wedding to Duncan Sandys, 1935. (Mary Evans Picture Library)

The Bystander

Sarah Churchill—Quietly Successful

Because Sarah Churchill is Winston Churchill's daughter she has not been allowed to develop her theatrical talent in the peaceful obscurity suitable to a young actress. Study the career of any top-liner and you will find they played a dozen or so small parts in which no one remembers them except their friends, and here and there a critic or manager. In those parts they learnt their art. Miss Churchill, on the other hand, has been good "copy" from the moment she went into a Cochran revue, and has escaped the limelight only by going on tour, as she did as young Mrs. Cherry in *Idiot's Delight*. Now she is in *Outward Bound* as one of the pair of lovers whose suicide makes them "half-way people" between life and death, and handles her not easy part with quiet success. The revival of Sutton Vane's play, with Louise Hampton, Cathleen Nesbitt, Stanley Lothbury and Terence De Marney in the chief roles, came from the "Q" to the New last Friday, and is being given every afternoon and on Wednesday and Saturday evenings.

On the cusp of fame: Sarah on the cover of *The Bystander*. (Mary Evans Picture Library)

Sarah and Vic Oliver arriving at Southampton. (Alamy)

The Transatlantic
Alliance: Gil
Winant signing
the Lend-Lease
Bill with Winston.
(Mary Evans Picture
Library)

The role model:
Mary in uniform
with Winston. (Mary
Evans Picture
Library)

Mary with Winston and his secretary on board ship as they cross the Atlantic to meet President Roosevelt. (Alamy)

Sarah with Roosevelt, Stalin and Winston at the Tehran Conference. (Alamy)

Winston, Duncan and Diana with their three children. (Alamy: W7DJYJ)

Mary, Clementine and Sarah at Buckingham Palace. (Mary Evans Picture Library)

A princess in the making? Clementine with Mary wearing a tiara. (Alamy)

THE TATLER

LONDON
NOVEMBER 20, 1946

and BYSTANDER

One Shilling and Sixpence

Postage: Inland 2d, Canada and Newfoundland 1d, Foreign 11d.

Vol. CLXXXII. No. 2369

Miss Mary Churchill Announces Her Engagement

Mary announces her engagement to Christopher Soames. (Mary Evans Picture Library)

The united foursome: Christopher, Mary, Winston and Clementine arrive in New York. (Mary Evans Picture Library)

The patriarch: Winston, Christopher and Mary with baby Jeremy. (Alamy)

Living the American dream: Sarah with Antony Beauchamp. (Alamy)

The American nightmare: Sarah being arrested in 1958. (Unknown source)

Under strain: Diana and Duncan near the end of their marriage. (Alamy)

Diana finds a new sense of purpose. (Alamy)

Surprised by joy: Sarah and Henry Audley find happiness at last. (Alamy)

The Churchill family at Winston's funeral in 1965. Clementine is supported by Randolph and followed by her daughters. (Mary Evans Picture Library)

The grandest of grande dames: Mary leads the Order of the Garter procession at Windsor with former prime minister, John Major. (Alamy)

Clementine's choice: The pictures she chose for her bedroom at Chartwell

Diana, young and serene. (National Trust Collection)

Looking regal: Mary wearing a headscarf. (National Trust Collection)

Sarah posing on a statue of a lion. (National Trust Collection)

18

Family Politics

By the early 1950s, the Churchills formed a formidable political dynasty. In the 1950 General Election both Diana and Mary were supporting their husbands. Duncan was elected in Streatham and Christopher in Bedford as Conservative Members of Parliament.

When the 1951 General Election was held, Sarah and Antony returned to England to make a documentary about it for American television. Sarah was with her father on election night and she was ecstatic when Winston became prime minister again. As Sarah and Antony were driving back to Hyde Park Gate from an election party at the Savoy, they saw their television crew filming from a scaffolding platform in Trafalgar Square. Pushing their way through the crowds, they clambered on to the platform to get a better view as the results were flashed up on a huge electric signboard. Antony described how, as each Conservative win came in, Sarah 'looking as wild and red-headed as I have ever seen her was leaping up and down like a sort of dervish'. Finally, the cameraman asked Antony if he could possibly hold Sarah down because she was practically bouncing the camera off the platform.[1]

Winston told Sarah that winning the election would be 'the last prize'. Back in America, she wrote to him:

I think it would be more, a fitting reward to those qualities in you which are not so quickly recognised – those of philosopher and humanitarian […] I just pray God that he will give you life and strength to achieve the last prize for the struggling world.[2]

Duncan and Christopher had been re-elected, but Randolph had once again failed to win a seat. Christopher was now more like a son to Winston. As the prime minister got older, he wanted peaceful, affectionate relationships with his family, not the argumentative explosions his son inflicted on him.[3] Randolph was jealous and referred to Christopher dismissively as 'The Master of the Horse'.[4]

Mary and Christopher always behaved with sensitivity to Randolph, even telling Winston and Clementine that they would not stay at Chartwell indefinitely because it might offend him. After divorcing Pamela at the end of the war, Randolph had remarried. He had a daughter, Arabella, with his second wife, June, but his home life was still unhappy. Increasingly bitter and often drinking too much, Randolph found it hard to sustain good relationships with many of the family.

Shortly after the election, Winston travelled to the United States to meet President Truman. Sarah and Antony were invited by their friend, the president's daughter, Margaret Truman, to stay at the presidential guest house, Blair House, in Washington.[5] They were present when Winston addressed a joint session of Congress. When his speech was over, the audience rose in their seats and it seemed as if the applause would never end.[6] The president, according to custom, did not attend but when Sarah and Antony returned to Blair House, they found Truman sitting in front of the television, with a gleam of admiration in his eye. 'I couldn't go,' he said to them. 'In any case, it was Winston's show and he was magnificent.'

While the prime minister dined at the British Embassy, Sarah and Antony had dinner with the Trumans. Exhilarated by her father's performance, Sarah was in one of her most vivacious moods, keeping the party amused with stories of the wartime conferences she attended.[7]

Although Sarah and Antony were living in America they wanted to be involved in Winston's premiership. They understood how important television would become in the promotion of politicians, so they offered Winston advice on how to capitalise on this new medium. Sarah even asked her father to consider a proposal for him to broadcast each week on American television and radio. She believed it could boost the special relationship between Britain and the United States and inspire and enlighten people.[8] Aware of the dangers of intervening in another country's affairs, her father explained that he could not do this as his position as prime minister fully occupied his time.[9]

Although all his son-in-laws were jockeying for position, throughout Churchill's 'Indian Summer' premiership the one who was closest to him was Christopher. He was made the prime minister's parliamentary private secretary. Using his position with discretion, he became one of his father-in-law's most trusted confidants.

In contrast, Duncan was relegated to the outer circles of power. In Churchill's new Cabinet, Sandys was hoping for promotion, but Clementine urged Winston not to make him Secretary of State for War as there might once again be charges of nepotism. Instead, he gave his son-in-law the lesser position of Minister of Supply.[10] Duncan's relationship with his father-in-law became less close than it had been previously. He was rarely invited to No. 10, Chartwell or Chequers.[11] When they did get together, unlike Christopher, Duncan could not follow Winston's moods. If they discussed politics, Winston did nothing to conceal his boredom with his son-in-law's arguments.[12]

No doubt her father's change of attitude to her husband did little to help Diana's marriage. However, the underlying problems were between the couple. Duncan often travelled abroad without Diana and her children were also growing up and beginning to lead their own lives.

Diana had built her life around supporting her husband and children. Although she had not been a hands-on mother – her children were largely brought up by a wonderful nanny – unlike her mother, she rarely left them for long periods and she usually looked after them on the nanny's day off.[13] As her family's needs changed, she found it hard to adapt. Sarah wrote to her mother fearing that there was a void in her older sister's life that she did not know how to fill.[14]

By 1953, Diana was suffering from mental health problems. Tensions that had festered beneath the surface for years now erupted. Although Diana's letters to her mother were usually warm and loving, when she was depressed the underlying resentments recurred. Mary wrote that their relationship which had, for many years, been 'a fragile construction', now sometimes came near 'breaking point'. Diana inflicted 'harsh, but forgivable verbal wounds' on Clementine.[15] On one occasion, Randolph was called to help when his sister was found hiding in some bushes near her house holding a carving knife. He afterwards told a friend that taking the knife away from her was 'like disarming a butterfly'.[16]

Diana was treated by the well-known psychiatrist Dr Carl Lambert. The 'society shrink', who looked rather like Aristotle Onassis, was renowned for his success in enabling his patients to cope with the pressures in their lives. He dealt with their symptoms first before spending time examining the underlying causes. He believed that psychological disorders were often reinforced by habitual responses to certain triggers, so if the response could be modified, the disorder could be held at bay.[17]

Under Lambert's care, Diana went into a London nursing home. All her family wanted to help, but it was hard to know what to do. Her father sent a sympathetic note, telling her that he was thinking of her and sending his love.[18]

After treatment in the nursing home, Diana recuperated in Alassio, in Italy, with her youngest daughter, Celia. The clinic was more like a luxury hotel than a hospital, the nurses were unobtrusive and Diana had a session with Dr Lambert every day. The treatment combined with the brilliant sunshine and blue sea helped her to relax. Having her daughter with her also made her feel better. She wrote to her parents, 'Celia is a great joy to me – she is so sweet and companionable.' Showing her usual thoughtfulness, even in her darkest hours she thanked Winston and Clementine for all they had done for her over the last months and apologised for being 'such a nuisance to everyone lately'.[19]

However, just as Diana seemed to be getting better, the stability of the whole family was rocked in June 1953 when Winston suffered a severe stroke. At the age of 78, the celebrations for the coronation of Queen Elizabeth had been a hectic and demanding time for him. Shortly afterwards, during a diplomatic dinner in Downing Street, he was taken ill. After making a speech he found himself unable to rise from his chair. Some guests thought he was drunk, but Christopher realised what had happened and immediately dealt with the situation, covering up for his father-in-law with the visitors.

The stroke involved a slow leak in the brain. It left Winston finding it difficult to speak and almost totally paralysed on the left side. There were fears he might not survive.

As soon as Sarah heard the news she flew back from America. When Mary collected her from the airport, she explained that Winston was alive, but Sarah should prepare herself for a shock. When Sarah first saw her father at Chartwell, she found it very distressing. She quickly went over to him and kissed him on the brow. Although he could not answer, his eyes flashed, and he managed to squeeze her hand.[20]

During those crucial days, Christopher's role was pivotal. With the help of Winston's press baron friends, the prime minister's true condition was kept secret from the public and all but a few trusted confidants. Assisted by Churchill's private secretary, Jock Colville, Christopher read his father-in-law's papers and made any unavoidable decisions for him.[21] Both men used their temporary powers with restraint, acting as they thought Winston would have done rather than imposing their own views.[22] It was an unconstitutional state of affairs but their actions allowed Winston to keep the premiership until he had recovered enough to resume the role.[23]

As Winston got better, his daughters were once again stalwartly by his side. Sarah wrote, 'It helps me to be near you. I wish I could do something more than just love – to help you regain completely your strength. But it is joyful and merciful to know that you will.'[24]

In September, Mary and Christopher went with Winston to Lord Beaverbrook's villa, La Capponcina, in the South of France. Winston was in low spirits and not sure whether he should carry on as prime minister. Although Mary and Christopher loved spending time with him, they felt impotent and Mary wrote to her mother, 'We yearn to be able to do more than be the mere witnesses (however loving) of his sadness.'[25]

The first test of the prime minister's health was his Conservative Conference speech at Margate, Kent, in October. When the old man passed with flying colours, Duncan and Diana were waiting for him at Downing Street to celebrate. Meanwhile, back in America, Sarah wrote to him that she cried with pride when she heard how well he had done, but she begged him not to overdo it, 'Since you pack more into a day than anyone else living'.[26]

Winston remained in office for the next eighteen months and, throughout that time, Christopher was by his side while Mary supported her mother. Her husband's illness left Clementine feeling very low and the demands of entertaining just added to the burden.

So that they could share the load, Christopher and Mary had a bedroom at No. 10 and often helped at Chequers weekends.[27] Then, when Winston went to the Commonwealth Prime Ministers' Conference in Bermuda in December 1953, Christopher went with him. It coincided with the presentation of the Nobel Prize in Literature to Churchill. Clementine went to Stockholm with Mary to receive the accolade for her husband, and mother and daughter stayed for several days in the royal castle as guests of the king and queen, then Clementine, looking regal in a tiara, spoke at the state banquet on behalf of Winston.

Although everything seemed to be getting back to normal, that illusion was soon shattered. Sarah and Diana were both near crisis point and no doubt Winston's illness had destabilised them further. Seeing him so close to death made them face the fact that their guiding star was not immortal. As Sarah told one interviewer, 'The time will come when I shall have to live in a world where he isn't – and I don't see how I can.'[28]

Adding to the pressures, Sarah's marriage to Antony was breaking down. The demands of their careers meant that they spent four or five months of the year apart. While Sarah was still working in America, Antony had returned to London to produce a new television series. When they were together it was 'dynamite', and they often argued as they both had such strong personalities.[29] Antony's mother, Vivienne, later said, 'She [Sarah] and Tony were far too much in love. I feel that they were too dynamic for each other. Neither would ever give in.'[30]

As their marriage deteriorated, Antony wrote to Winston setting out his side of the story. He admitted that he was not 'the easiest or most uncomplicated husband', but he added that although Sarah was 'a dear and lovable person', she had 'an incredibly obstinate streak to her nature which is terribly exhausting and which causes much unnecessary unhappiness for both of us'. Antony hoped for a reconciliation, but he believed that would only be possible if Winston was on his side. He wrote, 'You have an overwhelming influence upon her, and I can do nothing if you too stand against me.'[31]

Although Sarah was unhappy, repeating the pattern of the past, she still did not want to sever all links with her husband. There were several reconciliations, followed by rows, before they finally separated. Her parents were understanding, but she disliked acknowledging another failure to them. She admitted that the child in her wanted only one thing – for them to be proud of her.[32] She was unable to cope with her emotions and started to drink too much. There was an embarrassing incident in a Hollywood bar, where she had a disagreement with a waiter. He tried to take her beer away because under Californian law all drinks had to be removed by 2 a.m. She made a derogatory comment about American laws which sparked a heated debate in newspapers across the United States and Britain about her behaviour. As she was Churchill's daughter, a minor argument was turned into an international incident.

Diana's mental health problems also recurred at the end of this stressful year. In December, Dr Lambert suggested that she should become a patient at the Crichton Royal, a pioneering psychiatric hospital near Dumfries, Scotland. The hospital had become known for its outstanding contributions to psychiatric research under the leadership of German Jewish émigrés including Dr William Mayer-Gross. Diana went by her own wish to the hospital.

While she was there, she underwent insulin shock therapy.[33] It was physically and mentally gruelling, but as usual she put a brave face on the situation for everyone else's sake. At first, she felt in a daze but gradually she began to feel better.[34] She told her father that the nursing was excellent and she received 'every imaginable kindness'.[35] Her sense of humour survived the rigorous regime and she wrote to her mother that the insulin treatment was 'strenuous', joking that she was becoming 'a complete "Coma Queen"!', but she reassured Clementine that she was responding well to it.[36]

Although she was very impressed with the hospital, Diana was homesick. Duncan and the children spent Christmas at Chequers, then on Boxing Day he travelled to Scotland to see his wife. Celia made the long journey with her nanny and Clementine; Mary and

Sarah also visited.[37] It cannot have been an easy experience for any of them. After seeing her sister, Sarah wrote to Winston:

> It is bewildering and fearful – but still she has 'the courage of a lion' and is not giving in an inch. She wants to get well and believes there is a happy future for her. I believe there is too – only it will be a tight-rope of sense and sensibility we will all have to walk for some months to be of help to her.[38]

With their strained relationship, it must have been particularly difficult for Clementine to visit her daughter. However, Diana was delighted that her mother was coming and her only concern was that she should not tire herself out making the journey. The visit was a great success, and Diana wrote to Clementine that she enjoyed it 'tremendously'.

As Diana got better, she wrote warmly to her mother, calling her 'Darling Mummie' and thanking her for her thoughtful presents.[39] When she was well, Diana would never have wished to hurt her, but it was her depression which made her reopen old wounds. Always the peacemaker between the two women, Sarah told Clementine that she must forget what Diana said to her in 'her agony of despair'.[40] The nature of her illness meant historic resentments became irrationally intertwined with present grievances. Reflecting on this, after seeing Clementine, Diana had a happier visit with Duncan.[41]

In spring 1954, Diana was able to return home. Her family were delighted to have her back and Winston did everything he could to make her feel wanted and valued. She helped him host a weekend at Chequers and, according to her father, she coped admirably.[42] She was also given the task of organising the prime minister's party for the Trooping of the Colour in June.[43] The event went perfectly, and Sarah described her sister as looking her 'very best'.[44]

The last years of Churchill's premiership were difficult. His parliamentary colleagues, particularly Anthony Eden (who was married to Winston's niece, Clarissa), felt it was time for him to resign. Christopher was aware of the situation and acted with sensitivity. He did everything he could to protect his ageing father-in-law and make the administration as successful as possible.

When Winston finally left office in April 1955, it was a momentous event for the whole family. Mary wrote a letter to her mother full of understanding about the role she had played in the prime minister's life:

> It must seem like the end of a long, long journey, full of harassments and trials – and triumphs and bitter-sweet joys and anxieties. But what a story! And I know it would not have been such a splendid one if you had not been there.[45]

Looking back nostalgically to her childhood, Sarah wrote to her parents that she hoped they would now be able to have fun together, which she had missed since she grew up. She added that they should enjoy 'the wonderful things we have that other families don't have – we [are] most securely tied by our love for each other'.[46] Over the next few years, that love would be tested to the limits.

19

Sarah: From Hollywood to Holloway

The years after Winston resigned as prime minister were difficult for all the family. Clementine described leaving office as 'the first death and for him, a death in life'.[1] Without a sense of purpose, the former war leader gradually declined into old age and periods of depression were accentuated by his failing physical health. It was also very difficult for Clementine as her life had been dedicated to helping her husband fulfil his destiny. Their daughters tried to be supportive, but they were facing challenges of their own.

In 1955 both Sarah and Diana's mental health was unstable. After the problems of the previous year, Diana had a relapse and ended up in the Maudsley Hospital in London. According to Sarah, she felt she was an 'outcast'.[2] Her marriage was on the rocks and she did not feel that her place in Churchill family life was secure.[3] Sarah told Clementine that her sister had a feeling that she had been wronged; this did not relate to any one person or any specific time in her life, but the perception persisted. She also felt unfulfilled and believed that she had experienced a lack of recognition.[4]

During this crisis, Sarah did her best to help her sister. She wrote, 'She knows I believe in her grief and pain and that a way can be found to serenity and that while I am alive she will never be abandoned.'[5] Trying to help in practical ways, Sarah made enquiries in

America about the latest treatments for mental health problems. She discovered that they were moving away from electroconvulsive and insulin therapy towards powerful new sedatives.[6]

However, Sarah had to be careful not to get too involved in her sister's suffering for the sake of her own mental health. She found it very draining dealing with Diana because she was unable to distance herself emotionally from her distress.[7] As Sarah's marriage to Antony came to an end, she also felt 'a great void' inside her and 'a desperate sense of yet another failure'.[8] She suffered from panic attacks and felt an evil force around her. To calm herself, she thought about her great love for her parents. Like a child, she desperately longed to be in their arms. She wrote in her diary that she was having some very bad spells but, when she was with her father, she was all right.[9]

In November, both sisters joined Winston for a holiday at La Capponcina in the South of France. The villa was 'drenched in tranquillity' and the ideal place to escape from real life.[10] When Diana arrived, she still felt rather dazed from her medical treatments and was very quiet. At first, Sarah felt she was walking on 'egg-shells' and feared that she would say the wrong thing, but she found Diana was in an accepting frame of mind and jumped at any positive ideas she suggested to help her. Sarah decided that what her sister really required was 'a philosopher'. She explained, 'I mean "a thought", an "idea" that she can chew on helps her enormously.'[11]

Being with her father provided just the stimulation she needed. He was one of the few people who seemed able to help both his daughters. His rock-like presence made them feel more secure.[12] Sarah wrote to him, 'You can release tension and confusion in a person – in a few words – more than anyone – and you always give courage.'[13] She told one interviewer that her father was able to inspire in his children the same feeling he gave people in the war, 'It's a feeling that no matter how grim things are, if you hold on, and do your best, all will be well in the end'.[14]

As she gradually recovered, Diana appreciated her father and sister's loving care. She told Clementine that Sarah was 'quite angelic' and was looking after her 'most devotedly and imaginatively'. She added that Winston had been 'simply divine'.[15]

According to Mary, their father did not really understand psychological troubles.[16] However, during Diana's illness he did his best to help. He shared with her his own experience of 'Black Dog', his term for depression, when he was Home Secretary, four decades earlier.

Sarah believed that Diana suffered from '"inbred" melancholia'.[17] Some biographers have claimed that she had a similar depressive tendency to her father.[18] This is debatable as historians disagree about the extent of Winston's mental health problems.[19] His doctor, Lord Moran, believed that he had an inbuilt tendency to suffer from depression, which he inherited from his Churchill ancestors.[20] Developing this idea further, the distinguished psychiatrist Dr Anthony Storr claimed that Churchill had a prolonged and recurrent struggle with depression that was independent of events and circumstances.[21]

However, other biographers have been more cautious about the significance of depression in Winston's life. His official biographer, Sir Martin Gilbert, argued that although Churchill suffered from time to time from 'Black Dog', it was in reaction to serious misfortunes for himself or Britain. These episodes were usually brief and never significantly disabling until his cerebral circulation was impaired in advanced old age. They were not defining features of his life.[22]

Winston's recent biographer, Andrew Roberts, agrees. He believes that when there was a catastrophe, Winston got depressed, as anyone else would in the same circumstances. He dismisses as a myth amateur diagnoses that Churchill was a depressive or even bipolar.[23]

The latter biographers' arguments are convincing. Winston's experience of mental illness was on a totally different scale from Diana's. Although her problems were more extreme than either of her parents', it seems that they were more like her mother's lifelong bouts of anxiety and, at times, full-blown depression than her father's occasional 'Black Dog'.[24]

During this period, Clementine's own problems meant she was in no fit state to help her daughters. Now in her late sixties and exhausted by the stresses of family life, she was unhappy and suffering from neuritis which was very debilitating.[25] It was a vicious circle; all three women loved each other deeply, but they were fighting their own private emotional battles.

Once she was back from America, Sarah spent a great deal of time with her mother. She appreciated Clementine sharing her feelings because it made her feel closer to her. As in the past, she acted as a go-between with her mother and sister, helping them to heal their fractured relationship.[26] Sarah wrote to Clementine asking her to pray that 'we can all yet be happy', but she was not hopeful, adding, 'I am powerless and incapable in front of your despair.'[27]

Hope was in short supply in those dark years. Sarah's marriage to Antony was over, and although they did not get divorced, they separated and sold the Ebury Street house. Sarah went back to work in America while Antony remained in England. They both sought solace elsewhere, but Sarah found her flirtations with other men did nothing to lessen her sense of loneliness and defeat.

In August 1957 she returned to England to tell Antony she wanted a divorce. The night before she contacted him, she could not sleep and just walked up and down her room singing, 'I'm getting buried in the morning'. At seven the following morning, Clementine phoned to tell her that Antony had committed suicide. He had taken an overdose of sleeping tablets; he was only 39 years old.[28]

The reasons for a person taking their own life are complex and often unfathomable. Apparently, Antony had failed to get a television deal he had been working on and was in debt. However, there were underlying problems. Sarah wrote in her autobiography that there was a dark side to Antony's character and his emotional instability concerned her. There were several incidents that made her believe that he had a death wish. On one occasion, he drove to a cliff and said he thought he would drive the car over the edge, then he started laughing and said, 'But I didn't because I thought what the world would miss without me.'[29]

Although they had very little contact for the previous two years and Antony had been seeing other women, his mother, Vivienne, believed he only really loved Sarah.[30] After his death, Sarah identified his body and attended the inquest. At his funeral, many of the other women in his life sat sobbing in the pews behind her and his mother, but when the service was over Vivienne walked out of the chapel with her arm around a tearful Sarah. Throughout this ordeal, Diana was quietly there by her sister's side. Mary wanted to support her too, but at this time their relationship was not so close. Mary wrote to Clementine, 'Sometimes her unhappiness and my happiness have put a distance between us, that the difference in our ages never has.'[31]

Back in America, Sarah wrote a thoughtful letter to Antony's mother. She found it heart-breaking to think that even the people who loved him couldn't reach him in 'the terrible moments'. From her own experience, she understood his anguish, adding:

> I know how lonely and frightened he was – but his pride would not let anyone help him – and I understand so well, for I am proud too and when I am frightened I want to run away from my friends so that they shouldn't see my panic.[32]

This was exactly what Sarah did as she faced her latest crisis. No doubt Antony's suicide brought back painful memories of Gil's death just a decade before. Rather than staying close to her family and friends, she withdrew from them, instead choosing to live alone in a beach house in Malibu, near Los Angeles.

She always found being near the sea therapeutic. In a letter to her father, she described herself as sitting on a rock like a pelican just letting the waves splash over her.[33] However, alone with her thoughts, this self-imposed isolation was not good for her. She turned to drink and barbiturates to deaden her pain.

In January 1958, a telephone switchboard operator heard her on the phone for two hours using language heard 'only aboard ship and in barracks'.[34] He informed the police, who came around to complain that she was disturbing the peace. When she stepped outside her house, one of the police officers arrested her and charged her for being drunk. Since the traumatic experience of her childhood operation, she had always had a visceral reaction to being restrained. When the police officers pushed her into their patrol car, she struggled and kicked. After being questioned at a small police station, they took her to Los Angeles County Police Headquarters. According to Sarah, officers slapped her and when she fought back put her into a straitjacket. It seems someone tipped off the press, because on her arrival a barrage of photographers and television cameramen were there to greet her.[35] Photographs of a vulnerable-looking Sarah being restrained by policemen appeared in newspapers across the world.

Deeply concerned about her, the family rallied round. Her parents sent a telegram saying, 'Our thoughts are with you always.'[36] Clementine took it worse than Winston; she was very worried about Sarah but also upset by the embarrassing publicity.[37] When Diana went to see her father, he had all the press cuttings spread out on the floor and was on his hands and knees putting the various factors of the case in order. He told Diana he thought Sarah could win the case, but Diana replied she did not think Sarah wanted to. Randolph flew to Los Angeles to support her but as usual only made things worse by antagonising the press.[38] He told Sarah to plead guilty and that it would only be a 'nine days wonder'. However, he was wrong, as she wrote in her memoirs, it turned out to be 'a ten-year trauma for me and it was to leave an everlasting scar'.[39]

When Sarah appeared in court, she told the judge, 'I think I was more ill than drunk.' The London papers agreed. They were critical of the Los Angeles police for arresting her, arguing that doctors not the police should have been called.[40] The judge was also sympathetic. Although he fined Sarah $50, he commented, 'This matter has attracted great interest not because of the charges but because you are the daughter of the world's most famous statesman.'[41]

Showing characteristic courage, Sarah appeared in a television play shortly afterwards. As she gave one of the best performances of her life, everyone acknowledged it 'took guts'.[42] Many observers were aware of the pathos of the situation – just as she was reaching her peak as an actress, her talent was being undermined by her drinking problem. Her producer said, 'She has an extraordinary talent. She must be saved.' When asked if he believed she could be, he paused and then replied, 'She's Winston Churchill's daughter. Like him she may lose a few battles, but she'll win the war.'[43]

After completing her television work, Sarah escaped to join her father in the South of France. They stayed with Winston's literary agent, Emery Reves, and his American mistress, Wendy Russell, at their villa, La Pausa. Since 1956, Winston had spent up to a third of the year with them.

The former home of Coco Chanel, La Pausa was the ultimate in style. Its minimalist white décor showed off to perfection Reves' collection of Impressionist paintings.[44] Wendy, who was a former model, spoilt Winston, pandering to his every desire. Although Clementine rarely stayed, Sarah often visited and she became close friends with Wendy. In her hour of need, 'Pausaland' provided a much-needed haven for her.

When Winston developed pneumonia, Clementine flew out to join them. Sarah was grateful that her parents did not question her about what happened and were just quietly supportive. After a family discussion, she agreed to go to the Bircher-Benner clinic in Zurich, Switzerland. The centre had been founded in 1903 by Dr Maximilian

Bircher-Benner, the visionary pioneer in holistic natural healing who believed that diet, exercise, work and spiritual peace were essential to a healthy life and mind.[45] Feeling more like a health spa than a hospital, clients were offered a dietary and diagnostic regime while staying either on the campus or in a hotel nearby.

The whole family supported Sarah as she took the first steps to getting better. As with Diana during her illness, rather than pretending the problem was not happening the Churchills made sure their daughter got the best treatment available. The whole family showed a sensitivity to mental health problems and addiction which was unusual in a less well-informed era. Mary and Diana visited Sarah during her treatment and Winston told her, 'We are all in this adventure with you.'[46]

Sarah's doctor's reports from the clinic give a revealing insight into her character. She reported that Sarah possessed high intelligence, power of judgement and discipline. She was a personality of ethical depth and maturity, but she was sensitive and sought protection and security. She concluded that she needed psychological help not psychiatric treatment.[47]

When Sarah saw a psychoanalyst at the clinic, he found her unsure of herself, sometimes even helpless, and in great need of affection. He believed her alcohol problem was partly a chaotic protest against an order of things that was constantly being forced on her by the demands of public life with little consideration for her personal emotional needs. There was also a 'regressive shrinking' from the demands of her high position. It seemed that she tried to force the affection of her family to demonstrate the seriousness of her distress. Her father's fame made it difficult for her to discuss intimate family details, even with her analyst. One of the few things she would say was, 'My mother doesn't know her children, but she is alarmed by them'. The analyst noted how dependent she was on her parents' opinion. She wanted to free herself, but by her behaviour constantly renewed that dependence.[48]

It seems that the old dynamics of their childhood continued into adulthood. When they were unhappy, both Sarah and Diana became critical of their mother. Sarah complained in her diary that Clementine did not really expect her to succeed.[49] Winston's optimistic temperament had always made him see the best in his children but his wife's shakier self-esteem made her have more limited expectations. In recent years, Clementine had tried to support her daughters both emotionally and financially but, tragically for them all, she could not turn the clock back and rewrite history.

After staying at the clinic, Sarah improved. Off alcohol and feeling safely away from the outside world, she was calm and relaxed. However, any abstinence never lasted for long. After coming back to England, she starred in a production of *Peter Pan* in London's West End. She received rave reviews for her performance and her professional future looked promising. As one critic wrote, 'It seems that in her maturity her career is more full of possibilities than ever before.'[50]

Sadly, like the tragic heroine she had become, she could not overcome her fatal flaw. When *Peter Pan* was staged in Liverpool, in February 1959 she was arrested for being drunk and disorderly. Wearing a leopard skin coat and no shoes, she was carried into court by police officers. After a feisty performance in the witness box she was fined £2. However, determined that the show must go on, she appeared in the matinee of *Peter Pan*, flying across the stage on a high wire. She gave a flawless performance and was warmly applauded.

Once again, Sarah's family and friends did everything they could to support her. The Churchills' employees had always been particularly fond of Sarah because she was so friendly and unaffected. Now she was in trouble, they tried to protect her. When Sarah was staying at Chartwell, the policeman on duty came to Winston's bodyguard, Edmund Murray's room in the middle of the night to tell him that Sarah had gone out into the snow-covered garden. Murray found her barefooted in her nightdress in the freezing cold. He picked her up and carried her into the house, then he woke up Clementine and they called the doctor. To prevent any publicity, he asked the policeman not to talk to anyone about the incident or mention it in his diary.[51]

When Sarah was away from the family it was not so easy to protect her. Over the next few years there were to be more arrests for being drunk and disorderly which were covered in detail in the newspapers. These incidents really upset Clementine. Most mornings her secretary, Shelagh Montague Browne, used to go into her room and see her while she was still in her dressing gown. Lady Montague Browne said, 'I could tell by her demeanour if anything had transpired. One morning I went in and she said: "Sarah's been arrested." She was devastated by the news.'[52]

When Sarah was sober, she was charming, funny and talented, but when she was drunk it was another matter. One friend said, 'When she has a few drinks, she changes in the most extraordinary way. [...] She's nothing like the sweet person she normally is.'[53] The doctor who was treating her at the Priory clinic explained that intermittently he found her in a state of acute anxiety, tension and hysteria. Sometimes she would not sleep or eat for twenty-four hours.[54] Late at night she used to wander along the London Embankment barefoot and in blue jeans. She would get into a distressed state from drinking too much and then be picked up by the police.

After yet another incident in July 1961, Sarah was remanded in custody for a medical report. She was sent to the hospital section of Holloway Prison for ten days. She told the prison doctors that she was not an alcoholic, 'but things had happened that had built my resentment so high – that I could give way to hate – but I didn't. I just drank sometimes instead.'[55] Her explanation rings true: anyone faced with the number of tragedies she had experienced would have been damaged. Sarah needed to escape from her circumstances, and she found her escapism in alcohol.

Whether the crises in her life exacerbated a pre-existing genetic tendency to alcoholism is debatable. As both Sarah and Randolph had drink problems, it is certainly worth considering. Some biographers suggest that 'a drink gene' came from Clementine's family and was inherited from her mother, Lady Blanche. However, it might also have passed down through Winston's side. He enjoyed his drink, but his relationship with alcohol was very different from his two children's. According to people who worked with him, although he drank champagne, port and brandy with lunch and dinner, the whiskies he sipped throughout the day were diluted with large amounts of soda.[56] Winston's recent biographer, Andrew Roberts, explains that although he enjoyed depicting himself as a heavy drinker, there were very few occasions anyone considered him to be drunk.[57] His private secretary, Anthony Montague Browne, said that he never saw his boss 'the worse for wear'.[58] Sadly, the same could not be said for his son or daughter.

To her credit, Sarah made the best of being in Holloway Prison. Thanks to her ability to get on with all sorts of people, she made friends with the prostitutes, confidence tricksters and thieves she came across. She identified with many of them, realising that they were 'hot and angry like I am outside'. They made her feel like a real person and that her gifts were appreciated. When lesbian prisoners propositioned her, she took it in her stride. While politely turning down their advances, she joked with them. She also got on well with several young offenders because she was able to talk to them in their own language.[59]

After she was released from prison she went as a voluntary patient to the Maudsley Hospital, and feeling more optimistic because they treated her as if she was sane, she was very co-operative and willingly took part in extensive psychotherapy sessions.[60] Her considerable charm worked its magic even in hospital. She got on so well with her psychiatrist that he was soon joking and flirting with her.[61]

20

Surprised by Joy

After reaching such a low point in England, Sarah decided to move to Spain. She abandoned the stage for a while as she claimed it took so much out of her. Since returning from America she had appeared in a film with Anthony Quayle and a few plays but, with her recent track record, offers of work were in short supply.[1] She was a good actress but her drinking made her unreliable.[2] Intending to write poetry and paint, she hoped that living in Marbella, which was then a small fishing village, would give her a fresh start.

Although she was not looking for romance, to her surprise, she found it. Shortly after arriving, Sarah fell in love with Henry, Lord Audley, the man she considered to be the love of her life. They were both artistic and had a great deal in common. He had been an actor and then, after fighting in the war, he set up a glass factory in London which revived the art of hand-painted glass. He was a sensitive man who, like Sarah, wrote poetry. Both were in their late forties and neither expected to find love again, but they were immediately attracted to each other. Realising they had both found what they had been looking for all their lives, Henry soon moved into Sarah's villa and they decided to marry.

Reflecting Sarah's volatile mental state, when she sent a large envelope full of letters informing her family of her plans, her father's private secretary, Anthony Montague Browne, at first feared they were suicide notes. He was relieved to find it was happy news.[3] With characteristic wit, she joked to him, 'Hence forth my life will be more Audley.'[4]

In a more serious tone, Sarah wrote to her parents, 'I never ever believed I would ever find anyone ever again who could make me take heart and believe that happiness and love were yet ahead of me.'[5] She believed that Henry was very like her other great love, Gil Winant, writing, 'I suppose I must have been looking for him ever since.'[6]

However, there was a shadow on their horizon. Henry had been partially paralysed after suffering a massive stroke. He wrote to Sarah that she had brought him back to life again but, ominously, his letter was typed, and his signature was shaky.[7] During their courtship, he often got tired and needed to rest.

Unlike when Sarah introduced other boyfriends, this time Sarah's family approved. Lord Audley was more socially acceptable to them than her previous husbands. His title dated back to 1312 and the barony was one of the oldest in Britain. Her brother Randolph was impressed, saying, 'Well, *that* puts the Marlboroughs in their place.'[8] Hearing of the engagement, Clementine commented, 'Well, darling, at least you are finally marrying a man with his own name.'[9]

Her parents warmly welcomed Henry at Chartwell. It meant a great deal to Sarah that finally they believed she had found the right man. She described seeing the people she loved most getting on well together in the drawing room at Chartwell as 'like a dream'. She added, 'Yesterday evening the house glowed again for me – like in my happy childhood.'[10]

During their visit, Henry told Winston that he loved Sarah for her beauty, her sorrows and her instinctive goodness. He hoped to give her peace, but also excitement, and he promised to encourage her enthusiasms.[11] Winston replied that for a long time he had hoped that

Sarah would find peace and happiness and they felt she had done so with him.[12]

It was evident that Henry understood Sarah and loved her self-lessly and unconditionally. He was the first man in her life not to have ambitions of his own; he just wanted her to be happy and to feel free in their relationship. Recognising she always needed to leap around from one place to another, he nicknamed her 'the Cricket'.

In April 1962, the couple married in the ballroom of the Rock Hotel, in Gibraltar. The occasion was kept as simple as possible. Dressed in a blue wool suit and a white straw hat, which she had borrowed from her niece Celia, Sarah made her vows for the third time.[13] With few guests present, Diana was matron of honour.

After the wedding Sarah and Henry went on honeymoon to Tangiers, Casablanca and Marrakech. They travelled around in a red sports car and relished being alone together at last. Sharing a sense of humour, they found plenty to amuse them. As they were both redheads with pale skins, they painted each other head to toe in fake tan and they shrieked with laughter as they turned a streaky apricot colour.

It was a sentimental journey for Sarah as they revisited places she had been with her parents. They stayed at La Mamounia Hotel and enjoyed picnics in the valley where Winston had painted. As Henry could not walk far, they rode through the streets of Medina on mules. Henry wrote that he was completely happy with Sarah, while she added that they were 'at the rosy top of our cloud number seven!'[14]

After their honeymoon, Sarah felt London was haunted by ghosts for her so they returned to live in a villa in Marbella. Sarah described it as 'a tight little seashell of a world'.[15] Perhaps subconsciously realising time was precious, she did not want to spend a moment away from Henry. Creating the domestic idyll she had talked about with other men but never achieved, she bought Henry a black poodle puppy and created an outside study for him to write in, which they called 'The Cell'. Henry told her that he was proud of being so happy and he loved her completely.[16]

However, their happiness was short-lived. After visiting London, in the summer of 1963 the couple set off on a road trip through France to Spain. Full of enthusiasm, Henry knew France well and wanted to show Sarah the places he loved. It turned out to be an exhausting experience.

Just before they reached Granada, their car broke down. Finally, after a long wait in the stifling heat, they reached their hotel. After resting on their bed for a while, as they were going down the marble stairs, Henry stumbled. Sarah stopped him falling, but it shocked them both. He did not want to change their plans, so they got a taxi and looked around Granada before having dinner in a restaurant followed by singing and dancing.

Back at the hotel, Sarah continued talking to Henry while she went into the bathroom to clean her teeth. When she called something out and he did not answer, she put her head around the door. To her horror, she discovered Henry was dead. He had suffered a sudden, massive cerebral haemorrhage.[17]

Alone and in shock, the one person who, as always, was there for Sarah was Diana. She flew out immediately to join her. Diana calmed her sister and arranged the hurried funeral. When Sarah debated whether Henry's body should be returned to England, Diana said to her firmly, 'Remember, we are the daughters of a soldier. Where we fall, there we rest.'[18]

Henry was buried in the British Naval Cemetery at Malaga. As she sprinkled earth on to the coffin, Sarah took off her wedding ring and placed it in the grave. Alone once again, she wrote in a poem that after the 'momentary peace' of their marriage, once again she faced 'the endless barren plain'.[19]

After Henry's death Sarah was utterly heartbroken and desolate. However, as always, she tried to fight back and focus on the positive side. She turned to her faith, writing to her mother that her husband had 'died in the arms of God' and he had given her fifteen months of 'glorious happiness and unconditional love'. She added that he had left her 'a legacy of love'.[20]

Her family knew what a body blow this latest bereavement was to her. It seemed so unfair when she had finally found the man with whom she could happily have spent the rest of her life. When she returned to England and saw her father, Winston took her hand and said, 'We must close ranks and march on.'[21]

21

Diana: The Good Samaritan

The person who helped Sarah survive the tragedies in her life was Diana. As her support for her sister showed, she had great compassion for other people and the ability to do and say the right thing. Throughout her life, she had struggled with issues of low self-esteem which had culminated in her nervous breakdown in the mid-1950s. The illness had taken its toll on Diana. Sarah believed that 'the bright life had been rather successfully dimmed' by various experimental treatments, including insulin and electroconvulsive therapy.[1] Diana's daughter Celia remembers there always seemed to be a cloud over her mother.[2]

However, Diana's suffering had made her even more sensitive to the needs of others. From the latter part of the decade, Diana seemed better. Having searched for a fulfilling role outside her family all her life, she finally found a vocation which drew on her experiences and channelled her nurturing side.

In 1957 Diana separated from Duncan. For several years, they had been leading increasingly separate lives. He was very attractive to women and it seems that he had affairs. Rather than be judgemental, the Churchills tried to understand what had gone wrong. Sarah wrote that it was not possible for anyone 'to state categorically whether

Diana's developing neuroses destroyed her marriage or whether marriage difficulties created the neuroses'.[3]

Whatever the truth, at first Diana found it hard to come to terms with her failed marriage. She needed the support of her family in public and private.[4] With Diana's marriage ending, Winston and Clementine witnessed the breakdown of yet another of their children's marriages. Out of their four surviving children, only Mary was able to sustain a happy, long-term relationship. The divorces upset both Winston and Clementine, but they tried to be supportive. Happily married himself, Winston could never understand why the younger generation could not just 'make-it-up-and-have-another-try'.[5] Although she was quite strait-laced, Clementine was understanding about other people's marital problems. After Diana's separation, she was very sympathetic and often invited her to Chartwell with her children.[6] Out of loyalty to her daughter, she crossed Duncan off the guest list.

However, Winston had always liked Duncan and it seems the two men wanted to remain friends. Shortly after the separation, he decided to ask his former son-in-law to the Other Club, which was a small circle of Winston's personal friends. Diana rarely asked her father for any favour, but she asked him not to invite Duncan, as she considered this public display of support to be disloyal to her. Although she knew her father would not knowingly do anything hurtful to her, she believed it would give the impression that he either did not know, or did not care, about what was happening to her.[7] The last thing Winston wanted to do was upset his daughter at this difficult time, but he never totally severed links with his former son-in-law. He continued to write to him and called him 'my dear Duncan'.

Now she was single again, Diana went on several holidays with her father. She stayed with Winston in the South of France and joined him on a cruise on the Greek shipping tycoon Aristotle Onassis' yacht, *Christina*. Onassis had first invited Winston and Clementine in 1958 and for several years these trips became a regular feature in the Churchills' lives. The cruises brought some much-needed light relief into Winston's twilight years. Everything was done to please the elderly statesman; his wish was his host's command.

It was a sybaritic experience, as Onassis had created 'a floating mini palace'. There were eight luxurious guest cabins, a bar, a laundry and even an operating theatre. At dinner the finest food and wine were served. The floor of the swimming pool was a mosaic of bulls and acrobats taken from the fresco in Knossos, Crete. At night it could be raised hydraulically to become a dance floor. While guests danced, jets from the pool illuminated the scene.[8]

In 1959 Winston invited Diana and her daughter Celia to join him as they sailed from Monte Carlo down the Italian coast to the Greek Islands and then on to Istanbul. Winston's trips were like a royal progress and as well as his entourage there was a large quantity of luggage and his budgerigar, Toby, in a cage. When they landed at Nice airport, the red carpet was already out and a fleet of cars with a police escort was waiting for them.[9]

On the voyage, the Churchills watched as the Greek tycoon's wife, Tina, was usurped by the opera singer Maria Callas. Diana, Clementine and Celia liked Onassis' understated wife and were unimpressed with '*La Callas*', who Clementine described as 'shallow and common'.[10] The three generations of Churchill women met every night in Clementine's cabin to gossip about what was going on.[11]

The opera star's ego was as large as Winston's. When crowds assembled on the jetties of the places they visited, she remarked what a comfort it was to have some of the weight of popularity lifted from her shoulders. To Clementine's disgust, when two huge electric Vs were flashed up on the side of the Town Hall in Rhodes in Winston's honour, Maria had no idea what they meant.[12]

Despite the Callas/Onassis affair, it was a very happy trip for the Churchill family. Winston was stimulated by the sights and Diana also thoroughly enjoyed herself. Afterwards, she wrote to her father saying that she had 'a glorious time'.[13]

In 1960 Duncan and Diana divorced. Two years later, he married again. His new wife was French-born Marie-Claire, Viscountess Hudson. Diana was very distressed as, like her parents, she was naturally monogamous. Loyal to the core, her daughter Celia believes she never stopped loving Duncan.[14] Diana revealed her hurt feelings, asking her father if she could revert to her maiden name and be known as 'Mrs Diana Churchill'.[15]

With one era coming to an end, Diana needed something that would give her life more meaning and use her experiences. Because she understood mental health problems so well, she became involved in the Samaritans, an organisation that helped suicidal people. Quietly and unobtrusively, she worked often five days a week with Reverend Chad Varah, head of the Samaritans. She was regularly on call to talk to people who telephoned in a distressed state. Rather than be known as her father's daughter, while doing her voluntary work she used her middle name and was called 'Mrs Spencer'. She helped hundreds of people and found that she had a gift for the work.

Throughout her life, Diana's Christian faith had been important to her. During her worst periods of depression, she had felt cut off from God and unable to take Holy Communion. She spent a long period searching for a church that was right for her and believed that she had found it at the church where the Samaritans were based, St Stephen's, Walbrook, in the City of London. Here, she could put her Christianity into action.

She reassured one client, who knew her only as 'Diana', that 'she knew that things always work out right in the end if we trust in God'. The woman she helped wrote that she had 'a real faith' and 'a kinder person would be hard to imagine'.[16] While helping others, Diana found a serenity she had never known before. She frequently told Reverend Varah that she lived for the Samaritans.[17] He said, 'It had transformed her life, finding something to do which she felt was worthwhile and doing it as a member of a team of people who appreciated her.'[18]

During the two years she worked for the organisation, Diana's family thought that she was much happier. Her relationship with her mother improved and when Clementine went into hospital for treatment for nervous fatigue, depression and anxiety, Diana could not have been more loving and supportive. She reassured Clementine that she was doing the right thing and promised to do anything she could to help.[19]

Diana also tried to cheer up her father. In his final years, he suffered from bouts of melancholy or lethargy which were exacerbated by his increasing deafness.[20] Although he would suddenly rally and show flashes of his old self, sometimes he was silent and gloomy. Time passed very slowly for him and it seemed that he was just waiting for the end. His gradual decline was upsetting for his children to watch.[21] On one of his birthdays, when his two eldest daughters were visiting him, Diana spoke with admiration about all the things he had done in his life. To their surprise, he said, 'I have achieved a great deal to achieve nothing in the end.'

Trying to rally him, Diana replied, 'How can you say that?'

'There are your books,' Sarah added.

'And your painting,' Diana chipped in.

Then they both reminded him, 'And after all there is us. Poor comfort we know at times: and there are children who are grateful that they are alive.' Winston just smiled.[22]

Diana's children were the greatest joy of her life and she was immensely proud of them. Julian, who was a barrister, frequently visited his mother. Celia was also close to her mother but, although she could talk to her about her private life, they did not share everything. Celia explains, 'We were mother and daughter, not chums.'[23]

Recently married to Piers Dixon, the son of Britain's ambassador to Paris, Edwina gave Diana her first grandchild and Winston his first great-grandchild. At Christmas 1962, Clementine described a 'patriarchal luncheon', where there were four generations present: Winston, Clementine, Edwina, Diana and 5-week-old Mark.[24]

Just as Diana's family life reached a new level of fulfilment, her ex-husband was involved in a cause célèbre. Early in 1963, Duncan was named as one of Margaret, Duchess of Argyll's many lovers in her high-profile divorce case. Part of the evidence was explicit photographs, showing the duchess in a sex act with a lover, who became known as 'the headless man' because his face could not be seen. Sandys was one of several candidates rumoured to be the man in the erotic pictures. He offered to resign as Secretary of State for Commonwealth Relations, but the prime minister Harold Macmillan dissuaded him.

The Master of the Rolls, Lord Denning, was then asked to examine the case to discover the identity of 'the headless man'. Over the years, the debate about who he was has continued. According to recent biographers, it seems that Duncan was not the culprit, but he had been involved with the duchess before his remarriage.[25] As the photographs appeared in the same year as the Profumo scandal, they further undermined Harold Macmillan's government.[26] Diana was no longer directly involved in her ex-husband's life, but the gossip must have been an embarrassing reminder of the past.

During that fateful year, Diana's needs were not seen as a top priority. The tragedy of Lord Audley's death had devastated Sarah and, trying to cope with her grief, she divided her time between Spain, London and America. Diana was always ready to listen to her sister's feelings, but she recognised that they reacted very differently to traumatic experiences. She told Sarah, 'I am beginning to understand you. If anything awful happens to you, you go out and fight. If anything awful happens to me, I want to put my head under a pillow.'[27]

Then, in the summer, Winston suffered a vascular stoppage just above his left ankle and had to spend a great deal of time in bed.[28] The strain affected Clementine, who also became ill again, suffering from physical and mental exhaustion. Mary tried to look after her mother at her home, but doctors insisted that she needed expert care, so she was admitted to Westminster Hospital. From her own experience, Diana understood what her mother was going through. While her parents were ill, Diana was a sympathetic support to them and the rest of the family. She kept in close touch with Mary and provided sound advice.[29]

On 19 October 1963, Diana had lunch with her daughter Edwina. She seemed in a good mood and was intending to see her parents later that weekend, but that night it must have all just become too much for her. Normally, if she was feeling upset and needing 'to let off steam' there were a few close friends she could phone at any hour of the day or night. Unfortunately, several people in this support network were away from London that October weekend. Diana committed suicide by taking a massive overdose of sleeping tablets. Her death shocked everyone – even the head of the Samaritans, who dealt with mental illness every day, could not understand it. Reverend Varah said, 'The person we knew was not suicidal. I just do not know what happened to cause her to do this.'[30]

It was Mary's unenviable job to tell her parents, Sarah and Diana's daughter Celia the tragic news. Her parents were in no fit state to take in the tragedy – her father was increasingly fragile and her mother was still in hospital. When Winston heard the news he withdrew further into 'a great and distant silence'. Clementine's reaction was softened by the sedation but gradually, over a period of days, she absorbed the tragic news.[31] Winston and Clementine were too ill to attend their daughter's funeral but they went to her packed memorial service, which was held in St Stephen's, the church where Diana had worked for the Samaritans. As Winston sat in the front row in his wheelchair, head bowed, Chad Varah gave the address. He told the mourners:

> We knew her as a loyal and friendly, concerned person, warm and impulsive. Not all human beings are impulsive and those who are have advantages and disadvantages. Often they do and say things that more reserved people hesitate to do and say and those others are the losers because there are so many kind, impulsive things that one can say or do.[32]

Many of the condolence letters also referred to Diana's compassion. In her private life, as much as in her work with the Samaritans, she had given strength to many people. Her cousin, Anita Leslie, described her as 'the kindest, most gallant and touching person [...] All the philosophical things Diana ever said now come back to me.'[33] Randolph's second wife, June, recalled that Diana had been kinder than anyone else to her when she had suffered a nervous breakdown.[34] Diana's courage was also a constant theme. Her close friends realised that it had sometimes been a struggle for her to get through the day.

Friends and family worried about how Diana's children, and particularly Sarah, would cope with the loss. The two sisters had always been exceptionally close, but in recent years they had relied on each other. Sarah wrote that her sister always 'turned merciful eyes on my lapses which other people often could not understand'.[35] Having known them since they were children, the Churchill girls' nanny, Moppet, wrote to Mary about her concerns for Sarah. She felt Diana had been her 'only anchor'.[36]

In her grief, Sarah once again preferred the kindness of strangers to the support of friends. She spent time in America then Rome. Shortly after her sister's death, Sarah admitted that she still did not fully realise Diana was dead and she would often reach for the telephone to talk to her. She added:

I think of Diana - often – and with a terrible pang – not that I could have done anything OR she didn't know that I cared – but with a deep sense of the loss for the future – the future for me - without her.

Sarah dedicated the poems she had written to her, 'With love and – till we meet again. Your devoted sister.'[37]

As Moppet pointed out, Mary had a much more 'balanced and sane outlook on life' and was better able to cope with these blows than Sarah.[38] Due to their age difference, she had never been as close to her eldest sister. However, she was also devastated by Diana's death. In her grief, she found solace in her Christian faith, believing that her sister was now at peace.

22

Mary: The Calm at the Centre of the Storm

Through all the years of turbulence in her sisters' lives, Mary was the calm centre of the family. Christopher and Mary's evident happiness with their growing brood of five children brought much-needed relief to Winston and Clementine in those dark days. Mary became known to the Churchills' staff as 'Darling Mary', because whenever Clementine picked up the telephone and heard her youngest daughter's voice, she would say, 'Oh Mary, Darling Mary'.[1]

In 1957, after ten years living at Chartwell Farm, the Soameses moved to Hamsell Manor, near Tunbridge Wells in Kent. Although Mary was not moving far, as she had experienced such deep contentment at her childhood home she described leaving it as 'more than a sadness – it will be an up-rooting'.[2]

However, in their new home the family were soon living 'joyous country lives'.[3] Mary created a happy, secure world for her children. She found it particularly rewarding 'brewing the Christmas magic' for them in the same way her mother had cast her spell over Chartwell festivities.[4] Her parents visited often and enjoyed sharing the 'hurly burly' of the Soames' hectic lives.[5] To cheer her father up, Mary often wrote to him about what a full life she was living. She hoped that it gave him satisfaction to see their contentment because his generosity and love had helped to create it.

Christopher's political career was also advancing. In 1960 he was promoted to the Cabinet as Minister of Agriculture. Mary supported his political career while juggling the demands of her children and elderly parents. She was never as single-minded a political wife as Clementine and she gave her children higher priority. She worked hard in Christopher's Bedford constituency during term time but in the school holidays she hardly went there. Christopher joked, 'Your mother would never have let me alone in Bedford like this.'[6] Mary told one friend that Clementine annoyed her by saying that, for a Cabinet minister's wife, she was astonishingly ill-informed.[7] At one party conference she missed her husband's platform speech because she got the time wrong and was sitting on the pier sunbathing. She was so upset by her mistake she felt like crying.[8] However, it was rare for Mary to let anyone down.

Of course, the tribulations of the rest of the family worried her but rather than make a fuss she just quietly stepped in and picked up the pieces. In August 1964, the Soameses had a crisis of their own. Christopher had a serious riding accident. He was knocked unconscious and injured his pelvis. As he was in hospital for ten weeks, Mary fought the 1964 General Election campaign on his behalf, canvassing, visiting factories and giving his speeches in his Bedford constituency. Her daughter, Emma, who was a teenager at the time, recalls 'galloping in her wake around the constituency. [...] She was just up for anything.'[9] However, it seems she never regretted not having a political career of her own. She found canvassing an ordeal, admitting, 'I'm terror struck – it's such an intrusion into people's lives.'[10]

As Mary's children grew up, she continued to have a close relationship with them. Emma recalls:

She could be quite a tigress in protecting her cubs. She was very supportive but, like all selfish teenagers, one took it for granted. She was almost over-protective of her girls, not in a negative way but in wanting things to be just right for us, when all we wanted to do was go and listen to the Beatles.[11]

As Winston and Clementine grew older, one of Mary's main priorities was also protecting them. When they could no longer fight their own battles, she did it for them. In her biography of her mother, she described her sadness at seeing Winston's world closing in. As the whole family celebrated Winston's 90th birthday in November 1964, they knew time was running out.

In January 1965, Winston suffered a massive stroke. He survived for another fifteen days but slipped into unconsciousness. Mary supported her mother throughout those difficult days as her father lingered between life and death. They went for walks and the two women prayed together beside Winston's bed. Sarah flew from Rome to join them and stayed with her niece, Celia.

There was serenity as well as sadness in those final days. His children and grandchildren came to sit quietly with Winston as he slept peacefully. He died on 24 January, the anniversary of his father's death, with his family gathered around his bedside. Shortly afterwards, Sarah wrote to Anthony Montague Browne:

I don't have to tell you how much 'this child of the big animal' loved him – or how I have dreaded the day when inevitably he would go. But the whole of him and his life is too vast and inspiring for personal regret or loss. And somehow the majestic peace that seemed to surround him these last days is comforting.[12]

Acknowledging his role in British history, Winston was honoured with the first state funeral for a commoner since the Duke of Wellington. Sarah and Mary travelled with their mother in the queen's horse-drawn carriage to the funeral at St Paul's Cathedral. As the three women passed through the streets of London, lined with respectful crowds, they sat very still in the silent carriage. There was music outside, but they could not hear it. Only the steady beat of the drums, the clatter of the horses' hooves and the creak of the carriage permeated the silence.[13]

When they entered the cathedral, the congregation of 3,000 people, including world leaders and royalty, rose to their feet.[14] As sovereign, the queen did not attend non-family funerals, but she broke the precedent for Winston. As his family arrived, she was already in her pew just waiting quietly to pay her final respects to Britain's best-loved statesman. It was a proud and poignant moment for Winston's daughters, but it was also the end of an era. From their earliest childhood, they knew that their own lives came second to the great man's. He had been the centrifugal force in the family; now he was gone, there would be new dynamics. As Sarah wrote to a friend, 'The play is over and the actors have to say farewell.'[15]

23

Sarah Keeps on Dancing

Dressed in white boots, blue jeans and a casual black and white jumper, Sarah looked like a teenager as she snapped her fingers in time and swayed to the beat of the black jazz musician playing on her record player. There was no audience watching the elfin figure, just a journalist who had come to interview her. 'I'm still quite good, aren't I?' she asked him eagerly. 'You never forget your training.' As she tossed her long red hair around her fragile-looking face, she added, 'I live. I enjoy every minute of it.' Then, in a flash, her mood changed. Sombre again, she sat down, brandy and ginger in one hand, a cigarette in the other.[1]

Sarah could never win her battle with alcohol for long, but she refused to give in, and although at times it seemed more frenzied than graceful, she kept on dancing. After her father's death, she lived an increasingly bohemian life. She returned to Rome, which was the place to be after Fellini's iconic film, *La Dolce Vita*. As Hollywood stars descended on the eternal city, the battle between celebrities and paparazzi reached fever pitch.[2]

Inevitably, these voracious photographers often followed Sarah as she provided such good copy, but despite the threat of press intrusion, the hedonistic atmosphere suited her need for escapism. As one journalist observed, she had 'a Churchillian disregard for bores' and was 'at her best with poets, actors and the charmer type of social con-man'.[3]

There were plenty of those to choose from in 1960s Rome. As so often in her life, she turned to a man to save her and, once again, she chose the wrong one. Shortly before Winston's death she had thrown herself into an unconventional relationship with a black American artist and blues singer, Lobo Nocho.[4] He was dynamic and full of energy, and had appeared as the Devil in Dino De Laurentiis' film, *The Bible*. Exuding sex appeal, he was surrounded by adoring females who he called his 'Buddy Girls'. Sarah was happy to become one of the buddies, describing him as 'a vision in Levi's, a jet-age troubadour'.[5]

It was never going to be the most stable relationship, but she wrote that Lobo brought laughter back into her life. He moved her on from her grief for Henry Audley.[6] Their relationship was passionate, and she told Lobo, 'I love your fierceness – your unreasoning fury some-times – because I've had it too in my life – anything better than one drop of self-pity.'[7] However, there are hints that he was violent to her.[8] As their relationship came to an end she wrote, 'Perhaps he was too fierce and I too weak – and both disorganised.' It seems that after one incident the police were called, but she refused to press charges. However, she admitted, 'I was afraid that it was a situation domestic and heart I could no longer manage.'[9]

Their relationship followed the same trajectory as her marriages to Vic and Antony. She complained that Lobo undermined her, writing to him, 'Sometimes you have thought I needed cutting down – really I need loving and building up. I have never fooled myself or overestimated my talents.' However, even though their love affair was destructive, she did not want to cut all links with him. When it ended, she did not like being on her own. She told him, 'It is very difficult without a man on my side – who can protect me.'[10]

As a woman who had relied on her appearance for her career, getting older was not easy for Sarah. Although she was always slim and trendily dressed, drink had affected her looks. A journalist described her as having 'the same frail vulnerability' as the tragic film star Judy Garland.[11] As Sarah aged, acting roles were drying up. Still wanting to perform and needing to make some money, she put on one-woman shows, first 'A Matter of Choice' and then 'An Evening with Sarah Churchill', which she performed around Britain and abroad. An eclectic mixture of poetry, Shakespearian scenes and personal reminiscences, the choice seemed to entertain Sarah more than her audience. One critic wrote, 'She is a better actress than the evening suggested.'[12]

Following in her father's footsteps, she continued to paint. She did a series of pictures of Winston and Clementine, which skilfully captured her parents in their later years. She also learned how to create lithographs. And now finally having the time to support her daughter, Clementine always loyally attended Sarah's exhibitions.

As her acting career declined, Sarah's writing also flourished. She published two volumes of poetry which collected verse that she had written since she was a teenager. In 1966 *The Empty Spaces* was published; it was dedicated to Diana and one section was in memory of Henry Audley. The poems were often bleak in tone. 'Beyond Despair' described how 'nature wreaks her havoc on us'. In another one, she portrayed herself as a skeleton and asked people not to pick at her bones but instead to leave her alone.[13] The collection emphasised that she had pursued freedom, often at the cost of happiness. In 'A Matter of Choice', she wrote:

This is what I have chosen –
This moment bitter and free;
This is what I have chosen
From so much that was offered to me.[14]

In her poetry, the positive spin she often put on situations for the sake of loved ones' feelings was stripped away. Several years before her poems were published, she told one interviewer:

I have tried writing, but I tell too much of the truth – the truth about myself. The moment I begin the truth comes flowing down the veins of my arm into the pen and onto the paper. I read what I have written. 'Oh no,' I say, 'I have revealed too much.' And I tear it up.[15]

However, as she grew older, she felt more liberated to say what she really felt. *The Empty Spaces* was a great success, selling more than 40,000 copies in nine editions. Reviewers recognised the personal integrity and honesty of her writing. One critic wrote, 'It must have taken courage to write this book which tells not of events so much as the courage needed to face them.'[16] In 1969 she published a second volume, *The Unwanted Statue*. Her poetry attracted an eclectic collection of admirers. Even Britain's first female prime minister, Margaret Thatcher, loved her poems.[17]

Sarah's memoirs, *Keep on Dancing* and *A Thread in the Tapestry*, were also well written and honest. She did not avoid exposing her complicated love life or her drink problem. The only exception was her love affair with Gil Winant – perhaps it was still too painful for her to write about. She described her book as 'a living autopsy', the story of a woman who 'happened to be a daughter of one of the "greats" of history, who found the skies are not always so blue'.[18] However, in interviews there were no recriminations; she always said she felt privileged to have been the daughter of Winston Churchill.

The Churchill legacy had been even harder for his son. Although Randolph had finally found a degree of fulfilment in both his public and private life, he had not lived up to his father's expectations.[19] In June 1968, Randolph died aged only 57. He had been seriously ill for four years and, like Sarah, had a drink problem. Although his interventions had often made situations worse, he had always tried to protect his younger sister. Coming so soon after the loss of Diana and her father, Sarah felt the death of her 'unforgettable' brother deeply. She wrote to his daughter, Arabella, in words which seem intended for herself as much as her niece, 'Another oak tree has tumbled and you must go on.'[20] As she travelled back on the train to London from Randolph's funeral, all she wanted to do was look out of the window and remember him. She believed he was now finally at peace.[21]

After the funeral, Sarah contacted Randolph's children, offering love and support from 'old Aunt Sasa'. With Randolph and Diana dead, Sarah took on an increasingly important position in her nieces' and nephews' lives. Celia and Edwina Sandys were particularly fond of her. Edwina recalled that her aunt had always been 'a magical creature', who brought colour into her life and had a great sense of humour. Some of the funniest moments of Edwina's life were shared with her aunt and they often laughed until they cried.[22] Celia describes Sarah as 'like a fairy god-mother', who gave the most unsuitable presents, including a diaphanous gown from America. She also found her aunt great fun to be with, but the experience was rarely relaxing. She explains, 'She was enchanting then infuriating. It was nerve-wracking as you never knew what would happen. She could be very funny when she was drunk – if you weren't attached to her.'[23] Shelagh Montague Browne, who had known the family for many years, admired the way Celia treated her aunt. She said, 'Celia really looked after Sarah and was very attentive to her. She could deal with her.'[24]

In her later years, Sarah divided her time between London and New York. She said, 'I live in the middle of the Atlantic.'[25] She had always been a daddy's girl, but Sarah was also devoted to her mother and they had a special rapport which had eluded Diana. Although Sarah had occasionally blamed Clementine for her problems, that time was past. It seems mother and daughter forgave each other their failings, realising they were both human with the weaknesses and strengths that entailed.

When Sarah was in London, she used to meet Clementine for lunch once a week. Her friends noticed that was the one day she would always be sober.[26] When Sarah was in America, she sent affectionate and solicitous letters to Clementine. She wrote, 'So much love to you my darling mama. You are never out of my thoughts, Your loving and ever stubborn Mule.'[27]

Despite being so different, Mary also remained close to her sister. When Sarah was well, they still had fun together. They liked nothing better than spending a cosy evening watching television and gossiping. However, Mary was aware of the 'awful muddle' her sister's life was in. As Sarah would not listen to her suggestions, it made her feel helpless.[28] Showing sensitivity to the disparity in their circumstances, Mary wrote to Sarah:

> I am only sorry if I have not been able to be of more help and comfort to you - and I have minded so, so much that life has held so much unhappiness for you. You are splendid - because it has not embittered you - 'tho of course it has saddened you - and you are so wonderful the way you take joy in the happiness of others.[29]

The fact that the two sisters continued to have such a strong relationship, despite their divergent lifestyles, reflects well on them both. Their love for each other had always been generous and was never tainted by sibling rivalry. No doubt it helped that they wanted such different things out of life. Mary had seen all her dreams realised while fate had not treated Sarah so kindly.

Although her family and friends were devoted to her and saw her often, one observer described Sarah as 'the loneliest woman in London'.[30] It was not due to a lack of company but more an inner loneliness that had always plagued her. Assessing her life, she explained, 'the only complete and shadowless happiness' had come from her achievements. She had known 'ecstasy', but it was 'so momentary I can never recall it clearly - and am inclined to feel at times I missed it – and an abominable restlessness and loneliness descends on me'.[31]

In her final years, Sarah's faith gave her some comfort. She did not go to Sunday services, but she used to visit a Catholic church regularly. She enjoyed the silence and lit a candle in memory of the people she had loved and lost.[32]

Despite the dark times, Sarah always managed to pick herself up. She believed anything was better than self-pity. She said she did not want to look back, she was still looking to the future. She told one interviewer that her father had taught her 'you cannot stop tragedy, but that you can stop boredom. And he passed on to me some of his own enormous zest for living.' Life had shown her that 'there's always tomorrow' and 'to have a go'. [33] When friends came to her for advice, she told them her motto was to 'keep on dancing!'[34]

24

Mary's Golden Age

Looking regal in a midnight blue velvet mantle displaying the heraldic shield of St George's Cross encircled by the Garter, Mary Soames walked in the prestigious procession from Windsor Castle to St George's Chapel for the service of thanksgiving for the oldest order of chivalry in the country. Being appointed a Lady Companion of the Order of the Garter was the culmination of Mary's distinguished public life. Selected by the queen in 2005, she was part of an elite group that included former prime ministers, dukes and generals. Winston had been a Knight of the Garter and so, when Mary was appointed, the Churchills became the first non-royal father and daughter ever to have held the honour.

However, she had been chosen on her own merit, not because of Winston. The final decades of Mary's life were a golden era for her. No longer just a daughter, wife and mother, she came into her own, taking on major roles in her own right. As she paraded through Windsor, Mary was 'the grandest of *grande dames*', but there was nothing pompous about her.[1] Beneath the black velvet plumed hat, those twinkling blue eyes revealed the warmth and sense of humour that made her an adored matriarch as well as a pillar of the Establishment.

After Winston's death, there were subtle changes in the balance of family relationships and Mary got to know and understand her mother in a whole new way. The process began when they worked together with the National Trust to turn Chartwell from a family home into a house open to the public. It mattered to them both how posterity would view the family. It was decided to turn the clock back and recreate the golden age of Chartwell between the wars. To accurately recreate the atmosphere, Clementine and her daughter carefully curated exactly where every item should go.

Walking around Chartwell, a visitor gets a strong impression of what mattered most to them. Particularly moving is seeing the choice of pictures for Clementine's bedroom. In the corner of the room are clustered three pictures of her daughters at their peak. A youthful Diana, with her hair shingled, exudes serenity; posing on the statue of a lion, Sarah, in trendily tight trousers, smiles conspiratorially at the photographer; while in contrast, Mary, wearing a headscarf, looks self-assured but sensitive. These pictures showed the Churchill girls as their mother wanted to remember them – at their best before life took its toll on two out of the three sisters. Even more poignant are the two pictures on Clementine's desk. Beside the last known photograph of Winston is a snapshot of a smiling curly-haired toddler. It is Marigold on the beach at Broadstairs, taken just a few weeks before her death. It shows that although 'the Duckadilly' was not talked about by Clementine she was always in her thoughts.[2]

As well as remaining a dutiful daughter, the demands on Mary as a supportive wife were increasing. In 1966 Christopher lost his Bedford seat. Over the years he had won the admiration not only of the Conservative Party but of Labour politicians. In 1968 the Labour Prime Minister, Harold Wilson, made Christopher Britain's ambassador in Paris.

Mary was delighted with her husband's appointment. Returning to the embassy where they had first met two decades earlier revived romantic memories. However, Mary was worried about leaving her mother.[3] As Clementine grew older, her youngest daughter dedicated much of her time to her. Hamsell Manor became a refuge for Clementine and she stayed there often.

Although her mother would miss her, she did not stand in Mary's way. When the Soames family left for Paris, accompanied by their labrador and pug, Clementine gave them a tearful send-off at the station. As Mary's daughter Emma noted, it was as if they were going to Timbuktu rather than France.[4]

Christopher and Mary proved to be the perfect ambassadorial couple. It was a crucial time in Britain's relationship with France and the rest of Europe. Briefed to persuade General de Gaulle to end the French veto on Britain's European Economic Community membership, they played a vital part in the country's entry into the Common Market. The French, including President de Gaulle, were delighted to have Churchill's daughter in Paris.[5]

As well as diplomatic finesse, the Soameses brought style and charm to the British Embassy on the Faubourg St-Honoré. The beautiful eighteenth-century house, which had once been the home of Napoleon's sister, was fit for royalty – Mary slept in a huge gold-canopied bed – but they 'humanised' other rooms by bringing in their own furniture, pictures and books. Filled with 'flowers and laughter', the palatial embassy was soon transformed into a real home as family and friends descended on the hospitable couple.[6]

The new ambassador and his wife became known for their glamorous parties. You never knew who you might meet at the embassy. In a typical week, the dress designer Edward Molyneux came to lunch, the American Ambassador to tea and Mary's cousin, the author Nancy Mitford, to dinner. On another evening, Mary rushed off to a grand party given by the Aga Khan. She wrote to her mother, 'It should be fun – but I am panicky. Oh dear, oh dear – my life does seem to have changed.'[7]

Fortunately, Mary had learned from her mother how to be an accomplished hostess and, always the bon viveur, Christopher also took an interest in providing his guests with the finest cuisine.

Dressed in a vivid silk dressing gown, each morning he had a meeting with their chef in the *salon vert* to discuss the menu to be served at dinner.[8]

Due to their shared wartime memories, Mary got on very well with President de Gaulle. When he died in 1970, she attended his Requiem Mass in Notre-Dame Cathedral, wearing the gold *Croix de Lorraine* he had given her when she visited France with Winston in 1944. She wrote to Clementine that because of the French leader's long connection with her father, it felt like the end of an epoch.[9] There were also echoes of Winston when Mary and Christopher dined with his old friends, the Duke and Duchess of Windsor.

Mary and Christopher became used to socialising with royalty. Before taking up the Paris posting, they were invited to stay at Sandringham and Balmoral. Surrounded by members of the royal family and corgis, Mary found the atmosphere surprisingly relaxed. At Balmoral, she played the card game 'Racing Demon' with Prince Charles and visited Queen Elizabeth, the Queen Mother, at her neighbouring estate, Birkhall. Having known Mary since the war, the Queen Mother was particularly fond of her. After spending the afternoon together, they both nearly cried when the Queen Mother played 'Auld Lang Syne' on the gramophone as they said goodbye.[10]

In May 1972, it was Mary and Christopher's turn to host the queen when she made a state visit to France. The ambassador was determined to put on a spectacular show for his monarch. Not to be outdone by the splendour of President Pompidou's dinner for the queen at the Palace of Versailles, Mary and Christopher staged one of the grandest occasions in the British Embassy's history. The white-tie ball for 1,200 guests mixed the great and the good, the old and the young, with Prince Charles acting as host to the *jeunesse dorée*.

There was absolute silence as the queen, in full evening dress, entered the ball. Everyone wanted to be introduced to her, but Christopher skilfully steered her down the long line of guests. After the formalities were over, music played by the band filled the huge marquee and, shortly after midnight, the queen suggested to President Pompidou that they might lead the dancing. The one low point of the memorable evening was when he blushingly declined.

The bill for the event was estimated at £25,000, an amount equivalent to the annual salaries of two Cabinet ministers. Such extravagance was controversial but, showing his determination to make the party go with a swing, Christopher footed some of the bill himself. The ball was the grand finale of a very successful royal visit. *The Economist* commented, 'Britain has a particular part to play in the making of Europe and its French-speaking Queen has symbolised it well.'[11]

After four 'golden years' in Paris, which were to pave the way for Britain being admitted into the Common Market, the Soameses returned to England.[12] After waving goodbye to the embassy staff, as they drove away in their Bentley with the back seat piled high with luggage, including the symbolic gift of two live doves of peace in a cage, they could be proud of what they had achieved for Anglo-French relations.[13]

His mission accomplished, Christopher was now treated as a trusted statesman who was known as a safe pair of hands in difficult situations. Recognising his contribution, he was knighted, and then a few years later he was made a life peer. In 1973, Christopher was sent to Brussels as one of the first of two British Commissioners in Europe. As Mary's role was much smaller, she was able to return to England often to see her mother and children. Mary and Christopher sold Hamsell Manor and moved to a smaller house, Castle Hill House, near Odiham in Hampshire.

With more free time, Mary could at last concentrate on her mother's biography, which she had begun writing a decade earlier. Mary's book was a labour of love and showed the importance of Clementine in Winston's success. However, it was not a hagiography and, like Sarah, she wrote candidly about the tragedies as well as the triumphs of the Churchill family.

Writing about their past was a cathartic process for the Churchill sisters. Looking through family letters made them weep, laugh and remember. Sarah wrote to Mary, 'Out of it all comes a shining light for me – we were really sisters.'[14] Mary replied, 'I cling to our loving bond of sisterhood – and know that is one of the most precious things in my life.'[15]

From the start, Clementine had supported the idea of Mary writing her biography. Over the years mother and daughter spent much time together, talking as they never had before. At the end of her life, Clementine looked back at what she had done right and where she had gone wrong. There were a few regrets, not least about missing out on fun times with her children when they were small. However, she saw it in perspective, realising that she had behaved in the same way as many of her contemporaries. She explained to friends, 'Well I was an Edwardian.'[16] Overall, it had been an exceptional life which had been well lived.

As Clementine became increasingly frail, Mary used to enjoy having lunch or dinner alone with her. They did not talk much, but Mary found just being with her mother sustaining. Although she was now middle-aged, she still enjoyed being treated as a beloved child.[17] Just a few days after one of their lunches, on 12 December 1977, Clementine died peacefully and quickly, without pain. She was aged 92.

At their mother's service of thanksgiving in Westminster Abbey, Sarah and Mary placed a wreath of white flowers for both parents on the large marble slab engraved with the words, 'Remember Winston Churchill'. Her daughters were of course sad, but they were also thankful for their mother's long life.[18]

Sarah described Clementine as being like a chandelier who gave out great light and sparkle. She explained her mother was 'a crystal person – sparkling, ever clear and precise about every dimension of life. My father couldn't have chosen anybody better to accompany him on the long journey of life.'[19] After Clementine's death, Mary released her biography to widespread critical acclaim. It won the Wolfson Prize, Britain's top award for history, and became a bestseller.

The year Clementine died, Christopher's health was also a matter of concern. In January 1977, he had a major coronary bypass operation and his recovery took a long time. However, despite his health problems, Christopher was still active in public life.

Between December 1979 and April 1980, he was the Governor of Southern Rhodesia. With Mary by his side, he oversaw elections and the handover of power to Robert Mugabe. It was ironic that the champion of Empire, Winston's favourite son-in-law, should be Britain's last colonial governor in Rhodesia and play such an important part in the country's transition to independent Zimbabwe.[20]

When Christopher accepted the governorship, it was a volatile situation which could have become dangerous for the governor and his wife. Nobody really knew what was going to happen and, if things had gone wrong, Christopher would have had to take the consequences. Their old friend, the Foreign Secretary, Lord Carrington remembered saying goodbye to Christopher and Mary and wondering when and if they would all meet again. He prayed for their success and safety.[21]

As they flew out to Rhodesia, Mary felt nervous, but when they arrived they were treated like royalty. After the band had played 'God Save the Queen', the new governor and his wife drove in a motorcade to Government House. At her most regal, Mary waved to the enthusiastic crowd.

On arriving at Government House, the staff, dressed in gleaming white uniforms and bright green fezzes, were lined up to greet them. It was a large bungalow set in beautiful grounds, and one journalist described Government House as decorated 'in a manner which makes Versailles seem, well, middle class'.[22] The numerous staff were so keen to please Mary that she had to assure them she was perfectly capable of opening doors for herself.

Being 'Governess' of Rhodesia was a role Mary was born to fulfil, and despite some trepidation, she rose to the occasion with enthusiasm. The pressure was immense and every hour there seemed to be some crisis which involved Christopher making decisions. Mary was aware that one wrong step and it could all blow up. Security was tight and so whenever she went out, she was accompanied by a detective.

Capturing the atmosphere for her children, she sent home round-robin letters entitled, 'Despatch from the Governess'.[23] She wrote to her son Jeremy, 'We still live from hour to hour – and who knows whether we will leave with cheers or tears.'[24] When she was feeling daunted, however, Mary thought of what her father had said to the Harrow schoolboys in the war: 'These are not grim days – they are great days.'[25] His example inspired her to do her best in those crucial moments for Rhodesia's future.

During their short time in the country, Mary became very popular. As she visited schools, hospitals, orphanages and refugee camps, she was shocked by the damage done by the civil war. An estimated 20,000 lives had been lost and whole areas were living in a state of fear. Thousands of children had been deprived of education as the guerrillas shut the schools and thousands of other children had simply disappeared.[26] She organised a meeting at Government House for a deputation of women to tell her the horrifying facts about abducted children. Some were the parents and grandparents of the missing. She wrote to her son Nicholas, 'My dear – it's a different world.'[27]

On her visits to refugee camps, Mary was impressed by the way black and white people were working together, showing mutual understanding and respect. Young black Red Cross volunteers worked in teams to feed the children. Drawing on her recent experience as the United Kingdom's Chairman of the International Year of the Child, she set up a fund to help children's charities in Rhodesia/Zimbabwe.

While Christopher worked long hours to find agreement, Mary charmed Rhodesia's leaders. When she went to inspect a field hospital, she found herself addressing, off-the-cuff, 900 of Joshua Nkomo's ZIPRA guerrillas.[28]

Despite factional violence and intimidation, the elections proceeded and Robert Mugabe, a left-leaning nationalist, emerged as prime minister. Christopher and Mary became good friends with him and his wife, Sally. Christopher's skilful diplomacy and Mary's genuine warmth helped to create an atmosphere which allowed a reasonably smooth transfer of power.

After independence, the Soameses returned to England to a hero and heroine's welcome. Their time in Rhodesia/Zimbabwe was seen by many people as a personal triumph. Recognising Mary's contribution, she was made a Dame Commander of the Order of the British Empire.

Christopher became leader of the House of Lords in Margaret Thatcher's first Conservative Government. He enlivened dull Cabinet meetings with jokes, which did not go down well with 'the Lady'.[29] Nor were his politics to her taste. As a one-nation, Conservative grandee, Christopher had little in common with Mrs Thatcher. Considered 'a wet' in a Thatcherite government, in 1981 he was dismissed by the prime minister. Christopher complained that he would not have sacked his gamekeeper in the way Mrs Thatcher sacked him, while she later said that he had reacted as if a housemaid had fired him.[30] Two years later, Christopher and Mary's son, Nicholas, was to continue the family tradition by becoming a Conservative Member of Parliament.

25

Sarah and Mary
Leave the Stage

By the early 1980s, Sarah was increasingly unwell. Like her brother, Randolph, and sister, Diana, she did not live into old age. In September 1982 she died at the age of 67 from uraemia, cirrhosis of the liver and renal failure.[1] The night before her death, her old friend, the pianist Idris Evans, visited and played her favourite songs to her. Mary and Celia were with her at the end.

Her life had always been inextricably linked to her parents. In a letter written decades earlier, Sarah described her dream of eternity. She wrote to her father:

> I would like to holiday with you forever. I think my heaven would be somewhere like Marrakech – you and Mama presiding over all the people I love and of course the people you love too, picnics and long drawn out yellow mellow minutes, long enough so that one wasn't worried that they were going to end the whole time.[2]

Despite all her gifts, life had never been easy for Sarah. Although being Winston Churchill's daughter had opened doors for her, it also had disadvantages. Her niece, Celia explains, 'My aunt was almost too multi-talented, but she did not quite make it. She never knew if she was getting things because of her father or on her own merit.' Celia believes Diana and Mary did not suffer in the same way from the Churchill legacy because they were not trying to make a name for themselves.[3] Sarah, like Randolph, had great expectations for herself and, ultimately, she was to be disappointed.

The fate she had discussed as a young woman with Mary had not been kind to her. Born in a more sexist era, she had to make stark choices between her professional and private life, and being a free spirit in a world that expected her to conform had also created a tension that she never fully resolved. In death, she was finally free at last. In one of her poems, she imagined herself as a bird on the wing. She wrote:

> Into the unknown air I spring –
> Away from sunlit shore,
> Back on a stormlit sky
> Toward a Northern clime.
> No one shall have me –
> Child of earth's own turmoil,
> There is no rest for such as me.
> But my songs are for the singing
> And my heart is for the free.[4]

Winston's former private secretary, Jock Colville, who had known the Churchill girls since their youth, recognised how painful Sarah's death would be for Mary. He wrote:

> The loss of the last member of your family, and one whom you loved so deeply, must bite deeply into your heart. When others would have given up the struggle long, long ago, you plodded on with unfaltering perseverance and if ever there had been greater sisterly patience and affection, I have yet to hear of it. I know that all

you have done for Sarah, your generosity to her and your willingness to bear so many trials – and indeed sometimes abuse – would have gladdened your father's heart and made him still prouder of you than he anyhow was.[5]

With all her siblings dead, Mary was now the sole survivor of Winston's children. She admitted that it left her feeling like 'the last of the Mohicans'.

In September 1987, Mary suffered an even greater loss when Christopher died of cancer aged 66. They had enjoyed an exceptionally happy forty-year marriage. As Christopher had promised when they got engaged, whatever they did, they did it together. They hated being apart, but when they were separated their letters expressed their profound and lasting love for each other.

The funeral was a prestigious gathering and Prince Charles and Princess Diana attended. The heir to the throne was a close friend of Nicholas Soames, but he was also very fond of Mary. He first met the Soameses when he was a schoolboy and Mary felt that she had got to know him as a real 'person'.[6]

Robert and Sally Mugabe also showed their love and respect by flying to Britain to attend the funeral.[7] During the service, Mary impressed everyone with her calm dignity and remarkable serenity. As a committed Christian, she intended it to be a statement of faith and hope.

After Christopher's death, Mary wrote, 'A great hunk, perhaps three quarters, has fallen away from my life.'[8] However, like Sarah, she loathed self-pity. When her friend, the actor Robert Hardy, asked her if she felt up to all that she faced, she told him, 'Yes, if I concentrate on what I have to do, and on other people, all is pretty well, but you're right, it's miserable.'[9]

Mary needed a new role in her life. In 1989 she became Chairman of the Board of Trustees of the National Theatre. Initially, her appointment was not greeted with much enthusiasm by thespians. Mary was under no illusions about what they thought, and she later admitted it was 'the rummest appointment that was ever made'.[10] Mary and Christopher had rarely gone to the theatre, nor did she have any experience of management. In an early meeting, Mary sent a note to the National Theatre's Director, Sir Richard Eyre, asking, 'Who is Ian McKellen?'[11]

However, she threw herself into the new role with typical Churchillian energy and enthusiasm and had soon won over even her greatest critics. She was far more than just a figurehead, as her daughter Emma explained, 'She did not miss a single play and went to every meeting. She went around the National Theatre and visited every nook and cranny. She always checked the loos to make sure they were clean.'[12] Becoming an avid theatregoer, she saw the play *The Madness of George III* at least ten times and went on tour with it to America and Israel.

During her years at the National Theatre, she became good friends with Richard Eyre. He recalled, 'When we used to drive back late at night together through Parliament Square, as she passed the statue of her father, she would always turn towards it and say, "Night, Night Papa". It was very touching.'[13] At her farewell party in 1995, he told the audience that he would miss her 'gossip, guidance, champagne, 7.45 a.m. phone calls, enthusiasm, wisdom and friendship'. She replied, 'You go too far, but then you often do, dear Richard.'[14]

Like her mother before her, Mary now became the guardian of her father's legacy. Her house was full of Winston's paintings and memorabilia. She published more books about the family, including her parents' letters, a family album and her own memoir of her idyllic childhood at Chartwell and her wartime experiences. She was a great supporter of the archives centre at Churchill College, Cambridge, and attended many of the conferences of the International Churchill

Society. She believed that it was important 'to keep the memory green and the record accurate'.[15] However, she sometimes found herself answering the most obscure questions. When asked, 'Did Winston Churchill like spinach?', she replied, 'Well my father once threw a plate of it at my mother.'[16]

As well as her flourishing public life, Mary was a matriarch. Her son Nicholas described her as 'the head and heart of our family'.[17] She was loved and admired by her five children, many grandchildren and great-grandchildren, and her nieces and nephews.

As a self-deprecating person, she always slapped down any of the family if they got above themselves about being descendants of Winston Churchill.[18] However, while she was a formidable force, she was also great fun to be with. Like her father, she had a taste for the finer things in life. She had a penchant for Pol Roger Champagne and when she visited her niece, Celia, for New Year's Eve, she usually took a jar of caviar or foie gras.[19] However, it was the wonderful stories she told and her warmth and laughter which endeared her most to her family.[20] She had a good sense of humour and, like Winston, she openly expressed her emotions. She laughed a great deal, and if something moved her, she cried. Both father and daughter had the ability to talk and cry at the same time if they were telling a poignant story.[21]

Mary died on 31 May 2014, aged 91. She was a woman who really had managed to have it all, not necessarily *all* at the same time, but in different phases in her long and very full life. She had supported her family while also fulfilling her own potential and, most important of all, she had been happy. She once told a large audience, 'To have been my father's child was an enrichment […] beyond compare.'[22] For her, it was true; her experience of being the daughter of Winston Churchill had been so different from her siblings'. Her secure childhood, under Moppet's care, and the enduring religious faith she gained as a child sustained her throughout her life.

She had followed the middle path between the extremes of her two sisters. While Sarah had dedicated herself to her career, sacrificing the chance of having a family, Diana had devoted herself to a more conventional life as a wife and mother. Neither had found complete fulfilment in these roles, while Mary, who had both aspects in her life, enjoyed equilibrium.

However, the different life experiences of the three sisters were as much about nature as nurture. Mary's sanguine temperament protected her from the problems that tormented them. Certainly, she combined both her parents' best qualities in her personality. She inherited Winston's optimism and Clementine's charm. She was blessed with an inner confidence and stability that eluded her brother and sisters. Unlike them, a bright star had always shone for her.

Acknowledgements

I first knew that I wanted to write about the Churchill girls when I came across a letter from Sarah Churchill to her father. I was researching another project and I found it by chance but as soon as I read her eloquent words, I knew there was a fascinating story to be told. This was not an acolyte speaking to the great war leader, this was a daughter writing frankly to her father: the intimacy between them was tangible. The voice that came across immediately spoke to me. I heard a sensitive, passionate woman who was struggling with the dilemma of juggling the demands of her loved ones, while being true to herself. It made me want to know more.

Since starting my research, I have never been disappointed. The sisters' stories have entertained me, moved me and inspired me in equal measure. Their vulnerability, as much as their strength, has made them appealing characters to write about.

While delving into their lives, I have drawn on the wealth of published sources available. The richest source has been the memoirs of two of the Churchill girls themselves. Mary Soames' *A Daughter's Tale* and Sarah Churchill's *A Thread in the Tapestry* and *Keep on Dancing* provide invaluable detail. Both women wrote with great honesty about their lives and gave their perspective on what happened. The excellent biographies of Winston Churchill by Andrew Roberts and

Martin Gilbert, and of Clementine Churchill by her daughter Mary Soames, and more recently Sonia Purnell, have also been essential reading. I would like to thank Sonia Purnell for kindly granting me permission to quote from *First Lady: The Life and Wars of Clementine Churchill*. A revealing overview of the relationships between the whole Churchill family is given in *Citadel of the Heart* by John Pearson and *The Churchills* by Mary S. Lovell.

I also draw on the myriad memoirs of relatives, friends and staff, who observed the Churchill family at close quarters. I am very grateful to the following people/publishers for allowing me to quote from these sources: Rupert Colville and Harriet Bowes Lyon for their father, Jock Colville's books and letters; Gibson Square for Diana Mitford's *A Life of Contrasts*; Pan Macmillan for *The Diaries of Sir Robert Bruce Lockhart*. I have tried to contact all copyright holders – if there are any I have missed, I will rectify this omission in subsequent editions.

Even more enlightening than books has been the archival material from the Churchill Archives at Churchill College, Cambridge. This is one of the most comprehensive and full archives I have ever dealt with. The Mary and Christopher Soames Archives at Churchill College were opened in February 2019. They contribute immeasurably to my book, providing new material that has never been published before. I thank Emma Soames for generously granting me permission to quote from many of these letters and from her mother's books. The Soames' archives build on the already extensive material available in the Winston, Clementine and Sarah Churchill papers. These archives contain hundreds of letters to and from Diana, Sarah, Mary and their parents. The Churchill girls not only wrote in great detail about their experiences, their letters are also perceptive and beautifully written; at times they are very funny, at others heart-breaking.

I would also like to thank the wonderful, ultra-efficient librarians at the Churchill Archives, who made my trips to Cambridge so rewarding. The Director of the Churchill Archives Centre, Allen Packwood, has also been incredibly helpful. He has patiently acted as a go-between with members of the Churchill family and their friends and staff. I am particularly grateful to him for granting me permission to quote from Sarah and Clementine's letters, Sarah's published works and Patrick Kinna's taped oral histories.

Although the Churchill Archives is my main source, I have also used material from the Winant collection in the Franklin Delano Roosevelt Presidential Library in America. My thanks go to Christian Belena, who provided me with letters between Gil Winant, Clementine Churchill and Sarah Churchill, and allowed me to use them in my book. To create a rounded picture, I also refer to some of the thousands of newspaper articles that appeared about the Churchill girls, both in Britain and abroad, throughout their lives.

However, to understand the women I was writing about, nothing compares to talking to the people who really knew them. Celia Sandys and Emma Soames kindly spared time to talk to me about their mothers and aunts. Their candour and charm show that these Churchill qualities pass down the generations. I am very grateful to Celia Sandys for allowing me to quote from her mother's letters and for reading my manuscript.

I would also like to thank Shelagh Montague Browne for talking to me. Lady Montague Browne was Clementine Churchill's secretary during the early 1960s and she later married Winston Churchill's private secretary, Anthony Montague Browne. Not only has she allowed me to quote from her husband's witty and insightful memoir, she also provided me with a perceptive insider's view of the Churchill family during those tragic years.

Another experience that brought the Churchill girls alive for me was visiting their childhood home, Chartwell. Katherine Carter, the curator, kindly gave me a private tour of the house, pointing out things I would never have noticed on my own. Talking to her provided me with a whole new insight into the women. Her empathy and unrivalled knowledge of the family added greatly to my own understanding of them.

Lee Pollock and Andy Smith, from the International Churchill Society, have also been most supportive. It has been very stimulating bouncing ideas around with such unrivalled experts.

This book would not have come to fruition without the support of a fantastic team. Firstly, my agent Heather Holden Brown and Elly and Rob Dinsdale at HHB Agency have worked tirelessly to make this project a success. Once again, I have thoroughly enjoyed working with my publisher, Laura Perehinec, and her team at The History Press. From the moment I mentioned the idea of writing about the Churchill girls to her, Laura immediately understood exactly what I wanted to achieve and gave me the time and freedom to do it to my best ability. Katie Read has also been the perfect publicist, working hard even during the pressures of the COVID-19 lockdown to make sure this book reaches the widest possible audience. It has also been a pleasure working with my American publisher, Charles Spicer, and his team at St Martin's Press. Like Laura, he shared my vision for the book and how to turn that initial idea into reality.

Finally, as ever, I could not have written *The Churchill Sisters* without the love and support of my family, John, Christopher, Bridget, Becky and Teddy.

Select Bibliography

Attenborough, Wilfred, *Churchill and the Black Dog of Depression: Reassessing the Biographical Evidence of Psychological Disorder* (Basingstoke: Palgrave Macmillan, 2014).

Beauchamp, Antony, *Focus on Fame* (London: Odhams Press, 1958).

Bellush, Bernard, *He Walked Alone: A Biography of John Gilbert Winant* (The Hague and Paris: Mouton, 1968).

Browne, Anthony Montague, *Long Sunset: Memoirs of Winston Churchill's Last Private Secretary* (London: Indigo, 1996).

Castle, Charles, *The Duchess Who Dared: The Life of Margaret, Duchess of Argyll* (London: Pan Books, 1995).

Churchill, John Spencer, *Crowded Canvas: The Memoirs of John Spencer Churchill* (London: Odhams Press, 1961).

Churchill, Randolph, *Twenty-One Years* (Boston and Cambridge: Houghton Mifflin Co., 1965).

Churchill, Sarah, *A Thread in the Tapestry* (London: Andre Deutsch, 1967).

Churchill, Sarah, *Keep on Dancing: An Autobiography* (London: Weidenfeld and Nicolson, 1981).

Churchill, Sarah, *The Empty Spaces* (London: Leslie Frewin, 1966).

Churchill, Winston S., *His Father's Son: The Life of Randolph Churchill* (London: Phoenix, 1997).

Colville, John, *The Churchillians* (London: Weidenfeld and Nicolson, 1981).

Colville, John, *Footprints in Time: Memories* (London: Collins, 1976).

Colville, John, *The Fringes of Power: Downing Street Diaries 1939–1955* (London, Sydney, Auckland and Toronto: Hodder and Stoughton, 1985).

Danchev, Alex, and Daniel Todman (eds), *Field Marshal Lord Alanbrooke War Diaries 1939–45* (London: Weidenfeld and Nicolson, 2001).

Downing, Taylor, *Spies in the Sky: The Secret Battle for Aerial Intelligence During World War II* (London: Abacus, 2012).

Eden, Clarissa, *A Memoir from Churchill to Eden* (London: Weidenfeld and Nicolson, 2007).

Gilbert, Martin, *Churchill: A Life* (London: Pimlico, 2000).

Glueckstein, Fred, *Churchill and Colonist II: The Story of Winston Churchill and His Famous Race Horse* (Bloomington: iUniverse, 2014).

Graebner, Walter, *My Dear Mister Churchill* (London: Michael Joseph, 1965).

Grant Duff, Sheila, *The Parting of the Ways: A Personal Account of the Thirties* (London: Peter Owen, 1982).

Gray, Annie, *Victory in the Kitchen: The Life of Churchill's Cook* (London: Profile Books, 2020).

Halsall, Christine, *Women of Intelligence: Winning the Second World War with Air Photos* (Stroud: The History Press, 2017).

Hardman, Robert, *Queen of the World: The Global Biography* (London: Arrow Books, 2019).

Harriman, W. Averell, and Elie Abel, *Special Envoy to Churchill and Stalin 1941–1946* (New York, Random House: 1975).

Howells, Roy, *Churchill's Last Years* (New York: David McKay Co., 1966).

Ismay, General Lord, *The Memoirs of General Lord Ismay* (New York: The Viking Press, 1960).

James, Robert Rhodes (ed.), *'Chips': The Diaries of Sir Henry Channon* (London: Weidenfeld and Nicolson, 1993).

Jenkins, Roy, *Churchill* (London: Pan Macmillan, 2002).

King, Cecil, *With Malice Towards None: A War Diary By Cecil King* (London: Sidgwick and Jackson, 1970).

Lee, Celia, *Jean, Lady Hamilton 1861–1941: A Soldier's Wife* (London: Phoenix, 2001).

Lees-Milne, James, *Ancestral Voices* (London: Faber and Faber, 1984).

Leslie, Anita, *Cousin Randolph: The Life of Randolph Churchill* (London: Hutchinson, 1985).

Lovell, Mary S., *The Churchills: A Family at the Heart of History – From the Duke of Marlborough to Winston Churchill* (London: Abacus, 2011).

Lovell, Mary S., *The Mitford Girls: The Biography of an Extraordinary Family* (London: Little, Brown, 2001).

Lovell, Mary S., *The Riviera Set* (London: Little Brown, 2016).

McGowan, Norman, *My Years With Churchill* (Greenwich, Connecticut: Gold Medal Books, 1958).

Macmillan, Harold, *War Diaries: Politics and War in the Mediterranean 1943–1945* (London: Macmillan, 1984).

Martin, Sir John, *Downing Street: The War Years* (London: Bloomsbury, 1991).

Moir, Phyllis, *I Was Winston Churchill's Private Secretary* (New York: Wilfred Funk, 1941).

Moody, Joanna, *From Churchill's War Rooms: Letters of a Secretary 1943–45* (Stroud: The History Press, 2014).

Moran, Charles, *Winston Churchill: The Struggle for Survival, 1940–1965* (London: Constable, 1966).

Mosley, Diana, *A Life of Contrasts: The Autobiography of Diana Mosley* (London: Gibson Square, 2018).

Murray, Edmund, *I Was Churchill's Bodyguard* (London: W.H. Allen, 1987).

Nel, Elizabeth, *Mr Churchill's Secretary* (London: Hodder and Stoughton, 1958).

Nicolson, Nigel (ed.), *Harold Nicolson: Diaries and Letters 1939–1945* (London: Collins, 1967).

Norwich, John Julius (ed.), *The Duff Cooper Diaries* (London: Phoenix, 2006).

Oliver, Vic, *Mr Showbusiness: The Autobiography of Vic Oliver* (London: George G. Harrap and Co., 1954).

Olson, Lynne, *Citizens of London: The Americans Who Stood with Britain in Its Darkest, Finest Hour* (London: Scribe Publications, 2015).

Owen, David, *In Sickness and in Power: Illness in Heads of Government During the last 100 Years* (London: Methuen, 2008).

Payn, Graham, and Sheridan Morley (eds), *The Noël Coward Diaries* (London: Weidenfeld and Nicolson, 1982).

Pearson, John, *Citadel of the Heart: Winston and the Churchill Dynasty* (London: Macmillan, 1991).

Pender, Paul, *The Butler Did It: My True and Terrifying Encounters with a Serial Killer* (Edinburgh: Mainstream Publishing, 2012).

Pottle, Mark (ed.), *Champion Redoubtable: The Diaries and Letters of Violet Bonham Carter 1914–45* (London: Weidenfeld and Nicolson, 1998).

Purnell, Sonia, *First Lady: The Life and Wars of Clementine Churchill* (London: Aurum Press, 2015).

Roberts, Andrew, *Churchill: Walking With Destiny* (London: Allen Lane, 2018).

Robyns, Gwen, *Barbara Cartland: An Authorised Biography* (London: Sidgwick and Jackson, 1984).

Rose, Jill, *Nursing Churchill: Wartime Life from the Private Letters of Winston Churchill's Nurse* (Stroud: Amberley, 2018).

Sandys, Celia, *Chasing Churchill: The Travels of Winston Churchill by his Granddaughter* (London: Harper Collins, 2003).

Sandys, Celia, *Churchill by his Granddaughter, Celia Sandys* (London: Imperial War Museum, 2013).

Sandys, Jonathan, and Wallace Henley, *God and Churchill* (Illinois: Tyndale Momentum, 2015).

Soames, Mary, *A Churchill Family Album* (London: Allen Lane, 1982).

Soames, Mary, *A Daughter's Tale: The Memoir of Winston and Clementine Churchill's Youngest Child* (London: Transworld, 2011).

Soames, Mary, *Clementine Churchill* (London: Cassell, 1979).

Soames, Mary, *Speaking for Themselves: The Personal Letters of Winston and Clementine Churchill* (London: Transworld, 1998).

Spence, Lyndsy, *The Grit in the Pearl: The Scandalous Life of Margaret, Duchess of Argyll* (Stroud: The History Press, 2019).

Stelzer, Cita, *Working With Winston: The Unsung Women Behind Britain's Greatest Statesman* (London: Head of Zeus, 2019).

Storr, Anthony, *Churchill's Black Dog and Other Phenomena of the Human Mind* (London: Flamingo, 1991).

Thompson, Laura, *The Six: The Lives of the Mitford Sisters* (New York: Picador, 2015).

Thompson, Walter, *Beside the Bulldog: The Intimate Memoirs of Churchill's Bodyguard* (London: Apollo Publishing, 2003).

Winant, John G., *A Letter from Grosvenor Square* (London: Hodder and Stoughton, 1947).

Young, Caroline, *Roman Holiday: The Secret Life of Hollywood in Rome* (Stroud: The History Press, 2018).

Young, Kenneth (ed.), *The Diaries of Sir Robert Bruce Lockhart 1915–1938* (London: Macmillan, 1973).

Young, Kenneth (ed.), *The Diaries of Sir Robert Bruce Lockhart, Vol. 2: 1939–1965* (London: Macmillan, 1980).

Notes

Introduction

1   The Soames Papers at the Churchill Archives, Churchill College, Cambridge University, were opened in 2019.
2   'Sarah Churchill: What Life is to Me', 29 May 1961, *Amarillo Globe Times*.
3   Sarah Churchill to Winston Churchill, 6 March 1947. Churchill Archives, CHUR1/45.
4   Mary Soames to Sarah Churchill, 19 August 1975. Mary Soames Literary Papers, Churchill Archives, MCHL 5/7/70.
5   Sarah Churchill to Mary Soames, 12 August 1975. Mary Soames Literary Papers, Churchill Archives, MCHL 5/7/70.

1 Diana: The Gold Cream Kitten

1   Winston Churchill to Clementine Churchill, 12 September 1909, in Mary Soames (ed.), *Speaking for Themselves: The Personal Letters of Winston and Clementine Churchill* (London: Doubleday, 1998) p. 29.
2   Sonia Purnell, *First Lady: The Life and Wars of Clementine Churchill* (London: Aurum Press, 2015) p. 38.
3   Andrew Roberts, *Churchill: Walking With Destiny* (London: Allen Lane, 2018) p. 124.
4   For a full discussion of how Clementine juggled being a wife and mother, see Mary Soames, *Clementine Churchill* (London: Cassell, 1979) p. 235.
5   Mary S. Lovell, *The Churchills: A Family at the Heart of History – From the Duke of Marlborough to Winston Churchill* (London: Abacus, 2012) p. 254.
6   Mary Soames, *Speaking for Themselves*, p. 3.

7   Mary Soames, *Clementine Churchill*, p. 21.

8   Andrew Roberts, *Churchill: Walking With Destiny*, p. 13.

9   St George's near Ascot. Later he went to a school in Brighton and then Harrow.

10 Andrew Roberts, *Churchill: Walking With Destiny*, p. 23.

11 Winston Churchill to Clementine Churchill, 30–31 May 1909, in Mary Soames, *Speaking for Themselves*, p. 23.

12 Mary Soames, *Speaking for Themselves*, p. 19.

13 John Pearson, *Citadel of the Heart: Winston and the Churchill Dynasty* (London: Macmillan, 1991) p. 120.

14 Clementine Churchill to Winston Churchill, 29 August 1909, in Mary Soames, *Speaking for Themselves*, p. 25.

15 For a full discussion of Clementine's emotional needs, see Mary Soames, *Clementine Churchill* and Sonia Purnell, *First Lady*.

16 Winston Churchill to Clementine Churchill, 11 July 1911, in Mary Soames, *Speaking for Themselves*, p. 53.

17 Clementine Churchill to Winston Churchill, 11 September 1909, in Mary Soames, *Speaking for Themselves*, p. 27.

18 Clementine Churchill to Winston Churchill, 12 September 1909, in Mary Soames, *Speaking for Themselves*, p. 28.

19 Clementine Churchill to Winston Churchill, 16 September 1909, in Mary Soames, *Speaking for Themselves*, p. 30.

20 For instance, she would have protective edges put on tables to stop Marigold running into them and when Winston built a tree house for the children at Chartwell he had to reassure her that it was safe.

21 Martin Gilbert points out that, although the suffragettes saw Winston as an 'out-and-out' opponent of giving women the vote, this was not correct. He was in favour in principle of women being enfranchised but was unwilling to vote for a Bill which would give 'an undoubted preponderance to the property vote', or one which did not have the majority of the electorate behind it. Eventually, in the Commons vote in 1917, he voted in favour of votes for women. Martin Gilbert, *Churchill: A Life* (London: Pimlico, 2000) pp. 221–22.

22 'Guarding the Churchill Baby', 28 November 1910, *Dundee Evening Telegraph*.

23 Winston Churchill to Clementine Churchill, 11 July 1911, in Mary Soames, *Speaking for Themselves*, p. 53.

24 Reflecting his compassionate attitude, there were improvements in the treatment of political prisoners including the suffragettes. He supported the introduction of lectures and concerts and the provision of books for prisoners. He also reduced the number of young offenders being sent to prison. Anthony Storr, *Churchill's Black Dog and Other Phenomena of the Human Mind* (London: Flamingo, 1991) pp. 35–36.

25 Winston Churchill to Clementine Churchill, 29 June 1911, in Mary Soames, *Speaking for Themselves*, p. 50.

26 The case he was reviewing seems to have been about Mary Ann Nash. A domestic servant aged 33, Mary Ann had frequently moved her illegitimate son, Stanley, from one relative or friend's house to another, but she could no longer afford to pay them to keep him. The little boy went missing and, sometime later, the body of a child was found in a disused well. Mary Ann was found guilty of the murder of Stanley by drowning. However, the evidence against her was far from conclusive. She was sentenced to death, but early in July she was reprieved. Her sentence was commuted to penal servitude for life. In fact, Mary Ann's son was not 2, as Winston wrote in his letter to Clementine, but 5 years and 9 months when he went missing. Perhaps Winston's mistake suggests it made him think of his own child. Shortly afterwards, he dealt with a similar case in which a 22-year-old, penniless, illegitimate girl called Mabel Blackmore, who lived in Neath Workhouse, Wales, drowned her illegitimate child because she found it impossible to get work. Once again, in August 1911, Winston advised the king to respite the death sentence passed on her. It seems likely that both cases preyed on his mind.

27 Clementine Churchill to Winston Churchill, 4 July 1911, in Mary Soames, *Speaking for Themselves*, p. 52.

28 Winston Churchill to Clementine Churchill, 5 July 1911, in Mary Soames, *Speaking for Themselves*, p. 52.

29 Winston Churchill to Clementine Churchill, 23 July 1913, in Mary Soames, *Speaking for Themselves*, p. 75.

30 Mary Soames, *Clementine Churchill*, p. 236.

31 Randolph Churchill, *Twenty-One Years* (Boston and Cambridge: Houghton Mifflin, 1965) p. 4.

32 Mary Soames, *Clementine Churchill*, pp. 83–85.

33 Ibid., p. 84.

34 Randolph Churchill, *Twenty-One Years,* pp. 6–7.

2 Sarah: The Bumblebee

1 Winston S. Churchill, *His Father's Son: The Life of Randolph Churchill* (London: Phoenix, 1997) p. 10.

2 Mary Soames, *Speaking for Themselves*, p. 87

3 Andrew Roberts, *Churchill: Walking with Destiny*, p. 171.

4 Clementine Churchill to Winston Churchill, 1 June 1914, in Mary Soames, *Speaking for Themselves*, p. 89.

5 Mary S. Lovell, *The Mitford Girls: The Biography of an Extraordinary Family* (London: Little, Brown, 2001) p. 60.

6   Clementine Churchill to Winston Churchill, 5 June 1914, in Mary Soames, *Speaking for Themselves*, p. 91.

7   Winston Churchill to Clementine Churchill, 6 June 1914, in Mary Soames, *Speaking for Themselves*, p. 91.

8   John Spencer Churchill, *Crowded Canvas: The Memoirs of John Spencer Churchill* (London: Odhams Press, 1961) p. 27.

9   Mary Soames, *Clementine Churchill*, p. 103.

10 Randolph Churchill, *Twenty-One Years*, p. 7.

11 In December 1914, Scarborough, Whitby and Hartlepool were bombarded by German ships. Mary Soames, *Clementine Churchill*, p. 109.

12 Randolph Churchill, *Twenty-One Years*, p. 7.

13 Winston held the fort until General Sir Henry Rawlinson arrived and Antwerp capitulated on 10 October. Mary Soames, *Clementine Churchill*, p. 113.

14 Mary Soames, *Clementine Churchill*, p. 114.

15 Clementine Churchill to Lady Randolph Churchill, 7 October 1914. Churchill Archives, CHAR 28/80/10.

16 Sarah Churchill, *Keep on Dancing: An Autobiography* (London: Weidenfeld and Nicolson, 1981) p. 1.

17 Mary Soames, *Clementine Churchill*, p. 114.

18 Ibid., pp. 116–17.

19 Ibid., p. 237.

20 Ibid., p. 118.

21 Mary Soames, *Speaking for Themselves*, p. 107.

22 Anthony Storr, *Churchill's Black Dog and Other Phenomena of the Human Mind*, pp. 42–43.

23 John Spencer Churchill, *Crowded Canvas*, pp. 30–31.

24 See Mary Soames, *Clementine Churchill*, p. 237.

25 John Spencer Churchill, *Crowded Canvas*, p. 33.

26 Sarah Churchill, *A Thread in the Tapestry* (London: Andre Deutsch, 1967) p. 29.

27 Randolph Churchill, *Twenty-One Years*, p. 8.

28 Sarah Churchill, *Keep on Dancing*, p. 2.

29 Randolph Churchill, *Twenty-One Years*, p. 8.

30 Clementine Churchill to Winston Churchill, 28 November 1915, in Mary Soames, *Speaking for Themselves*, p. 122.

31 Clementine Churchill to Winston Churchill, 1 December 1915, in Mary Soames, *Speaking for Themselves*, p. 123.

32 Winston Churchill to Clementine Churchill, 1–2 January 1916, in Mary Soames, *Speaking for Themselves*, pp. 143,145.

33 Mary Soames, *Speaking for Themselves*, p. 131.

34 Clementine Churchill to Winston Churchill, 7 February 1916. Churchill Archives, CHAR1/118A/63.

35 Clementine Churchill to Winston Churchill, 9 February 1916. Churchill Archives, CHAR1/118A/63.

36 Mary Soames, *Clementine Churchill*, p. 169.

37 Randolph Churchill, *Twenty-One Years*, p. 11.

38 John Spencer Churchill, *Crowded Canvas*, p. 34.

39 Anita Leslie, *Cousin Randolph: The Life of Randolph Churchill* (London: Hutchinson, 1985) p. 4.

40 Mary S. Lovell, *The Mitford Girls*, p. 22.

41 Sarah Churchill, *A Thread in the Tapestry*, p. 27.

42 Diana Mosley, *A Life of Contrasts: The Autobiography of Diana Mosley* (London: Gibson Square, 2018) p. 73.

43 Sarah's diary, 1955, Sarah Churchill Personal Papers, Churchill Archives, SCHL 2/2/2.

44 Sarah Churchill, *A Thread in the Tapestry*, p. 27.

45 John Pearson, *Citadel of the Heart*, p. 156.

46 Randolph Churchill, *Twenty-One Years*, pp. 9–10.

47 Sarah Churchill, *Keep on Dancing*, p. 2.

48 John Pearson, *Citadel of the Heart*, p. 157.

49 Written by Richmal Crompton, *Just William* was first published in 1921. The schoolboy, William, leads his band of friends called the Outlaws on a series of adventures. William's escapades usually go wrong, getting him into trouble with his parents.

50 John Spencer Churchill, *Crowded Canvas*, pp. 36–37.

51 Randolph Churchill, *Twenty-One Years*, p. 11.

52 Ibid., p. 12.

53 Mary S. Lovell, *The Mitford Girls*, p. 53.

54 Sarah Churchill, *Keep on Dancing*, p. 3.

55 Ibid., p. 3

56 Mary Soames, *Clementine Churchill*, p. 243.

57 The effect on the Churchill children was, perhaps, rather like Winston's reaction to his childhood. Andrew Roberts believes that his nephew Peregrine was perhaps correct to think that Winston was not more neglected by his parents than most Victorian children but 'his sensitive nature rebelled against it more than most'. Andrew Roberts, *Churchill: Walking with Destiny*, p. 13.

3 Marigold: The Duckadilly

1 As the military commander who led the Gallipoli campaign, Sir Ian's career had been effectively ended by the disaster. The two couples went through the damaging experience together, but Jean and Clementine had never

become real friends. Jean wrote critical comments about Clementine in her diary just a month before their intimate conversation.

2   The 16-month-old little boy had been left outside the door of the Paddington Creche, of which Jean was president, with a note pinned to his clothing that read, 'Harry'. No one claimed him so Jean agreed to foster him. Celia Lee, *Jean, Lady Hamilton 1861–1941: A Soldier's Wife* (London: Phoenix, 2001) p. 196.

3   21 June 1918, Jean Hamilton's diary in Celia Lee, *Jean, Lady Hamilton 1861–1941. A Soldier's Wife*, pp. 198–99.

4   Mary Soames to Mrs C.M. Lee, 6 December 1999. Mary Soames Literary Papers, Churchill Archives, MCHL 5/2/15.

5   Suggesting Jean never took the idea seriously, she mused in her diary about whether she would really like a son of Winston's. She wrote that she would have to smack him when young to instil some manners into him as she considered that Winston lacked any, although she thought he had a good heart. Jean Hamilton's diaries, 21 June 1918. Notes in Mary Soames Literary Papers, Churchill Archives, MCHL 5/2/15.

6   Jean Hamilton did not mention the matter again in her diary, and merely commented on the 13 November 1918 that Clementine was going to have a baby. Evidently, there were no hard feelings between Jean and Clementine and, in fact, afterwards they got on much better. The Hamiltons soon had a child of their own as they adopted Harry. Only a few months after Marigold's birth, they visited the Churchills at Lullenden. Jean now liked Clementine, writing that she was very attractive. They lunched together with Randolph and Diana, who Jean described as 'the gentle little maid' with 'white eyelashes'. Jean Hamilton's diaries, 16 March 1919. Notes in Mary Soames Literary Papers, Churchill Archives, MCHL 5/2/15.

7   Clementine Churchill to Lady Randolph Churchill, 10 July 1918. Churchill Archives, CHAR 28/128/3-4.

8   Mary Soames, *Speaking for Themselves*, p. 220.

9   Mary Soames, *Clementine Churchill*, p. 195.

10 Ettie Desborough to Winston and Clementine Churchill, 24 August 1921. Churchill Archives, CHAR 1/141/34.

11 Sonia Purnell, *First Lady*, p. 21.

12 Sarah's school report, April 1925. Sarah Churchill Personal Papers, Churchill Archives, SCHL 2/1/1.

13 Clementine Churchill to Winston Churchill, 4 August 1922. Churchill Archives, CHAR 1/158/42-43.

14 John Colville, *The Churchillians* (London: Weidenfeld and Nicholson, 1981) p. 21.

15 Winston Churchill to Clementine Churchill, 27 January 1922, in Mary Soames, *Speaking for Themselves*, p. 248.

16 Winston Churchill to Charles Sims, 16 May 1922. Churchill Archives, CHAR 1/157/31-34.

17 Mr Sims stood by his image and suggested that Winston ask someone who knew the girls well whether it was like them before saying anything further. Charles Sims to Winston Churchill, 11 July 1922. Churchill Archives, CHAR1/157/51.

18 Mary Soames, *Clementine Churchill*, p. 236.

19 John Pearson, *Citadel of the Heart*, p. 187.

20 Martin Gilbert, *Churchill: A Life*, p. 432.

21 Winston Churchill to Clementine Churchill, 6 February 1921, in Mary Soames, *Speaking for Themselves*, p. 225.

22 Winston Churchill to Clementine Churchill, 27 February 1921, in Mary Soames, *Speaking for Themselves*, p. 234.

23 Mary Soames, *Speaking for Themselves*, p. 235.

24 Mary Soames, *Clementine Churchill*, p. 199.

25 Randolph Churchill, *Twenty-One Years*, pp. 17–19.

26 Sarah wrote to Clementine, 'Baba is very sweet and quite well now.' Sarah Churchill to Clementine Churchill, no date. Mary Soames Literary Papers, Churchill Archives, MCHL 5/1/57.

27 Diana Churchill to Clementine Churchill, 20 August 1921. Mary Soames Literary Papers, Churchill Archives, MCHL 5/1/57.

28 Mary Soames, *Clementine Churchill*, p. 202.

29 Winston Churchill to Clementine Churchill, 19 (18) September 1921, in Mary Soames, *Speaking for Themselves*, p. 242.

30 Winston Churchill to Lord Crewe, 3 September 1921. Quoted in Winston S. Churchill, *His Father's Son*, p. 29.

31 Mary Soames, *Speaking for Themselves*, p. 241.

32 Clementine Churchill to Winston Churchill, 22 September 1921. Churchill Archives, CHAR 1/139/75-77.

33 Clementine Churchill to Winston Churchill, 4 January 1922, in Mary Soames, *Speaking for Themselves*, pp. 245–46.

34 Mary Soames, *A Daughter's Tale: The Memoir of Winston and Clementine Churchill's Youngest Child* (London: Doubleday, 2011) p. 3.

4 Mary: The Chartwell Child

1 Clementine Churchill to Winston Churchill, 3 February 1922, in Mary Soames, *Speaking for Themselves*, p. 252.

2 Clementine Churchill to Winston Churchill, 8 August 1922, in Mary Soames, *Speaking for Themselves*, p. 260.

3   Sir Henry Wilson, a prominent Ulsterman, was assassinated by Irish gunmen on the steps of his house on 22 June 1922. Mary Soames, *Clementine Churchill*, p. 237.

4   Randolph Churchill, *Twenty-One Years*, p. 20.

5   Clementine Churchill to Winston Churchill, 8 August 1922, in Mary Soames, *Speaking for Themselves*, p. 260.

6   Mary Soames, *A Daughter's Tale*, p. 12.

7   Maryott was the daughter of Lady Maude Whyte, a daughter of the Earl and Countess of Airlie. She had to work for her living so trained as a Norland nanny.

8   For Mrs Everest's influence on Winston Churchill's Christianity, see Jonathan Sandys and Wallace Henley, *God and Churchill* (Illinois: Tyndale Momentum, 2015) pp. 7–9.

9   Winston Churchill to Clementine Churchill, 28 March 1926, in Mary Soames, *Speaking for Themselves*, p. 298.

10 Conversation with Katherine Carter, curator at Chartwell, 21 October 2019.

11 Sarah Churchill, *A Thread in the Tapestry*, p. 22.

12 Mary Soames, *Clementine Churchill*, p. 223.

13 Mary Soames, *A Daughter's Tale*, p. 14.

14 Ibid., pp. 13–14.

15 Conversation with Katherine Carter, curator at Chartwell, 21 October 2019.

16 Mary Soames, *A Daughter's Tale*, pp. 13–15.

17 Mary Soames, *Clementine Churchill*, p. 233.

18 Conversation with Katherine Carter, curator at Chartwell, 21 October 2019.

19 Mary Soames, *A Daughter's Tale*, pp. 12–13.

20 In the portrait by William Nicholson of Winston and Clementine having breakfast together, which was painted for their silver wedding, Tango the cat is on the table and a chicken has just wandered into the dining room. Admittedly, there was some poetic licence as Winston and Clementine rarely breakfasted together, but the portrayal of the animals captured the atmosphere.

21 Mary Soames, *A Daughter's Tale*, p. 22.

22 'Tango' was painted by William Nicholson, who often stayed at Chartwell. Mary Soames, *A Daughter's Tale*, p. 24.

23 26 September 2011, 'Mary Soames Interview', BBC Radio 4, *Woman's Hour*.

24 Winston Churchill to Clementine Churchill, 10 August 1928, in Mary Soames, *Speaking for Themselves*, p. 327.

25 John Spencer Churchill, *Crowded Canvas*, p. 201.

26 Mary Soames, *A Daughter's Tale*, p. 65.

27 Sarah Churchill, *Keep on Dancing*, p. 2.

28 26 September 2011, 'Mary Soames Interview', BBC Radio 4, *Woman's Hour*.

29 Mary Soames, *A Daughter's Tale*, pp. 69–70.

30 Diana Mosley, *A Life of Contrasts*, p. 22.

31 Ibid., p. 48.

32 Anita Leslie, *Cousin Randolph*, p. 8.

33 Diana Mosley, *A Life of Contrasts*, p. 225.

34 Ibid., p. 44.

35 Sarah Churchill, *A Thread in the Tapestry*, p. 29.

36 Clementine Churchill to Winston Churchill, 30 September 1929, in Mary Soames, *Speaking for Themselves*, p. 348.

37 Talks with Peregrine in Mary Soames Literary Papers, Churchill Archives, MCHL 5/2/12.

38 Mary Soames, *A Daughter's Tale*, p. 67.

39 Clementine was not unique in abiding by these old-fashioned rules. In the 1920s young girls were not expected to go out in London without a chaperone. In the country, different rules applied: girls could walk and ride out alone. Mary S. Lovell, *The Mitford Girls*, p. 69.

40 Clementine Churchill to Winston Churchill, 10 September 1926, in Mary Soames, *Speaking for Themselves*, p. 300.

41 Diana Mosley, *A Life of Contrasts*, p. 42. Diana was right, there was an unfounded rumour that Brendan Bracken was Winston's illegitimate son because little was known about his parentage and he had thick red hair.

42 John Spencer Churchill, *Crowded Canvas*, p. 102.

43 Mary Soames, *A Daughter's Tale*, pp. 79–80.

44 Sarah Churchill, *A Thread in the Tapestry*, p. 31.

45 Mary Soames, *Clementine Churchill*, p. 231.

46 Sarah's diary 1955, Sarah Churchill Personal Papers, Churchill Archives, SCHL 2/2/2.

47 Sarah Churchill, *A Thread in the Tapestry*, p. 33.

5 The Chancellor's Daughters

1 Mary Soames, *A Daughter's Tale*, p. 26.

2 Winston Churchill to Clementine Churchill, 27 September 1927, in Mary Soames, *Speaking for Themselves*, p. 311.

3 Mary Soames, *A Daughter's Tale*, p. 38.

4 Winston Churchill to Clementine Churchill, 22 October 1927, in Mary Soames, *Speaking for Themselves*, p. 314.

5 Sarah Churchill, *Keep on Dancing*, p. 18.

6 'Casualty', Sarah Churchill, *The Empty Spaces* (London: Leslie Frewin, 1966) p. 25.

7 Note from Sarah Churchill in Sarah Churchill Personal Papers, Churchill Archives, SCHL 1/1/3.

8   Sarah's school reports 1927–28, Sarah Churchill Personal Papers, Churchill Archives, SCHL 2/1/1.

9   Sarah Churchill, *Keep on Dancing*, p. 5.

10 Note from Sarah Churchill in Sarah Churchill Personal Papers, Churchill Archives, SCHL 1/1/3.

11 Sarah Churchill, *Keep on Dancing*, p. 5.

12 25 November (no year given), Sarah Churchill Personal Papers, Churchill Archives, SCHL 1/1/2.

13 Winston Churchill to Clementine Churchill, 20 March 1926, in Mary Soames, *Speaking for Themselves*, p. 296.

14 Laura Thompson, *The Six: The Lives of the Mitford Sisters* (New York: Picador, 2015) p. 98.

15 Diana Churchill to Winston Churchill, 28 November 1926. Churchill Archives, CHAR 1/88/69.

16 Diana Churchill to Clementine Churchill, 17 October 1926. Mary Soames Literary Papers, Churchill Archives, MCHL 5/1/268.

17 Diana Churchill to Winston Churchill, no date, Venice. Mary Soames Literary Papers, Churchill Archives, MCHL 5/1/268.

18 'Two Interesting Debs', 7 February 1928, *Leeds Mercury*.

19 'Winston's Eldest', 19 January 1927, *Exeter and Plymouth Gazette*.

20 Diana Churchill to Clementine Churchill, April 1928. Mary Soames Literary Papers, Churchill Archives, MCHL 5/1/268.

21 Mary Soames, *A Daughter's Tale*, p. 28.

22 Sarah Churchill, *Keep on Dancing*, p. 16.

23 She had two operations on a mastoid.

24 Clementine Churchill to Winston Churchill, 6 August 1928, in Mary Soames, *Speaking for Themselves*, p. 325.

25 Ibid.

26 Diana Churchill to Winston Churchill, 4 April 1928. Churchill Archives, CHAR 1/199/79-80.

27 She married Bryan Guinness in 1929. Diana Churchill was one of the bridesmaids at the wedding.

28 Diana wrote to Clementine in 1928 that she was 'thrilled' with *Orlando*, Virginia Woolf's latest novel. Diana Churchill to Clementine Churchill, 8 November 1928. Mary Soames Literary Papers, Churchill Archives, MCHL 5/7/1.

29 Diana Churchill to Winston Churchill, 17 October 1929. Churchill Archives, CHAR 1/205/45-46.

30 Diana Churchill to Winston Churchill, 2 October 1929. Mary Soames Literary Papers, Churchill Archives, MCHL 5/7/1.

31 Clementine Churchill to Winston Churchill, 28 September 1927, in Mary Soames, *Speaking for Themselves*, p. 310.

32   Interview with Celia Sandys, 21 January 2020.

33   Sarah Churchill, *Keep on Dancing*, p. 15.

34   Anita Leslie, *Cousin Randolph*, p. 13.

35   Sonia Purnell, *First Lady*, p. 167.

36   Sarah Churchill, *Keep on Dancing*, p. 16.

37   Shelagh Montague Browne, who was Clementine's secretary in the early 1960s, says Clementine was 'very witty but she had no sense of humour', and she could not laugh at herself. Interview with Shelagh Montague Browne, 27 February 2020.

38   Talks with Peregrine in Mary Soames Literary Papers, Churchill Archives, MCHL 5/2/12.

39   'A London Diary: Looking Forward', 3 April 1929, *Portsmouth Evening News.*

40   Diana Churchill to Winston Churchill, 4 December 1923. Mary Soames Literary Papers, Churchill Archives, MCHL 5/1/268.

41   Winston Churchill to Clementine Churchill, 20 March 1925, in Mary Soames, *Speaking for Themselves*, p. 296.

42   Diana Churchill to Clementine Churchill, 2 December 1923. Mary Soames Literary Papers, Churchill Archives, MCHL 5/1/268.

43   'Diana Goes to See', 4 December 1923, *Yorkshire Evening Post.*

44   In 1928 she led the procession to Disraeli's house, Hughenden Manor, to celebrate Primrose Day and made a well-received speech.

45   Violet Bonham Carter and Megan Lloyd George both became politicians.

46   Clementine's secretary in the 1960s, Shelagh Montague Browne, thinks that if Clementine had not married Winston, she might have become an MP herself. She told Shelagh that when she met Gertrude Bell she envied her ability to be independent. When she was young, she never had the money to be able to live that sort of life. Interview with Shelagh Montague Browne, 27 February 2020.

47   He hoped the vote would not be extended to women because they were 'less able than men'. Echoing his father's view of Lady Astor, the first woman in Parliament, he wrote, 'Although only one percent of the House of Commons consists of females it is a woman who is by far the most unpopular member.' Anita Leslie, *Cousin Randolph*, p. 9.

48   In a *Sunday Times* interview in about 1964, Randolph said, 'Obviously the women's vote is here to stay. It's always struck me as a great mistake on their part. The influence of women is only successful when it's indirect.' He agreed that women's influence should be 'exercised in country houses, at the dining-room table in the boudoir and the bedroom [...] But I believe with Dr Johnson: "A woman talking is like a dog walking on its hind legs. It is not done well, Sir, but one marvels that it's done at all". Curiously enough, the better a woman speaks the more embarrassing I always find it. It makes

me feel quite uncomfortable.' Quoted in Randolph Churchill, *Twenty-One Years*, p. 132.

49 Anita Leslie, *Cousin Randolph*, p. 1.

6 Diana in the Limelight

1   'Diana Churchill "Mobbed": Wedding Crowd Break Through Cordon', 13 December 1932, *Dundee Courier*.

2   Sarah Churchill, *Keep on Dancing*, p. 17.

3   Phyllis Moir, *I Was Winston Churchill's Private Secretary* (New York: Wilfred Funk, 1941) pp. 42, 57–61.

4   Miriam Morrell to Clementine Churchill, 30 December 1931. Churchill Archives, CHAR 1/398A/2.

5   'Engagement to MP', 24 August 1935, *The Scotsman*.

6   John Pearson, *Citadel of the Heart*, p. 227.

7   Interview with Celia Sandys, 21 January 2020.

8   Mary Soames, *A Daughter's Tale*, p. 98.

9   John Pearson, *Citadel of the Heart*, p. 228.

10 Interview with Celia Sandys, 21 January 2020.

11 Mary Soames, *Clementine Churchill*, p. 245.

12 For a full description of life at Maxine's villa, see Mary S. Lovell, *The Riviera Set* (London: Little Brown, 2016).

13 Winston Churchill to Clementine Churchill, 31 December 1934, in Mary Soames, *Speaking for Themselves*, p. 368.

14 Winston Churchill to Clementine Churchill, 23 February 1935, in Mary Soames, *Speaking for Themselves*, p. 384.

15 Winston Churchill to Clementine Churchill, 31 December 1934, in Mary Soames, *Speaking for Themselves*, p. 368.

16 Maryott Whyte to Clementine Churchill, 12 February 1935. Mary Soames Literary Papers, Churchill Archives, MCHL 5/7/4.

17 Diana Churchill to Clementine Churchill, 19 March 1935. Mary Soames Literary Papers, Churchill Archives, MCHL5/1/80.

18 Sarah Churchill to Clementine Churchill, 17 February 1935. Sarah Churchill Personal Papers, Churchill Archives, SCHL1/1/4.

19 Clementine Churchill to Winston Churchill, 20 January 1935, in Mary Soames, *Speaking for Themselves*, p. 375.

20 Interview with Celia Sandys, 21 January 2020.

21 Winston Churchill to Clementine Churchill, 2 March 1935, in Mary Soames, *Speaking for Themselves*, p. 388.

22 Sarah Churchill to Clementine Churchill, 17 February 1935. Sarah Churchill Personal Papers, Churchill Archives, SCHL1/1/4.

23 Winston Churchill to Clementine Churchill, 23 January 1936, in Mary Soames, *Speaking for Themselves*, p. 378.

24 Clementine Churchill to Winston Churchill, 22 February 1935, in Mary Soames, *Speaking for Themselves*, p. 382.

25 Maryott Whyte to Clementine Churchill, 31 January 1935. Mary Soames Literary Papers, Churchill Archives, MCHL 5/7/4.

26 Sarah Churchill to Mary Churchill, 17 November 1935. Sarah Churchill Personal Papers, Churchill Archives, SCHL 1/3/1.

27 Maryott Whyte to Clementine Churchill, 31 January 1935. Mary Soames Literary Papers, Churchill Archives, MCHL 5/7/4.

28 Sarah Churchill to Clementine Churchill, 17 February 1935. Sarah Churchill Personal Papers, Churchill Archives, SCHL1/1/4.

29 Winston Churchill to Clementine Churchill, 2 March 1935, in Mary Soames, *Speaking for Themselves*, p. 388.

30 Clementine Churchill to Margery Street, 21 August 1935. Mary Soames Literary Papers, Churchill Archives, MCHL5/1/78.

31 Winston Churchill to Clementine Churchill, 20 January 1937. Churchill Archives, CHAR 1/298/20-23.

32 'Duncan Sandys Wedding', 16 September 1935, *Dundee Evening Telegraph*.

33 'Bridegroom MP a Rival at By-Election', 17 September 1935, *Western Daily Press*.

34 'Panorama', 20 January 1937, *The Tatler*.

7 Sarah Takes Centre Stage

1 Sarah Churchill to Mary Churchill, 17 November 1935. Sarah Churchill Personal Papers, Churchill Archives, SCHL 1/3/1.

2 Clementine Churchill to Margery Street, 8 November 1933. Mary Soames Literary Papers, Churchill Archives, MCHL5/1/78.

3 Sarah Churchill, *Keep on Dancing*, p. 7.

4 Ibid., p. 8.

5 Mary Soames, *A Daughter's Tale*, p. 53.

6 Ibid., p. 54.

7 Allegedly, Doris Castlerosse slept with both Randolph and Winston. Whether Winston was unfaithful to Clementine with Doris is disputed by his biographers. Mary S. Lovell sets out some of the evidence in *The Riviera Set*, pp. 142–44. Andrew Roberts also examines the evidence and he comes to the conclusion that it is impossible to believe that Churchill had an affair with Lady Castlerosse, or anyone else (*Churchill: Walking with Destiny*, pp. 385–86).

8 John Pearson, *Citadel of the Heart*, p. 235.

9 Ibid., p. 241.

10 Sarah Churchill, *Keep on Dancing*, p. 16.

11 Ibid., p. 15.

12 Clementine Churchill to Margery Street, 9 June 1933. Mary Soames Literary Papers, Churchill Archives, MCHL5/1/78.

13 Clementine Churchill to Margery Street, 8 November 1933. Mary Soames Literary Papers, Churchill Archives, MCHL5/1/78.

14 Mary Soames, *A Daughter's Tale*, p. 55.

15 Clementine Churchill to Margery Street, 18 September 1934. Mary Soames Literary Papers, Churchill Archives, MCHL 5/1/78.

16 C.B. Cochran to Winston Churchill, 7 November 1935. Churchill Archives, CHAR 1/272/41-42.

17 Sarah Churchill, *Keep on Dancing*, p. 30.

18 Cecil Beaton was to become one of the most famous portrait photographers of his era and Frederick Ashton later became director of the Royal Ballet.

19 As well as Sarah, his young ladies included Gertrude Lawrence's daughter, Pamela.

20 Called 'The First Shoot', it sounds utterly bizarre, but it was the creation of the best in the business, written by Osbert Sitwell with music by William Walton and choreographed by Frederick Ashton. 'Eight Nations Star in Cochran Revue', 5 February 1936, *Daily Herald*.

21 Clementine Churchill to Margery Street, 30 December 1935. Mary Soames Literary Papers, Churchill Archives, MCHL 5/1/78.

22 Sarah Churchill, *Keep on Dancing*, p. 32.

23 Clementine Churchill to Winston Churchill, 27 February 1936, in Mary Soames, *Speaking for Themselves*, p. 413.

24 Winston Churchill to Clementine Churchill, 21 February 1936, in Mary Soames, *Speaking for Themselves*, p. 412.

25 Martin Gilbert, *Churchill: A Life*, pp. 181, 429.

26 Andrew Roberts, *Churchill: Walking with Destiny*, pp. 363–65.

27 Accounts of his age differ, some state Vic was sixteen years older than Sarah, others eighteen. The number of times he was divorced also differs. Winston thought he had been married twice and the evidence from his lawyers, which is now in the Churchill Archives, seems to support this. However, Mary Soames claimed this was not true and he had only been married once before he met Sarah.

28 Vic Oliver, *Mr Showbusiness: The Autobiography of Vic Oliver* (London: George G. Harrap and Co., 1954) p. 95.

29 Winston Churchill to Clementine Churchill, 21 February 1936, in Mary Soames, *Speaking for Themselves*, p. 412.

30 Sarah Churchill to Clementine Churchill, 12 October 1936. Sarah Churchill Personal Papers, Churchill Archives, SCHL 1/1/5.

31 Sarah Churchill, *Keep on Dancing*, pp. 35–36.

32 Ibid., p. 36.

8 Sarah Follows Her Star

1   Mary Soames, *A Daughter's Tale*, p. 58.

2   Sarah Churchill to Clementine Churchill, October 1936. Sarah Churchill Personal Papers, Churchill Archives, SCHL 1/1/5.

3   Mary Soames, *A Daughter's Tale*, pp. 59–60.

4   Mary Soames to Sarah Churchill, 26 October 1936. Mary Soames Literary Papers, Churchill Archives, MCHL 5/7/5.

5   Winston Churchill to Sarah Churchill, 25 October 1936. Mary Soames Literary Papers, Churchill Archives, MCHL 5/7/5.

6   Alice, Lady Wimborne to Winston Churchill, 21 September 1936. Churchill Archives, CHAR 1/286/1-2.

7   Sarah Churchill, *Keep on Dancing*, pp. 56–57.

8   Vic Oliver to Sarah Churchill, no date. Sarah Churchill Personal Correspondence, Churchill Archives, SCHL 1/8/1.

9   Vic Oliver, *Mr Showbusiness*, p. 101.

10 'Vic Oliver Says: "No, No, No"', 17 September 1936, *Daily Herald*.

11 Nancy Astor was the first woman Member of Parliament to take her seat in the House of Commons. She often clashed with Winston.

12 Sarah Churchill to Mary Churchill, no date. Mary Soames Literary Papers, Churchill Archives, MCHL 5/7/5.

13 Apparently, in Boston she was paid $300 a week, while in New York she earned $750. She had been paid £4 a week in Cochran's Revue.

14 Sarah Churchill to Winston Churchill, November 1936. Churchill Archives, CHAR 1/288/71-72.

15 Winston Churchill to Clementine Churchill, 7 January 1937, in Mary Soames, *Speaking for Themselves*, p. 422.

16 Clementine Churchill to Sarah Churchill, 25 October 1936. Mary Soames Literary Papers, Churchill Archives, MCHL 5/7/5.

17 Ibid.

18 Winston Churchill to Sarah Churchill, 25 October 1936. Mary Soames Literary Papers, Churchill Archives, MCHL 5/7/5.

19 Vic Oliver, *Mr Showbusiness*, pp. 107–09.

20 Ibid., p. 110.

21 Clementine Churchill, 5 January 1937, in Mary Soames, *Speaking for Themselves*, p. 422.

22 Winston Churchill to Sarah Churchill, 2 February 1937. Churchill Archives, CHAR 1/303/21-22.

23 'The Affair Churchill Tried to Wreck', 20 November 1982, *Liverpool Echo*.

24 'The Sarah Churchill Story', 1 December 1958, *Liverpool Echo*.

25 She appeared in the film *Who's Your Lady Friend?* with Vic in the lead role. In the theatre, she played Mrs Manningham in *Gas Light*.

26 Vic Oliver to Sarah Churchill, no date. Sarah Churchill Personal Correspondence, Churchill Archives, SCHL 1/8/1.

27 Sarah Churchill to Winston Churchill, 13 March 1939. Churchill Archives, CHAR 1/344/26-27. Cecil Beaton mentioned her cosmetic surgery in a conversation with James Lees-Milne. He said, 'Perhaps I should not tell tales out of school, but if her nose were only her own.' When asked whose it was, he replied, 'Gillies's', 8 February 1942. James Lees-Milne, *Ancestral Voices* (London: Faber and Faber, 1984) p. 19.

28 Vic Oliver, *Mr Showbusiness*, p. 122.

29 Ibid., p. 132.

9 Mary Faces the Gathering Storm

1   William Nicholson, the famous artist, said the depressing conversation made him feel quite sick. John Spencer Churchill, *Crowded Canvas*, pp. 101–02.

2   Mary Soames, *Speaking for Themselves*, p. 438.

3   Clarissa Eden, *A Memoir from Churchill to Eden* (London: Weidenfeld and Nicolson, 2007) p. 5.

4   John Spencer Churchill, *Crowded Canvas*, pp. 101–05.

5   Mary Soames, *A Daughter's Tale*, p. 61.

6   'A Childhood: Mary Soames', Ray Connolly, 10 November 1990, *The Times*.

7   Mary Soames, *A Daughter's Tale*, p. 47.

8   Clementine Churchill to Margery Street, 18 September 1934. Mary Soames Literary Papers, Churchill Archives, MCHL5/1/78.

9   Mary Soames to Clementine Churchill, 8 March 1935. Mary Soames Literary Papers, Churchill Archives, MCHL 5/7/4.

10 Mary Soames, *A Daughter's Tale*, p. 111.

11 Sonia Purnell, *First Lady*, p. 190.

12 Mary Soames, *A Daughter's Tale*, p. 86.

13 Mary Soames, *Clementine Churchill*, p. 248.

14 Mary Soames, *A Daughter's Tale*, pp. 89–90.

15 Celia Sandys, *Chasing Churchill: The Travels of Winston Churchill* (London: Harper Collins, 2003) p. 110.

16 Duncan Sandys to Winston Churchill, 29 January 1937. Churchill Archives, CHAR 1/298/34.

17 Clementine Churchill to Winston Churchill, 27 December 1937. Churchill Archives, CHAR 1/322/12-15.
18 Winston Churchill to Duncan Sandys, 31 March 1938. Churchill Archives, CHAR 1/323/31.
19 Mary Soames, *Speaking for Themselves*, p. 38.
20 'A Childhood: Mary Soames', Ray Connolly, 10 November 1990, *The Times*.
21 Mary Soames, *A Daughter's Tale*, p. 122.
22 Ibid., p. 64.
23 Clementine Churchill to Margery Street, 6 April 1939. Mary Soames Literary Papers, Churchill Archives, MCHL5/1/78.
24 Laura Thompson, *The Six: The Lives of the Mitford Sisters*, p. 119.
25 For a full discussion of the dynamics between the Mitford sisters, see Laura Thompson, *The Six*.
26 Mary S. Lovell, *The Churchills*, p. 399.
27 Winston Churchill to Clementine Churchill, 8 January 1939. Churchill Archives, CHAR 1/344/7-11.
28 Martin Gilbert, *Winston Churchill: A Life*, p. 563.
29 Winston Churchill to Sir Alexander Maxwell, 18 June 1938. Churchill Archives, CHAR1/326/2.
30 Andrew Roberts, *Churchill: Walking with Destiny*, p. 444.

10 The Churchill Girls at War

1 Vic Oliver, *Mr Showbusiness*, pp. 124–27.
2 Mary Soames, *A Daughter's Tale*, p. 135.
3 Sarah Churchill, *Keep on Dancing*, p. 56.
4 Mary Soames, *Clementine Churchill*, p. 283.
5 'Miss Churchill's Visit', 27 October 1939, *Chatham News*.
6 Sarah Churchill to Winston Churchill, 4 April 1940. Churchill Archives, CHAR 1/355/24.
7 Mary Soames, *A Daughter's Tale*, p. 135.
8 Ibid., pp. 139–40.
9 Cecil King, *With Malice Towards None: A War Diary by Cecil H. King* (London: Sidgwick and Jackson, 1970) p. 20.
10 11 August 1940, John Colville, *The Fringes of Power: Downing Street Diaries 1939–1955* (London: Hodder and Stoughton, 1985) p. 219.
11 9 May 1940, John Colville, *The Fringes of Power*, p. 120.
12 Mary Soames, *A Daughter's Tale*, p. 151.
13 'Wartime Debutantes Communal Coming Our Party on Leap Year Night', 13 March 1940, *The Sketch*.
14 Mary Soames, *A Daughter's Tale*, p. 151.

15 Ibid., pp. 152–53.

16 Ibid., p. 158.

17 Mary Soames, *Clementine Churchill*, p. 305.

18 For a full discussion of Mrs Landemare's role, see Annie Gray, *Victory in the Kitchen: The Life of Churchill's Cook* (London: Profile Books, 2020).

19 Mary Soames, *A Daughter's Tale*, pp. 137–39.

20 For a full discussion of her role see Sonia Purnell, *First Lady*.

21 Mary Soames, *Clementine Churchill*, p. 294.

22 Mary Soames, *A Daughter's Tale*, p. 241.

23 A week later, Marshal Pétain formally signed the Armistice with Germany on 22 June 1940.

24 15 June 1940, John Colville, *Footprints in Time: Memories* (London: William Collins, 1976) pp. 86–87.

25 29 June 1940, John Colville, *The Fringes of Power*, p. 177.

26 14 June 1940, John Colville, *The Fringes of Power*, p. 156.

27 13 October 1940, John Colville, *The Fringes of Power*, pp. 264–66.

28 Unity died in 1948. Diana Mosley, *A Life of Contrasts*, p. 167.

29 29 June 1940, John Colville, *The Fringes of Power*, p. 177.

30 When Diana's mother, Sydney Mitford, appealed to her, Clementine told her she believed the Mosleys were better off in prison because, if they were released, they might be lynched. Winston was more sympathetic. He disliked the suspension of habeas corpus. He was also particularly unhappy that his former favourite, Diana, who had an unweaned baby, was imprisoned in Holloway Prison. However, he would not go against the coalition government. Mary S. Lovell, *The Churchills*, p. 435.

31 Mary Soames, *A Daughter's Tale*, p. 158.

32 Sonia Purnell, *First Lady*, p. 233.

33 Mary Soames, *A Daughter's Tale*, p. 185.

34 Ibid., p. 175.

35 Ibid., p. 193.

36 Lynne Olson. *Citizens of London: The Americans Who Stood with Britain in its Darkest, Finest Hour* (London: Scribe Publications, 2015) p. xvi.

37 Quoted in Andrew Roberts, *Churchill: Walking With Destiny*, p. 576.

11 Transatlantic Alliances

1 Andrew Roberts, *Churchill: Walking With Destiny*, p. 634.

2 John Pearson, *Citadel of the Heart*, p. 278.

3 Ibid., p. 300.

4 Lynne Olson, *Citizens of London*, p. 54.

5   Sonia Purnell, *First Lady*, p. 252.

6   17 April 1941, John Colville, *The Fringes of Power*, p. 375.

7   Lynne Olson, *Citizens of London*, p. 101.

8   Ibid., p. 103.

9   Sonia Purnell, *First Lady*, p. 254.

10 Mary Soames, *A Daughter's Tale*, pp. 227–28.

11 John Pearson, *Citadel of the Heart*, p. 302.

12 Anthony Eden to Winston Churchill, 16 July 1941. Churchill Archives, CHAR 20/34/6.

13 16 July 1941, John Colville, *The Fringes of Power*, p. 415.

14 31 March 1946, Kenneth Young (ed.), *The Diaries of Sir Robert Bruce Lockhart, Vol. 2, 1939–1965* (London: Macmillan, 1980) p. 534.

15 'A New Star', 23 September 1940, *Liverpool Echo*.

16 Charles L. Epting, *Bebe Daniels: Hollywood's Good Little Bad Girl* (Google Books: McFarland & Co., 2016).

17 25 July 1940, John Colville, *The Fringes of Power*, p. 200.

18 Sarah to Clementine, 30 June 1940. Sarah Churchill Personal Correspondence, Churchill Archives, SCHL 1/1/6.

19 Vic Oliver to Sarah Churchill, no date. Sarah Churchill Personal Correspondence, Churchill Archives, SCHL 1/8/1.

20 Vic Oliver, *Mr Showbusiness*, p. 131.

21 It seems Phyllis was not the only threat to the Olivers' marriage. A recent book suggests that Vic was bisexual and enjoyed trysts with young men. The source for these stories was not the most reliable witness. The claim appears in Paul Pender's book, *The Butler Did It: My True and Terrifying Encounters with a Serial Killer* (Edinburgh and London: Mainstream Publishing, 2012) pp. 81–84. Roy Fontaine, also known as Archie Hall, who was butler to British aristocracy, alleged that when he was 17, Vic Oliver had a fling with him. According to Roy, he was in the Central Hotel in Glasgow when Vic asked him if he could buy him a drink. Within an hour of meeting they were in bed together. When Vic offered to pay for him to come down to London for a few months, all expenses paid, Roy readily agreed. During the Blitz, Vic took him to all-male parties in Ivor Novello's flat. Apparently, at one soiree, the playwright Terence Rattigan chatted him up while Novello played the grand piano. Whether Roy's story can be believed is open to question as he was a serial killer who, after he had told his story to Paul Pender, threatened to kill him.

22 'The Affair Churchill Tried to Wreck', 20 November 1982, *Liverpool Echo*.

23 Ibid.

24 Sarah to Clementine, no date. Sarah Churchill Personal Correspondence, Churchill Archives, SCHL 1/1/6.

25 Sarah Churchill, *Keep on Dancing*, p. 58.

26 Mary Churchill to Sarah Churchill, no date. Sarah Churchill Personal Correspondence, Churchill Archives, SCHL 1/3/1.

27 Mary Soames, *A Daughter's Tale*, p. 62.

28 Sarah Churchill, *Keep on Dancing*, p. 58.

29 Interview with Shelagh Montague Browne, 27 February 2020.

30 Sarah Churchill to Clementine and Winston Churchill, no date. Sarah Churchill Personal Correspondence, Churchill Archives, SCHL 1/1/7.

31 Sarah to Clementine, 5 November 1941. Sarah Churchill Personal Correspondence, Churchill Archives, SCHL 1/1/6.

32 Mary Soames, *A Daughter's Tale*, p. 164.

33 26 September 2011, 'Mary Soames Interview', BBC Radio 4, *Woman's Hour*.

34 Mary Soames, *A Daughter's Tale*, p. 144.

35 'Mary Churchill is Engaged to Lord Duncannon', 15 May 1941, *Lincoln Evening State Journal*.

36 Mary Soames, *A Daughter's Tale*, p. 192.

37 3–4 May 1941, John Colville, *The Fringes of Power*, pp. 382–83.

38 Rudolf Hess had just been arrested after flying to Scotland in the hope that he could obtain a compromise peace.

39 Clementine Churchill to Lord Beaverbrook, 10 May 1941. Mary Soames Literary Papers, Churchill Archives, MCHL 5/1/116.

40 Mary Soames, *A Daughter's Tale*, p. 194.

41 Lynne Olson, *Citizens of London*, p. 95.

42 Mary Soames, *A Daughter's Tale*, pp. 195–97.

43 John G. Winant, *A Letter from Grosvenor Square* (London: Hodder and Stoughton, 1947) p. 6.

44 Bernard Bellush, *He Walked Alone: A Biography of John Gilbert Winant* (The Hague and Paris: Mouton, 1968) p. vii.

45 John G. Winant, *A Letter From Grosvenor Square*, p. 3.

46 Lynne Olson, *Citizens of London*, p. 78.

47 James O. Freedman, *Liberal Education and the Public Interest* (Google Books: University of Iowa Press, 2005) p. 85.

48 Usually very formal, refusing to use Christian names with even long-standing friends, Clementine was soon addressing him in her letters as 'My dear Mr Winant' and later 'Gil'. Shortly after he arrived in England, she arranged a lunch for him to meet the social reformer Dame Rachel Crowdy, at No. 10 Downing Street. She told the ambassador that she had particularly picked a Tuesday because that was the day Winston usually lunched with the king. She explained, 'This sounds as though I was trying to prevent you and Winston getting together! This is not really my wicked intention, but it did occur to me that if he were not there to engross your attention Dame Rachel and I would enjoy your company even more!' Clementine Churchill

to Gil Winant, 2 April 1941. John Gil Winant Collection, Franklin Delano Roosevelt Library, Box 190.

49   In one letter, he chose a poem by Robert Browning specially for her. She valued his presents, keeping the carved jade he gave her on her dressing table. Clementine Churchill to Gil Winant, 3 January 1943. John Gil Winant Collection, Franklin Delano Roosevelt Library, Box 190.

50   Sonia Purnell, *First Lady*, p. 249.

51   Mary Soames, *Clementine Churchill*, p. 353.

52   'Brides, Bridegroom', 16 July 1941, *The Sketch*.

53   Sarah Churchill's diary, 1955. Sarah Churchill Personal Papers, Churchill Archives, SCHL 2/2/2.

54   7 May 1941, Robert Rhodes James (ed.), *'Chips': The Diaries of Sir Henry Channon* (London: Weidenfeld and Nicolson, 1993) p. 304.

55   Bernard Bellush, *He Walked Alone*, p. 161.

56   Lynne Olson, *Citizens of London*, p. 104.

57   30 March 1941, Robert Rhodes James, *'Chips'*, p. 297.

58   Quoted in Lynne Olson, *Citizens of London*, p. 109.

59   Lynne Olson, *Citizens of London*, p. 99.

60   Mary Soames to Alex Beam, 30 May 2002. Mary Soames Literary Papers, Churchill Archives, MCHL 52/34.

61   Quoted in Sonia Purnell, *First Lady*, p. 250.

62   'Copy of a note made about the announcement of the Japanese attack on Pearl Harbour', in the John Gil Winant Collection, Franklin Delano Roosevelt Library, Box 189.

63   Andrew Roberts, *Churchill: Walking with Destiny*, p. 692.

64   Lynne Olson, *Citizens of London*, p. xviii.

12 Doing Their Duty on the Home Front

1   'Miss Sarah Churchill Joins WAAFs', 30 October 1941, *Liverpool Daily Post*.

2   'Sarah Churchill', 10 April 1960, *Corpus Christi Caller Times*.

3   Mary Soames, *A Daughter's Tale*, p. 199.

4   John G. Winant, *A Letter From Grosvenor Square*, p. 167.

5   Judy was Clementine's cousin Venetia Montagu's (née Stanley's) daughter.

6   Mary Soames, *A Daughter's Tale*, pp. 207–08.

7   'US Soldier Spanks Mary Churchill', 1 August 1942, *The New York Times*. Churchill Archives, CHAR 20/64/46.53.

8   Mary Soames, *A Daughter's Tale*, p. 235.

9   Mary Churchill to Sarah Churchill, no date. Sarah Churchill Personal Correspondence, Churchill Archives, SCHL 1/3/1.

10   Mary Soames, *A Daughter's Tale*, p. 260.

11 Ibid., p. 286.

12 'London Defended by Guns Manned with Girl Crews', 4 February 1944, *Troy Times*.

13 Christine Halsall, *Women of Intelligence: Winning the Second World War With Air Photos* (Stroud: The History Press, 2017) p. 42.

14 Sarah to Clementine, no date, Morecambe. Sarah Churchill Personal Correspondence, Churchill Archives, SCHL 1/1/6.

15 Sarah to Clementine, no date, Nuneham. Sarah Churchill Personal Correspondence, Churchill Archives, SCHL 1/1/6.

16 They were introduced to the principles of stereoscopic viewing, which involved looking at two photographs slightly out of alignment to create a three-dimensional effect. They had to work out the scale of the photographs using a slide rule and logarithms, and calculate measurements of the objects they were viewing. Christine Halsall, *Women of Intelligence*, p. 50.

17 Christine Halsall, *Women of Intelligence*, p. 50.

18 Taylor Downing, *Spies in the Sky: The Secret Battle for Aerial Intelligence During World War II* (London: Abacus, 2012) p. 9.

19 Christine Halsall, *Women of Intelligence*, p. 1.

20 By the end of the war, there were about 550 officers and 3,000 other ranks working there. Taylor Downing, *Spies in the Sky*, p. 93.

21 Taylor Downing, *Spies in the Sky*, p. 83.

22 Sarah Churchill to Winston Churchill, 18 September 1942. Churchill Archives, CHAR 1/369/68-70.

23 Sarah to Clementine, no date, Morecambe. Sarah Churchill Personal Correspondence, Churchill Archives, SCHL 1/1/6.

24 Christine Halsall, *Women of Intelligence*, p. 65.

25 Ibid., p. 28.

26 Ibid., p. 50.

27 Ibid., p. 64.

28 Their aircraft carried no weapons so that they could carry more fuel. If a plane was damaged there was no way to communicate with base. Some of the pilots crashed in the sea to prevent the enemy getting their film. Christine Halsall, *Women of Intelligence*, p. 65.

29 Sarah Churchill, 'The Bombers', *The Empty Spaces*, p. 43.

30 John Pearson, *Citadel of the Heart*, p. 338.

31 Christine Halsall, *Women of Intelligence*, p. 100.

32 Sarah Churchill to Winston Churchill, 18 September 1942. Churchill Archives, CHAR 1/369/68-70.

33 Taylor Downing, *Spies in the Sky*, p. 101.

34 Ibid.

35 Ibid., p. 103.

36 John Pearson, *Citadel of the Heart*, p. 336.

37 Christine Halsall, *Women of Intelligence*, p. 27.

38 Winston Churchill to Randolph Churchill, 30 October 1941. Churchill Archives, CHAR 1/362/43-45.

39 John Colville, *The Churchillians*, pp. 119–23.

40 'A Bright Evening in the Blackout: On Leave with Winston Churchill's Fighting Daughters', Donn Sutton, 29 July 1942, *Xenia Evening Gazette*.

41 Mary Soames, *A Daughter's Tale*, p. 261.

42 Ibid., pp. 237–40.

43 Taylor Downing, *Spies in the Sky*, pp. 105–06.

44 6 June 2014, 'Interview Emma Soames', BBC Radio 4, *Last Word*.

45 Mary Churchill to Sarah Churchill, 7 July 1942. Sarah Churchill Personal Correspondence, Churchill Archives, SCHL 1/3/1.

46 Mary Soames, *A Daughter's Tale*, pp. 247–49.

47 Although, her own family had to come first, Diana remained very close to her father. He particularly valued her sense of humour. While she was working as a voluntary helper in a West End Hospital, she collected remarks people made about him which she thought would amuse him. John Pearson, *Citadel of the Heart*, p. 324.

48 Diana Sandys to Clementine Churchill, 8 January 1944. Mary Soames Literary Papers, Churchill Archives, MCHL 5/1/268.

49 Clementine Churchill to Winston Churchill, 20 May 1943, in Mary Soames, *Speaking for Themselves*, p. 481.

50 Diana Sandys to Winston Churchill, 6 June 1943. Churchill Archives, CHAR 1/375/3-4.

51 Mary Soames, *A Daughter's Tale*, p. 261.

13 Travels with Their Father

1 Modern medical analysis suggests it may have been a muscle strain or a strain of the bony and cartilaginous chest wall. However, at the time, Moran believed it to be a heart attack. Andrew Roberts, *Churchill: Walking with Destiny*, p. 703.

2 During the war, he made twenty-five return trips covering more than 110,000 miles. They were hazardous journeys often in noisy, unpressurised planes. The risk of crashing or being shot down was high; a number of prominent people died in flights in the war. Andrew Roberts, *Churchill: Walking With Destiny*, p. 970.

3 Cecil King wrote that taking Mary to Quebec caused 'great resentment here. We have made no comment in the papers, but have received a lot of letters. Why does the Prime Minister do these things?' 23 August 1943, Cecil King, *With Malice Towards None*, p. 229.

4   General Lord Ismay, *The Memoirs of General Lord Ismay* (New York: The Viking Press, 1960) p. 304.

5   Mary Churchill to Sarah Churchill and Maryott Whyte, 15 August 1943. Sarah Churchill Personal Correspondence, Churchill Archives, SCHL 1/3/1.

6   Mary Churchill to Sarah Churchill and Maryott Whyte, ibid.

7   Ibid.

8   Andrew Roberts, *Churchill: Walking With Destiny*, p. 791.

9   She found it particularly interesting as the CWAC was the counterpart of the British ATS. 'Mary Churchill – Broadcast from Quebec. September 1943. To Celebrate Third Birthday of Canadian Women's Army Corps', Sarah Churchill Personal Correspondence, Churchill Archives, SCHL 1/3/1.

10 Mary Soames' 'Report on Canada 1943', Mary Soames Literary Papers, Churchill Archives, MCHL 5/1/108.

11 'Mary Churchill – Broadcast from Quebec. September 1943. To Celebrate Third Birthday of Canadian Women's Army Corps', Sarah Churchill Personal Correspondence, Churchill Archives, SCHL 1/3/1.

12 Mary Soames, *A Daughter's Tale*, p. 307.

13 Clementine Churchill to Sarah Churchill, 22 August 1943. Sarah Churchill Personal Correspondence, Churchill Archives, SCHL 1/2/1.

14 Mary Soames, *A Daughter's Tale*, pp. 275–76.

15 Sonia Purnell, *First Lady*, pp. 286–87.

16 18 August 1943, Sir John Martin, *Downing Street: The War Years* (London: Bloomsbury, 1991) p. 112.

17 Quoted in Mary Soames, *A Daughter's Tale*, pp. 277–78.

18 Celia Sandys, *Chasing Churchill*, p. 170.

19 Mary Soames, *A Daughter's Tale*, p. 279.

20 Sarah Churchill to Clementine Churchill, 19 November 1943. Sarah Churchill Personal Correspondence, Churchill Archives, SCHL 1/1/7.

21 Sarah Churchill to Clementine Churchill, 19 November 1943. Sarah Churchill Personal Correspondence, Churchill Archives, SCHL 1/1/7.

22 Sarah Churchill to Clementine Churchill, 20 November 1943. Sarah Churchill Personal Correspondence, Churchill Archives, SCHL 1/1/7.

23 Sarah Churchill to Clementine Churchill, 24 November 1943. Sarah Churchill Personal Correspondence, Churchill Archives, SCHL 1/1/7.

24 Andrew Roberts, *Churchill: Walking With Destiny*, p. 804.

25 Sarah Churchill to Clementine Churchill, 26 November 1943. Sarah Churchill Personal Correspondence, Churchill Archives, SCHL 1/1/7.

26 Celia Sandys, *Chasing Churchill*, p. 172.

27 Sarah Churchill to Clementine Churchill, 26 November 1943. Sarah Churchill Personal Correspondence, Churchill Archives, SCHL 1/1/7.

28 Quoted in Sonia Purnell, *First Lady*, p. 291.

29 Sarah Churchill to Clementine Churchill, 4 December 1943. Sarah Churchill Personal Correspondence, Churchill Archives, SCHL 1/1/7.

30 Sarah Churchill, *A Thread in the Tapestry*, p. 63.

31 Sarah Churchill to Clementine Churchill, 4 December 1943. Sarah Churchill Personal Correspondence, Churchill Archives, SCHL 1/1/7.

32 Andrew Roberts, *Churchill: Walking With Destiny*, p. 807.

33 Lord Moran arranged for a pathologist and two nurses from Cairo to care for his patient. He started giving him M and B tablets (an early form of antibiotic sulphonamide) and digitalis for his heart. With the right medication, he began to recover. Charles Moran, *Winston Churchill: The Struggle for Survival, 1940–1965* (London: Constable, 1966) pp. 148–49.

34 Sarah Churchill, *A Thread in the Tapestry*, p. 69.

35 Sarah Churchill to Winston Churchill, 28 March 1944. Churchill Archives, CHAR 1/381/59-61.

36 17 December 1943, John Colville, *The Fringes of Power*, p. 455.

37 Mary Soames, *Clementine Churchill*, pp. 344–45.

38 Lady Diana Cooper, quoted in Andrew Roberts, *Churchill: Walking With Destiny*, p. 810.

39 Sarah Churchill to Winston Churchill, 28 March 1944. Churchill Archives, CHAR 1/381/59-61.

40 Charles Moran, *Winston Churchill*, pp. 156–57.

41 Mary Soames, *Clementine Churchill*, p. 348.

42 From Patrick Kinna's taped oral histories at the Churchill Archives. Quoted in Cita Stelzer, *Working With Winston: The Unsung Women Behind Britain's Greatest Statesman* (London: Head of Zeus, 2019) p. 91.

43 Sarah to Gil Winant, 22 December 1943. Sarah Churchill Personal Correspondence, Churchill Archives, SCHL 1/8/1.

44 Clementine Churchill to Sarah Churchill, 12 December 1943. Sarah Churchill Personal Correspondence, Churchill Archives, SCHL 1/2/1.

45 Bernard Bellush, *He Walked Alone*, p. 194.

46 Ibid., p. 180.

47 22 February 1944, Robert Rhodes James, *'Chips'*, p. 386.

14 Onwards to Victory

1 Mary Soames, *A Daughter's Tale*, p. 297.

2 The V1s were pilotless aircraft carrying a high-explosive warhead. They flew at speeds of up to 400 miles per hour and were difficult targets for anti-aircraft guns.

3 They left over 6,000 civilians dead and 18,000 injured. When Clementine came to visit Mary on 18 June, a flying bomb made a direct hit on the

Guards Chapel in Wellington Barracks during a packed Sunday service. Tragically, 121 people were killed and 141 seriously wounded. Mary Soames, *A Daughter's Tale*, pp. 299–303.

4   Mary Soames, *A Daughter's Tale*, pp. 293–94.

5   Ibid., pp. 299–300.

6   Ibid., pp. 301–03.

7   Mary Soames to Clementine Churchill, 19 July 1944. Mary Soames Literary Papers, Churchill Archives, MCHL 5/1/109.

8   Winston Churchill to Mary Churchill, 25 August 1944. Churchill Archives, CHAR 20/149/21.

9   'The Victory of London', 8 September 1944, *Daily Sketch*.

10 Winston had asked Lord Portal to resign so that the Minister of Works could be a member of the House of Commons. Portal was very hurt. 4 December 1944, Harold Macmillan, *War Diaries: Politics and War in the Mediterranean 1943–1945* (London: Macmillan, 1984) p. 596.

11 Sarah Churchill to Clementine Churchill, December 1944. Sarah Churchill Personal Correspondence, Churchill Archives, SCHL 1/1/7.

12 'Armistice Day 1944 in France', 29 December 1944, *Muscatine Journal and New Tribune*.

13 Andrew Roberts, *Churchill: Walking with Destiny*, p. 848.

14 Mary Soames, *A Daughter's Tale*, pp. 321–22.

15 Mary Churchill to Clementine Churchill, 19 November 1944. Mary Soames Literary Papers, Churchill Archives, MCHL 5/1/109.

16 Mary Churchill to Maryott Whyte, 26 February 1945. Sarah Churchill Personal Correspondence, Churchill Archives, SCHL 1/3/1.

17 She kept any celebrations low key. She wanted just the people who mattered most to her there. Her father was away but she asked her mother to invite Gil to a 'cosy party' with Diana and Mary.

18 Sarah to Clementine, 31 January 1945. Sarah Churchill Personal Correspondence, Churchill Archives, SCHL 1/1/8.

19 Sarah Churchill, *A Thread in the Tapestry*, p. 76. The president had been diagnosed with high blood pressure and coronary artery disease.

20 Sarah to Clementine, 4 February 1945. Sarah Churchill Personal Correspondence, Churchill Archives, SCHL 1/1/8.

21 3 February 1945, Charles Moran, *Winston Churchill*, p. 219.

22 Sarah to Clementine, 6 February 1945. Sarah Churchill Personal Correspondence, Churchill Archives, SCHL 1/1/8.

23 Sarah Churchill, *Keep on Dancing*, pp. 74–75.

24 General Lord Ismay, *The Memoirs of General Lord Ismay*, p. 387.

25 They did not meet until 4 in the afternoon, then they held a four- or five-hour session. After the meeting was over, Winston usually dined quietly with Sarah and Anthony Eden.

26 Sarah Churchill, *Keep on Dancing*, p. 76.

27 Ibid., p. 75.

28 Sarah to Clementine, 12 February 1945. Sarah Churchill Personal Correspondence, Churchill Archives, SCHL 1/1/8.

29 Sarah to Clementine, 9 February 1945. Sarah Churchill Personal Correspondence, Churchill Archives, SCHL 1/1/8.

30 Sarah Churchill, *Keep on Dancing*, p. 77.

31 For a full discussion of the rivalry between Harriman and Winant, see Bernard Bellush, *He Walked Alone*, pp. 175–76.

32 Bernard Bellush, *He Walked Alone*, pp. 205–06.

33 Sarah Churchill to Gil Winant, 13 February 1943. John Gil Winant Collection, Franklin Delano Roosevelt Library, Box 190.

34 Sarah to Clementine, 1 February 1945. Sarah Churchill Personal Correspondence, Churchill Archives, SCHL 1/1/8.

35 Clementine Churchill to Mary Churchill, 17 February 1945. Mary Soames Literary Papers, Churchill Archives, MCHL 5/1/117.

36 General Lord Ismay, *The Memoirs of General Lord Ismay*, p. 388.

37 Sarah to Clementine, 12 February 1945. Sarah Churchill Personal Correspondence, Churchill Archives, SCHL 1/1/8.

38 Sarah Churchill, *A Thread in the Tapestry*, p. 83.

39 On Christmas Eve, Winston had flown out to Athens to deal with the crisis that had developed with the culmination of the Greek Civil War. He presided over a conference to bring about a settlement.

40 Mary Soames, *Speaking for Themselves*, p. 517.

41 Sarah to Clementine, 15 February 1945. Sarah Churchill Personal Correspondence, Churchill Archives, SCHL 1/1/8.

42 Sarah Churchill to Winston Churchill, 28 March 1944. Churchill Archives, CHAR 1/381/59-61.

43 'Walsall Girl at Belsen went with Commander Mary Churchill in ATS Rhine Crossing', 21 July 1945, *Walsall Observer*.

44 Mary Churchill to Clementine Churchill, 4 March (no year given). Sarah Churchill Personal Correspondence, Churchill Archives, SCHL 1/3/1.

45 Mary Churchill to Clementine Churchill, 21 June 1945. Sarah Churchill Personal Correspondence, Churchill Archives, SCHL 1/3/1.

46 Sarah Churchill to Winston Churchill, 6 March 1947. Churchill Archives, CHUR 1/45.

47 Sarah to Clementine, 7 April 1945. Sarah Churchill Personal Correspondence, Churchill Archives, SCHL 1/1/8.

48 Mary Soames, *Clementine Churchill*, p. 367.

49 In the early months of 1945, photo reconnaissance aircraft photographed German railway marshalling yards and factories, some of which had now gone underground to escape the Allied bombing offensive. Sarah's section

had been up most nights checking the ground information about these factories, which were potentially points of resistance. Spotting underground factories was not difficult for the photo interpreters because the piles of earth or rocks that had been dug out for their construction were visible on the landscape. The fans and air ducts they needed could also be clearly seen from the air. Taylor Downing, *Spies in the Sky*, p. 324.

50 Sarah Churchill to Winston Churchill, April 1945. Churchill Archives, CHAR 1/387/24-25.

51 Sarah to Clementine, 7 April 1945. Sarah Churchill Personal Correspondence, Churchill Archives, SCHL 1/1/8.

52 'Emma Soames: "My Mother's Mercy Dash to Comfort her Father Winston in Victory"', 9 May 2020, *Daily Mail*.

53 Victory in Europe was celebrated by two days of national holiday, VE plus 1 and VE plus 2, on 9 and 10 May.

54 Mary Soames, *A Daughter's Tale*, p. 334.

55 Ibid., p. 335.

56 'Emma Soames: "My Mother's Mercy Dash to Comfort her Father Winston in Victory"', 9 May 2020, *Daily Mail*.

57 Mary Soames, *A Daughter's Tale*, p. 336.

58 The Germans were handing in their military equipment and Mary's regiment was assisting in mothballing their armaments.

59 Mary Soames, *A Daughter's Tale*, pp. 337–38.

60 Mary Churchill to Clementine Churchill, 21 June 1945. Sarah Churchill Personal Correspondence, Churchill Archives, SCHL 1/3/1.

61 'Walsall Girl at Belsen Went with Commander Mary Churchill in ATS Rhine Crossing', 21 July 1945, *Walsall Observer*.

62 Mary Soames, *A Daughter's Tale*, p. 341.

63 Mary Churchill to Clementine Churchill, 16 July 1945. Sarah Churchill Personal Correspondence, Churchill Archives, SCHL 1/3/1.

64 Ibid.

65 Ibid.

66 Ibid.

67 Mary Churchill to Clementine Churchill, 19 July 1945. Sarah Churchill Personal Correspondence, Churchill Archives, SCHL 1/3/1.

68 Mary Soames, *Clementine Churchill*, p. 385.

69 Mary Churchill to Winston Churchill, 24 September 1945. Churchill Archives, CHUR 1/42.

70 Sarah to Clementine, 7 April 1945. Sarah Churchill Personal Correspondence, Churchill Archives, SCHL 1/1/8.

71 Mary Soames, *A Daughter's Tale*, p. 324.

15 The Aftermath

1   Sarah Churchill to Winston Churchill, 27 July 1945. Sarah Churchill Personal Correspondence, Churchill Archives, SCHL 1/1/8.

2   Elizabeth Nel, *Mr Churchill's Secretary* (London: Hodder and Stoughton, 1958) p. 179.

3   Sarah Churchill to Winston Churchill, 5 June 1945. Churchill Archives, CHAR 1/387/18-23.

4   Clementine Churchill to Sarah Churchill, 12 June 1945. Sarah Churchill Personal Correspondence, Churchill Archives, SCHL 1/2/1.

5   Martin Gilbert, *Churchill: A Life*, pp. 847–49.

6   The Common Wealth Party was founded in 1942. Its leaders included the writer J.B. Priestley and the Liberal Party MP, Richard Acland.

7   Clementine Churchill to Mary Churchill, 27 January 1945. Mary Soames Literary Papers, Churchill Archives, MCHL 5/1/117.

8   Andrew Roberts, *Churchill: Walking with Destiny*, p. 884.

9   Sarah Churchill, *A Thread in the Tapestry*, p. 86.

10 Sarah Churchill to Winston Churchill, 27 July 1945. Sarah Churchill Personal Correspondence, Churchill Archives, SCHL 1/1/8.

11 Ibid.

12 Sarah Churchill to Clementine Churchill, 3 September 1945. Sarah Churchill Personal Correspondence, Churchill Archives, SCHL 1/1/9.

13 Picnics were an essential part of any Churchill holiday and Sarah's favourite way of eating. Normally, she ate very little, sometimes only one meal a day or only every other day but at picnics she ate as much as anyone. Eggs in aspic, cold roast beef or chicken, cucumber salad, celery and radishes followed by Stilton cheese and biscuits were prerequisites for a Churchillian picnic. Sarah Churchill, *A Thread in the Tapestry*, p. 93.

14 Sarah Churchill to Clementine, 8 September 1945. Sarah Churchill Personal Correspondence, Churchill Archives, SCHL 1/1/9.

15 8 September 1945, Charles Moran, *Winston Churchill*, p. 302.

16 Sarah Churchill to Clementine Churchill, 15 September 1945. Sarah Churchill Personal Correspondence, Churchill Archives, SCHL 1/1/9.

17 Clementine Churchill to Sarah Churchill, 12 September 1945. Sarah Churchill Personal Correspondence, Churchill Archives, SCHL 1/2/1.

18 Clementine Churchill to Winston Churchill, 11 September 1945. Churchill Archives, CHUR 1/41.

19 Sarah Churchill to Clementine Churchill, 3 September 1945. Sarah Churchill Personal Correspondence, Churchill Archives, SCHL 1/1/9.

20 Mary Soames, *A Daughter's Tale*, p. 368.

21 Clementine Churchill to Mary Soames, 14 August 1945. Mary Soames Literary Papers, Churchill Archives, MCHL 5/1/117.

22 Mary Churchill to Clementine Churchill, 20 January 1946. Mary Soames Literary Papers, Churchill Archives, MCHL 5/1/130.

23 Mary Churchill to Clementine Churchill, 27 January 1946. Mary Soames Literary Papers, Churchill Archives, MCHL 5/1/130.

24 Mary Soames, *A Daughter's Tale*, p. 371.

25 Clementine Churchill to Sarah Churchill, 12 October 1946. Sarah Churchill Personal Correspondence, Churchill Archives, SCHL 1/2/2.

26 Caroline Young, *Roman Holiday: The Secret Life of Hollywood in Rome* (Stroud: The History Press, 2018) p. 26.

27 Sarah Churchill to Clementine Churchill, 5 October 1946. Sarah Churchill Personal Correspondence, Churchill Archives, SCHL 1/1/10.

28 Shelagh Montague Browne interview, 27 February 2020.

29 Mary Soames, *A Daughter's Tale*, p. 372.

30 Mary Churchill to Sarah Churchill, 16 October 1946. Mary Soames Personal Correspondence, Churchill Archives, MCHL 2/1.

31 Mary Soames to Clementine and Winston Churchill, 26 October 1946. Mary Soames Personal Correspondence, Churchill Archives, MCHL 2/1.

32 Mary Soames to Clementine Churchill, 29 October 1946. Mary Soames Personal Correspondence, Churchill Archives, MCHL 2/1.

33 Christopher Soames to Mary Churchill, no date. Mary Soames Personal Correspondence, Churchill Archives, MCHL 2/2.

34 Mary Soames to Clementine and Winston Churchill, 26 October 1946. Mary Soames Personal Correspondence, Churchill Archives, MCHL 2/1.

35 Mary Soames to Clementine Churchill, 29 October 1946. Mary Soames Personal Correspondence, Churchill Archives, MCHL 2/1.

36 Mary Soames to Clementine and Winston Churchill, 26 October 1946. Mary Soames Personal Correspondence, Churchill Archives, MCHL 2/1.

37 Mary Soames to Clementine Churchill, 29 October 1946. Mary Soames Personal Correspondence, Churchill Archives, Cambridge MCHL 2/1.

38 Christopher Soames to Mary Churchill, no date. Mary Soames Personal Correspondence, Churchill Archives, MCHL 2/2.

39 Sarah Churchill to Winston and Clementine Churchill, 27 October 1946. Sarah Churchill Personal Correspondence, Churchill Archives, SCHL 1/1/10.

40 Ibid.

41 Christopher Soames to Winston Churchill, 16 November 1946. Churchill Archives, CHUR 1/42.

42 Mary Soames, *Clementine Churchill*, p. 415.

43 Charles Moran, *Winston Churchill*, p. 317.

44 Mary Churchill to Sarah Churchill, 20 November 1946. Mary Soames Personal Correspondence, Churchill Archives, MCHL 2/1.
45 Sarah Churchill to Clementine Churchill, 19 December 1946. Sarah Churchill Personal Correspondence, Churchill Archives, SCHL 1/1/10.
46 Mary Soames, *Clementine Churchill*, p. 416.
47 Mary Churchill to Sarah Churchill, 29 December 1946. Mary Soames Personal Correspondence, Churchill Archives, MCHL 2/1.

16 Love and Marriage

1   In fact, Princess Elizabeth was to marry Prince Philip later the same year.
2   Although Attlee and Churchill were political adversaries they were friends and the Labour prime minister was invited to the wedding.
3   Sarah Churchill to Winston Churchill, 20 February 1947. Churchill Archives, CHUR 1/42.
4   Sarah Churchill to Mario Soldati, 5 August 1947. Sarah Churchill Personal Correspondence, Churchill Archives, SCHL 1/5/2.
5   Ibid.
6   Sarah Churchill to Winston Churchill, 6 March 1947. Churchill Archive, CHUR 1/45.
7   John Pearson, *Citadel of the Heart*, p. 349.
8   Sarah Churchill to Clementine Churchill, 10 March 1947. Sarah Churchill Personal Correspondence, Churchill Archives, SCHL 1/1/11.
9   His memoirs were called *A Letter from Grosvenor Square* (London: Hodder and Stoughton, 1947).
10 Sarah Churchill to Winston and Clementine Churchill, 11 November 1947. Churchill Archives, CHUR 1/45.
11 Sarah Churchill, *Keep on Dancing*, p. 95.
12 Sarah Churchill's diary 1955. Sarah Churchill Personal Papers, Churchill Archives, SCHL 2/2/2.
13 Clementine Churchill to Mary Soames and Diana Churchill, 4 January 1948. Sarah Churchill Personal Correspondence, Churchill Archives, SCHL 1/2/2.
14 Mary Soames to Winston Churchill, 15 September (no year given). Churchill Archives, CHUR 1/46.
15 Sarah Churchill to Mary Soames, 17 February 1948. Mary Soames Personal Correspondence, Churchill Archives, MCHL 2/10.
16 Antony Montague Browne, *Long Sunset: Memoirs of Winston Churchill's Last Private Secretary* (London: Indigo, 1996) p. 150.
17 Mary Soames to Clementine Churchill, 29 August 1954. Mary Soames Literary Papers, Churchill Archives, MCHL 5/7/47.

18 Interview with Emma Soames, 19 February 2020.

19 Mary Churchill to Winston Churchill, 10 November 1951. Churchill Archives, CHUR 1/52 B.

20 6 June 2014, 'Interview Emma Soames', BBC Radio 4, *Last Word*.

21 Winston Churchill to Clementine Churchill, 19 August 1954, in Mary Soames, *Speaking for Themselves*, p. 586.

22 Andrew Roberts, *Churchill: Walking with Destiny*, p. 899.

23 Juliet Rhys Williams to Mary Soames, 21 October 1963. Mary Soames Personal Correspondence, Churchill Archives, MCHL 2/13.

17 Sarah Goes to Hollywood

1 Antony Beauchamp, *Focus on Fame* (London: Odhams Press, 1958) p. 35.

2 Ibid., pp. 85–86.

3 Ibid., p. 72.

4 Sarah Churchill to Clementine Churchill, 3 October 1953. Sarah Churchill Personal Correspondence. Churchill Archives, SCHL 1/1/15.

5 Antony Beauchamp, *Focus on Fame*, p. 74.

6 This was said when Princess Margaret married another society photographer, Antony Armstrong-Jones.

7 Antony Beauchamp, *Focus on Fame*, p. 75.

8 Sarah Churchill to Winston Churchill, no date. Churchill Archives, CHUR 1/46.

9 These were often large, very professional theatres, seating between 600 and 1,400 people.

10 Sarah Churchill to Clementine Churchill, 29 August 1949. Sarah Churchill Personal Correspondence, Churchill Archives, SCHL 1/1/12.

11 Sarah Churchill to Antony Beauchamp, no date. Sarah Churchill Personal Correspondence, Churchill Archives, SCHL 1/6/1.

12 Harry S. Truman to Winston Churchill, 21 October 1949. Churchill Archives, CHUR 2/158.

13 Winston Churchill to Harry S. Truman, 10 October 1949. Churchill Archives, CHUR 2/158.

14 Sarah Churchill to Antony Beauchamp, no date. Sarah Churchill Personal Correspondence, Churchill Archives, SCHL 1/6/1.

15 Antony Beauchamp to Clementine Churchill, 11 September 1949. Churchill Archives, CHUR 1/46.

16 Sarah Churchill to Clementine Churchill, no date. Sarah Churchill Personal Correspondence, Churchill Archives, SCHL 1/1/13.

17 Winston Churchill to Sarah Churchill, 16 September 1949. Churchill Archives, CHUR 1/46.

18 Sarah Churchill to Clementine Churchill, 29 August 1949. Sarah Churchill Personal Correspondence, Churchill Archives, SCHL 1/1/12.
19 Antony Beauchamp, *Focus on Fame*, p. 88.
20 Sarah Churchill to Diana Sandys, 29 October 1949. Sarah Churchill Personal Correspondence, Churchill Archives, SCHL 1/3/2.
21 Clementine Churchill to Sarah Churchill, 21 December 1949. Sarah Churchill Personal Correspondence, Churchill Archives, SCHL 1/2/2.
22 Sarah Churchill to Clementine Churchill, 19 May 1950. Sarah Churchill Personal Correspondence, Churchill Archives, SCHL 1/1/13.
23 Sarah Churchill to Clementine Churchill, 30 June 1950. Sarah Churchill Personal Correspondence, Churchill Archives, SCHL 1/1/13.
24 Sarah Churchill to Clementine Churchill, no date. Sarah Churchill Personal Correspondence, Churchill Archives, SCHL 1/1/13.
25 Sarah Churchill, *Keep on Dancing*, p. 133.
26 Antony Beauchamp, *Focus on Fame*, p. 144.
27 Sarah Churchill, *Keep on Dancing*, p. 132.
28 'The Churchills', 20 May 1951, *The People*.
29 'Earl Wilson the Man of the Hour (After Midnight)', 20 May 1951, *Syracuse Herald Journal*.
30 Diana Churchill to Winston Churchill, 12 July 1951. Churchill Archives, CHUR 1/49.
31 Instead, they fixated on whether Mrs Roosevelt had travelled on a battleship or a destroyer during a wartime trip to England. Antony Beauchamp, *Focus on Fame*, pp. 122–23.
32 Sarah Churchill, *Keep on Dancing*, p. 139.
33 John Crosby, 'Avon Wonderful Time', 25 May 1953, *Cumberland News*.
34 Sarah Churchill, *Keep on Dancing*, p. 143.
35 Sarah Churchill to Clementine Churchill, no date. Sarah Churchill Personal Correspondence, Churchill Archives, SCHL 1/1/13.

18 Family Politics

1 Antony Beauchamp, *Focus on Fame*, pp. 170–75.
2 Sarah Churchill to Winston Churchill, 20 November 1951. Churchill Archives, CHUR 1/50 A-B.
3 Anthony Montague Browne, *Long Sunset*, p. 148.
4 John Colville, *The Churchillians*, p. 28.
5 The president and his wife were living there while the White House was renovated.
6 John Colville, *The Churchillians*, p. 103.
7 Antony Beauchamp, *Focus on Fame*, p. 177.

8   Sarah Churchill to Winston Churchill, 7 January 1951. Churchill Archives, CHUR 4/8.

9   Winston Churchill to Sarah Churchill, February 1951. Churchill Archives, CHUR 4/8.

10   Sonia Purnell, *First Lady*, p. 333.

11   John Colville, *The Churchillians*, p. 26.

12   Charles Moran, *Winston Churchill*, pp. 539–40.

13   Interview with Celia Sandys, 21 January 2020.

14   Sarah Churchill to Clementine Churchill, Christmas Day 1950. Sarah Churchill Personal Correspondence, Churchill Archives, SCHL 1/1/13.

15   Mary Soames, *Clementine Churchill*, p. 443.

16   Mary S. Lovell, *The Churchills*, p. 520.

17   Carl Lambert was a fashionable psychiatrist. A German emigre, he had fled Berlin in 1939. He saw private patients for psychoanalysis at his consulting rooms off Harley Street. His wife, Grace, was leading lady to the Crazy Gang at Jack Hylton's Victoria Palace. Jane Perry, *Different Drummer: The Life Of Kenneth Macmillan* (Google Books) p. 399.

18   Winston Churchill to Diana Churchill, 5 April 1953. Churchill Archives, CHUR 1/52 B.

19   Diana Sandys to Winston and Clementine Churchill, 5 May 1953. Mary Soames Literary Papers, Churchill Archives, MCHL 5/1/160.

20   Sarah Churchill, *Keep on Dancing*, pp. 146–47.

21   John Colville, *The Fringes of Power*, p. 670.

22   Roy Jenkins, *Churchill* (London: Pan Macmillan, 2002) p. 886.

23   Andrew Roberts, *Churchill: Walking with Destiny*, p. 939.

24   Sarah Churchill to Winston Churchill, 9 July 1953. Churchill Archives, CHUR1/50 A-B.

25   Mary Soames to Clementine Churchill, 22 September 1953. Mary Soames Literary Papers, Churchill Archives, MCHL 5/7/46.

26   Sarah Churchill to Winston Churchill, 19 October 1953. Churchill Archives, CHUR 1/50 A-B.

27   Mary Soames, *Clementine Churchill*, p. 440.

28   Adela Rogers St Johns, 'Sarah Churchill Talks', 30 March 1958, *Corpus Christi Caller Times.*

29   'The Women Who Wept for Tony Beauchamp But Mother Says He Loved Only One', 23 August 1957, *Daily Herald.*

30   'Sarah Churchill', 10 April 1960, *Corpus Christi Caller Times.*

31   Antony Beauchamp to Winston Churchill, 15 November (no year given). Churchill Archives, CHUR 1/50 A-B.

32   Sarah Churchill to Clementine Churchill, 8 March 1955. Sarah Churchill Personal Papers, Churchill Archives, SCHL 1/1/15.

33 Insulin shock therapy or insulin coma therapy was a form of psychiatric treatment in which patients were repeatedly injected with increasingly large doses of insulin, which reduce the sugar content of the blood and bring on a state of coma. Usually, the coma would be allowed to persist for about an hour, at which time it would be terminated by administering warm salt solution via a stomach tube or an intravenous injection of glucose. Typically, injections were administered six days a week for about two months. This therapy was used extensively in the 1940s and 1950s but fell out of favour in the 1960s (*Britannica Online Encyclopaedia*).

34 Diana Churchill to Clementine Churchill, 4 January 1954. Mary Soames Literary Papers, Churchill Archives, MCHL 5/1/268.

35 Diana Churchill to Winston Churchill, 8 February 1954. Churchill Archives, CHUR 1/52 B.

36 Diana Sandys to Clementine Churchill, 3 January 1954. Mary Soames Literary Papers, Churchill Archives, MCHL 5/1/268.

37 Interview with Celia Sandys, 21 January 2020.

38 Sarah Churchill to Winston Churchill, 9 January 1954. Mary Soames Literary Papers, Churchill Archives, MCHL 5/7/47.

39 Diana Sandys to Clementine Churchill, 3 January 1954. Mary Soames Literary Papers, Churchill Archives, MCHL 5/1/268.

40 Sarah Churchill's diary, 1955. Sarah Churchill Personal Papers, Churchill Archives, SCHL 2/2/2.

41 Sarah Churchill to Clementine Churchill, 28 February 1954. Mary Soames Literary Papers, Churchill Archives, MCHL 5/7/47.

42 Winston Churchill to Clementine Churchill, 25 May 1954. Churchill Archives, CHUR 1/50 B.

43 Diana Sandys to Clementine Churchill, 8 June 1954. Mary Soames Literary Papers, Churchill Archives, MCHL 5/1/268.

44 Sarah Churchill to Clementine Churchill, 10 June 1954. Sarah Churchill Personal Correspondence, Churchill Archives, SCHL 1/1/15.

45 Mary Soames to Clementine Churchill, 24 March 1955. Mary Soames Literary Papers, Churchill Archives, MCHL 5/7/48.

46 Sarah Churchill to Clementine Churchill, 3 May 1955. Sarah Churchill Personal Correspondence, Churchill Archives, SCHL 1/1/15.

19 Sarah: From Hollywood to Holloway

1 Quoted in Andrew Roberts, *Churchill: Walking with Destiny*, p. 948.

2 Sarah Churchill to Mary Soames, 12 August 1975. Mary Soames Literary Papers, Churchill Archives, MCHL 5/7/70.

3   Sarah Churchill's diary, 19 November 1955. Sarah Churchill Personal Papers, Churchill Archives, SCHL 2/2/2.

4   Sarah Churchill to Clementine Churchill, 5 November 1955. Sarah Churchill Personal Correspondence, Churchill Archives, SCHL 1/1/15.

5   Sarah Churchill's diary, 19 November 1955. Sarah Churchill Personal Papers, Churchill Archives, SCHL 2/2/2.

6   Sarah Churchill to Clementine Churchill, 1 September 1955. Sarah Churchill Personal Correspondence, Churchill Archives, SCHL 1/1/5.

7   Sarah Churchill's diary, 1955. Sarah Churchill Personal Papers, Churchill Archives, SCHL 2/2/2.

8   Sarah Churchill to Clementine Churchill, 8 March 1955. Sarah Churchill Personal Correspondence, Churchill Archives, SCHL 1/1/15.

9   Sarah Churchill's diary, 1955. Sarah Churchill Personal Papers, Churchill Archives, SCHL 2/2/2.

10 Mary Soames to Winston and Clementine Churchill, 1 October 1955. Mary Soames Literary Papers, Churchill Archives, MCHL 5/7/50.

11 Sarah Churchill to Clementine Churchill, 5 November 1955. Sarah Churchill Personal Correspondence, Churchill Archives, SCHL 1/1/15.

12 Mary Soames, *Clementine Churchill*, p. 443.

13 Sarah Churchill to Winston Churchill, 9 January 1954. Mary Soames Literary Papers, Churchill Archives, MCHL 5/7/47.

14 'Sarah Churchill: What Life is to Me', 29 May 1961, *Amarillo Globe Times*.

15 Diana Churchill to Clementine Churchill, 8 November 1955. Mary Soames Literary Papers, Churchill Archives, MCHL 5/1/268.

16 Mary Soames, *Clementine Churchill*, p. 443.

17 Sarah Churchill to Mary Soames, 12 August 1975. Mary Soames Literary Papers, Churchill Archives, MCHL 5/7/70.

18 John Pearson, *Citadel of the Heart*, p. 368.

19 For a detailed overview of the debate, see Wilfred Attenborough, *Churchill and the Black Dog of Depression: Reassessing the Biographical Evidence of Psychological Disorder* (Basingstoke: Palgrave Macmillan, 2014).

20 Winston's friend, Brendan Bracken, told Moran that according to the historian A.L. Rowse, out of the last seven Dukes of Marlborough, five suffered from melancholia. However, although Moran thought there was a depressive strain in the Churchill inheritance, he believed that it was balanced in Winston by the physical and mental robustness of the Jeromes, his mother's family. To a degree, it cast out the Churchill melancholy in him, but not entirely (Charles Moran, *Winston Churchill*, pp. 745–46).

21 For his full assessment, see Anthony Storr, *Churchill's Black Dog and Other Phenomena of the Human Mind*.

22 Wilfred Attenborough, *Churchill and the Black Dog of Depression*, p. 3.

23 Andrew Roberts, *Churchill: Walking with Destiny*, p. 224.

24 For a full discussion of Clementine's anxiety, see Sonia Purnell, *First Lady*.
25 Shelagh Montague Browne says that throughout her life Clementine also suffered from terrible headaches which were unbelievably painful.
26 Mary Soames, *Clementine Churchill*, pp. 456–57.
27 Sarah Churchill to Clementine Churchill, 5 November 1955. Sarah Churchill Personal Correspondence, Churchill Archives, SCHL 1/1/5.
28 Sarah Churchill, *Keep on Dancing*, p. 163.
29 Ibid., pp. 160–61.
30 'The Women Who Wept For Tony Beauchamp But Mother Says He Loved Only one', 23 August 1957, *Daily Herald*.
31 Mary Soames to Clementine Churchill, 6 September 1957. Mary Soames Literary Papers, Churchill Archives, MCHL 5/7/50.
32 Sarah Churchill to Vivienne Entwistle, October 1957. Sarah Churchill Chronological Correspondence, Churchill Archives, SCHL 1/8/2.
33 Sarah Churchill to Winston Churchill, 1 October 1957. Churchill Archives, CHUR 1/55.
34 'Sarah Churchill in Jail', 14 January 1958, *Daily Herald*.
35 Sarah Churchill, *Keep on Dancing*, pp. 165–66.
36 'Sarah Churchill Talks', 30 March 1958, *Corpus Christi Caller Times*.
37 Mary Soames, *Clementine Churchill*, p. 464.
38 In a television interview he got angry when the interviewer, John Wingate, asked indirectly about Sarah. This set Randolph off for ten minutes, saying that he never discussed his family with strangers. He then said to Wingate, 'I don't even know if you had a father.' Wingate considered taking legal action for the comment.
39 Sarah Churchill, *Keep on Dancing*, p. 167.
40 'Sarah Churchill Makes It For Television', 15 January 1958, *Gastonia Gazette*.
41 'Miss Sarah Churchill Fined $50', 17 January 1958, *Birmingham Daily Post*.
42 'Sarah Churchill Makes It For Television', 15 January 1958, *Gastonia Gazette*.
43 'Sarah Churchill Talks', 30 March 1958, *Corpus Christi Caller Times*.
44 Mary S. Lovell, *The Riviera Set*, pp. 326–28.
45 Dr Bircher-Benner created the world-renowned Swiss muesli.
46 Sarah Churchill to Winston Churchill, 21 March 1958. Churchill Archives, CHUR 1/55.
47 Health Report by Dr Liechti on Sarah from Zurich, 27 March 1958. Sarah Churchill Financial Papers, Churchill Archives, SCHL 4/2.
48 Dr Med. F. Meerwein to Dr Liechti, 16 June 1958. Sarah Churchill Financial Papers, Churchill Archives, SCHL 4/2.
49 Sarah's diaries, 24 January 1957. Churchill Archives, SCHL 2/2/2.
50 'Limelight', 6 November 1958, *The Stage*.
51 Edmund Murray, *I was Churchill's Bodyguard* (London: W.H. Allen, 1987) pp. 138–39.

52 Interview with Shelagh Montague Browne, 27 February 2020.

53 'Sarah Churchill', 10 April 1960, *Corpus Christi Caller Times*.

54 'Sarah Churchill Staggering Bare-footed in Main Road', 14 July 1960, *Liverpool Echo*.

55 'Extract from a letter I wrote to a friend written from Maudsley Hospital', 27 July 1961. Sarah Churchill Personal Chronological Correspondence, Churchill Archives, SCHL 1/8/3.

56 Walter Graebner, *My Dear Mister Churchill* (London: Michael Joseph, 1965) p. 38.

57 Andrew Roberts, *Churchill: Walking with Destiny*, p. 45.

58 Anthony Montague Browne, *Long Sunset*, p. 115.

59 'Extract from a letter I wrote to a friend, written from Maudsley Hospital', 27 July 1961. Sarah Churchill Personal Chronological Correspondence, Churchill Archives, SCHL 1/8/3.

60 Ibid.

61 D.L. to Sarah Churchill, 19 December 1961. Sarah Churchill Personal Chronological Correspondence, Churchill Archives, SCHL 1/8/3.

20 Surprised by Joy

1 The film was *Serious Charge*. Reflecting the quality of the plays she was offered, one had the bizarre name 'The Night Life of a Virile Potato'.

2 Interview with Shelagh Montague Browne, 27 February 2020.

3 Sarah Churchill, *Keep on Dancing*, p. 194.

4 Anthony Montague Browne, *Long Sunset*, p. 221.

5 Sarah Churchill to Winston and Clementine Churchill, 22 March 1962. Sarah Churchill Papers, Churchill Archives, SCHL 1/1/17.

6 Sarah Churchill to Clementine Churchill, no date. Churchill Archives, SCHL 1/1/17.

7 Henry Audley to Sarah Churchill, 22 March 1962. Sarah Churchill Personal Correspondence, Churchill Archives, SCHL 1/7/1.

8 The Churchills were descended from the Dukes of Marlborough. Sarah Churchill, *Keep on Dancing*, p. 194.

9 Vic Oliver was born Samek and Antony Beauchamp was originally Entwistle. Anthony Montague Browne, *Last Sunset*, p. 221.

10 Sarah Churchill to Henry Audley, 2 April 1962. Sarah Churchill Personal Correspondence, Churchill Archives, SCHL 1/7/1.

11 Henry Audley to Winston Churchill, 3 April 1962. Sarah Churchill Papers, Churchill Archives, SCHL 1/1/17.

12 Winston Churchill to Henry Audley, 4 April 1962. Sarah Churchill Personal Correspondence, Churchill Archives, SCHL 1/2/5.

13 The dress was Celia's Ascot outfit. Interview with Celia Sandys, 21 January 2020.

14 Sarah Churchill to Clementine Churchill, 7 June 1962. Sarah Churchill Papers, Churchill Archives, SCHL 1/1/17.

15 Sarah Churchill, *Keep on Dancing*, p. 196.

16 Henry Audley to Sarah Churchill, 20 January 1963. Sarah Churchill Personal Correspondence, Churchill Archives, SCHL 1/7/1.

17 Sarah Churchill, *Keep on Dancing*, pp. 199–201.

18 Quoted in Mary S. Lovell, *The Churchills*, p. 552.

19 'Five Poems in Memory of Henry Audley', Sarah Churchill, *The Empty Spaces*, p. 88.

20 Sarah Churchill to Clementine Churchill, 15 July 1963. Sarah Churchill Personal Correspondence, Churchill Archives, SCHL 1/1/18.

21 Sarah Churchill, *Keep on Dancing*, p. 204.

21 Diana: The Good Samaritan

1 Sarah Churchill, *Keep on Dancing*, p. 205. Electroshock therapy, electroconvulsive therapy, or ECT uses electric currents to treat psychiatric disorders. The technique involves passing an alternating current through the head between two electrodes placed over the temples. The passage of the current causes an immediate cessation of consciousness and the induction of a convulsive seizure. Typically, electroconvulsive treatments are given three times a week for a period ranging from two to six weeks. Following the treatment, there is usually some impairment of memory (*Britannica Online Encyclopaedia*).

2 Interview with Celia Sandys, 21 January 2020.

3 Sarah Churchill, *Keep on Dancing*, p. 205.

4 Diana Churchill to Winston Churchill, 3 April 1957. Churchill Archives, CHUR 1/56.

5 Mary Soames, *Clementine Churchill*, p. 414.

6 Ibid., p. 480.

7 Diana Churchill to Winston Churchill, 3 April 1957. Churchill Archives, CHUR 1/56.

8 Antony Montague Browne, *The Last Sunset*, pp. 243–45.

9 Celia Sandys, *Chasing Churchill*, pp. 2–4.

10 Clementine Churchill to Mary Soames, 3 August 1959. Mary Soames Literary Papers, Churchill Archives, MCHL 5/7/52.

11 Celia Sandys, *Chasing Churchill*, p. 11.

12 Clementine Churchill to Mary Soames, 3 August 1959. Mary Soames Literary Papers, Churchill Archives, MCHL 5/7/52.

13 Diana Churchill to Winston Churchill, 16 June 1960. Churchill Archives, CHUR 1/135.

14 Interview with Celia Sandys, 21 January 2020.

15 Diana Churchill to Winston Churchill, 6 March 1962. Churchill Archives, CHUR 1/135.

16 Maud Lindsay, 'Diana of the Samaritans' (no date), *The Surrey Advertiser.*

17 'Diana Churchill, Samaritan', 25 October 1963, *Daily Mail.*

18 'Suicide of Mrs Diana Churchill', 25 October 1963, *Birmingham Daily Post.*

19 Diana Churchill to Clementine Churchill, 28 February 1961. Mary Soames Literary Papers, Churchill Archives, MCHL 5/1/268.

20 Mary Soames, *Clementine Churchill*, p. 464.

21 Sarah Churchill, *A Thread in the Tapestry*, p. 19.

22 Ibid., p. 17.

23 Interview with Celia Sandys, 21 January 2020.

24 Clementine Churchill to Sarah Churchill, 26 December 1962. Sarah Churchill Personal Correspondence, Churchill Archives, SCHL 1/2/5.

25 Lyndsy Spence, *The Grit in the Pearl: The Scandalous Life of Margaret, Duchess of Argyll* (Stroud: The History Press, 2019) p. 205.

26 The Cabinet minister John Profumo admitted that he had lied to the House of Commons about his affair with Christine Keeler. He resigned in June 1963.

27 Sarah Churchill, *Keep on Dancing*, p. 205.

28 Mary Soames, *Clementine Churchill*, p. 479.

29 Ibid., pp. 480–81.

30 'Suicide of Mrs Diana Churchill', 25 October 1963, *Birmingham Daily Post.*

31 Mary Soames, *Clementine Churchill*, p. 481.

32 'Memorial Service "Loyal Diana Churchill"', 1 November 1963, *Daily Telegraph.* Mary Soames Literary Papers, Churchill Archives, MCHL 5/1/196.

33 Anita Leslie to Mary Soames, 29 October 1963. Mary Soames Personal Correspondence, Churchill Archives, MCHL 2/13.

34 June Churchill to Mary Soames, 21 October 1963. Mary Soames Personal Correspondence, Churchill Archives, MCHL 2/13.

35 Sarah Churchill, *Keep on Dancing*, p. 207.

36 Maryott Whyte to Mary Soames, no date. Mary Soames Personal Correspondence, Churchill Archives, MCHL 2/13.

37 'Memo on death of Kennedy and Diana', Sarah Churchill Personal Papers, Churchill Archives, SCHL 2/2/4.

38 Maryott Whyte to Mary Soames, no date. Mary Soames Personal Correspondence, Churchill Archives, MCHL 2/13.

22 Mary: The Calm at the Centre of the Storm

1   Interview with Shelagh Montague Browne, 27 February 2020.
2   Mary Soames to Winston Churchill, 3 December 1951. Churchill Archives, CHUR 1/52 B.
3   Clementine Churchill to Winston Churchill, 2 February 1958. Churchill Archives, CHUR 1/55.
4   Mary Soames to Sarah Churchill, 27 December 1960. Mary Soames Literary Papers, Churchill Archives, MCHL 5/7/53.
5   Mary Soames to Winston Churchill, 12 August 1958. Churchill Archives, CHUR 1/55.
6   'Interview with Mary Soames', in *Finest Hour: The Journal of Winston Churchill and His Times*, No. 116 (Autumn 2002).
7   Mary Soames to Judy Montagu, 2 February 1963. Mary Soames Literary Papers, Churchill Archives, MCHL 5/7/46.
8   16 October 1962, *Daily Mirror.*
9   6 June 2014, 'Interview with Emma Soames', BBC Radio 4, *Last Word*.
10 'Memories of a Churchill Generation', 1 March 1983, *Illustrated London News.*
11 Interview with Emma Soames, 19 February 2020.
12 Sarah Churchill to Anthony Montague Browne, no date. Sarah Churchill Personal Chronological Correspondence, Churchill Archives, SCHL 1/8/3.
13 Sarah Churchill, *A Thread in the Tapestry*, pp. 15, 70, 99.
14 Mary Soames, *Clementine Churchill*, p. 496.
15 Sarah Churchill to Anthony Montague Browne, no date. Sarah Churchill Personal Chronological Correspondence, Churchill Archives, SCHL 1/8/3.

23 Sarah Keeps on Dancing

1   'Sarah Churchill Writes Book', 24 June 1967, *El Paso Herald Post.*
2   Caroline Young, *Roman Holiday*, p. 197.
3   'The Poetry of Sarah Churchill', 2 July 1966, *The Tatler.*
4   His real name was Ernest Leroy Nocho. He was born in America and had served in the Second World War.
5   Sarah Churchill, *Keep on Dancing*, pp. 210–11.
6   Ibid., p. 212.
7   Sarah Churchill to Lobo Nocho, 3 December 1966. Sarah Churchill Personal Correspondence, Churchill Archives, SCHL 1/8/3.
8   Attached to Sarah's letters in the Churchill Archives is a post-it note, possibly in Mary's handwriting, which says, 'I think this is about Sarah's

relationship with Lobo – who was violent to her.' Sarah Churchill Personal Correspondence, Churchill Archives, SCHL 1/8/3.

9 Note by Sarah, no date. Sarah Churchill Personal Correspondence, Churchill Archives, SCHL 1/8/3.

10 Sarah Churchill to Lobo Nocho, 3 December 1966. Sarah Churchill Personal Correspondence, Churchill Archives, SCHL 1/8/3.

11 'Happily Alone – That's Sarah the Poetess', 9 November 1969, *The People*.

12 'Theatre', 8 October 1966, *Illustrated London News*.

13 Sarah Churchill, *The Empty Spaces*.

14 'A Matter of Choice', *The Empty Spaces*, p. 9.

15 'The Sarah Churchill Story', 1 December 1958, *Liverpool Echo*.

16 'Sarah Churchill's *Empty Spaces*', 22 July 1966, *Kensington Post*.

17 Margaret Thatcher to Sarah Churchill, 3 August 1982. Sarah Churchill Personal Correspondence, Churchill Archives, SCHL 1/8/4.

18 Sarah Churchill, *Keep on Dancing*, pp. x–ix.

19 He was working on Winston's biography and had fallen in love at first sight with a married woman, who spent part of her time with him.

20 Sarah Churchill to Arabella Churchill, 11 June 1968. Sarah Churchill Personal Correspondence, Churchill Archives, SCHL 1/3/2.

21 Sarah Churchill to Michael, 11 June 1968. Sarah Churchill Personal Correspondence, Churchill Archives, SCHl1/3/2.

22 Lynne Olson, *Citizens of London*, p. 117.

23 Celia Sandys interview, 21 January 2020.

24 Shelagh Montague Browne interview, 27 February 2020.

25 'Flamboyant, Tenacious Sarah Churchill: Past and Present', 14 March 1976, *Victoria Advocate*.

26 John Pearson, *Citadel of the Heart*, p. 427.

27 Sarah Churchill to Clementine Churchill, no date. Sarah Churchill Personal Correspondence, Churchill Archives, SCHL 1/1/18.

28 Mary Soames to Clementine Churchill, 13 June 1976. Mary Soames Literary Papers, Churchill Archives, MCHL 5/7/71.

29 Mary Soames to Sarah Churchill, 19 August 1975. Mary Soames Literary Papers, Churchill Archives, MCHL 5/7/70.

30 'Happily Alone – That's Sarah the Poetess', 9 November 1969, *The People*.

31 Note by Sarah at the Savoy Hotel, no date. Sarah Churchill Personal Correspondence, Churchill Archives, SCHL 1/8/5.

32 'Sarah Churchill Rebuilds Her Life', 10 January 1973, *Salina Journal*.

33 'Happily Alone – That's Sarah the Poetess', 9 November 1969, *The People*.

34 Sarah Churchill, *Keep on Dancing*, p. 233.

24 Mary's Golden Age

1   Geoffrey Wheatcroft, 'Winston Churchill's Last Surviving Daughter was the Grandest of Grand Dames', 7 June 2014, *The New Republic*.

2   Katherine Carter drew my attention to these pictures and explained Clementine and Mary's process of selection, 21 October 2019.

3   Mary Soames, *Clementine Churchill*, p. 513.

4   Emma Soames, 'My Dear Mama', in *Finest Hour: The Journal of Winston Churchill Special Edition*, No. 164 (September 2014).

5   Ibid.

6   Ibid.

7   Mary Soames to Clementine Churchill, 23–30 September 1968. Mary Soames Literary Papers, Churchill Archives, MCHL 5/7/63.

8   'Lord Carrington's Speech at Christopher Soames's Memorial Service', 29 October 1987. Mary Soames Personal Correspondence, Churchill Archives, MCHL 2/23.

9   Mary Soames to Clementine Churchill, 9 November 1970. Mary Soames Literary Papers, Churchill Archives, MCHL 5/7/65.

10 Mary Soames to Clementine Churchill, 4 September 1968. Mary Soames Literary Papers, Churchill Archives MCHL 5/7/63.

11 Robert Hardman, *Queen of the World: The Global Biography* (London: Arrow Books, 2019) pp. 291–305.

12 Britain joined the EEC in January 1973.

13 'The Amateur Diplomat Who Took France by Storm', 10 November 1972, *The Times*.

14 Sarah Churchill to Mary Soames, 12 August 1975. Mary Soames Literary Papers, Churchill Archives, MCHL 5/7/70.

15 Mary Soames to Sarah Churchill, 19 August 1975. Mary Soames Literary Papers, Churchill Archives, MCHL 5/7/70.

16 Shelagh Montague Browne interview, 27 February 2020.

17 Mary Soames, *Clementine Churchill*, p. 523.

18 Ibid., p. 524.

19 'Sarah Churchill Rebuilds Her Life', 10 January 1973, *Salina Journal*.

20 John Pearson, *Citadel of the Heart*, p. 428.

21 'Lord Carrington's Speech at Christopher Soames's Memorial Service', 29 October 1987. Mary Soames Personal Correspondence, Churchill Archives, MCHL 2/23.

22 Simon Hoggart, 'Ironing the Lawn in Salisbury', 9 February 1980, *The Guardian*.

23 '1st Despatch from the Governess', 13 December 1979. Mary Soames Diplomatic Life, Churchill Archives, MCHL 4/1.

24 Mary Soames to Jeremy Soames, 9 February 1980. Mary Soames Literary Papers, Churchill Archives, MCHL 5/7/75.

25 '2nd Despatch from the Governess', 19 December 1979. Mary Soames Diplomatic Life, Churchill Archives, MCHL 4/1.

26 Ibid.

27 Mary Soames to Christopher Soames, 17 January 1980. Mary Soames Diplomatic Life, Churchill Archives, MCHL 4/1.

28 'Lady Soames Obituary', 1 June 2014, *The Telegraph*.

29 'Lord Carrington's Speech at Christopher Soames's Memorial Service', 29 October 1987. Mary Soames Personal Correspondence, Churchill Archives, MCHL 2/23.

30 'Winston Churchill's Last Surviving Daughter was the Grandest of Grand Dames', 7 June 2014, *The New Republic*.

25 Sarah and Mary Leave the Stage

1 Death certificate, 24 September 1982. Sarah Churchill Personal Papers, Churchill Archives, SCHL 2/1/4.

2 Sarah Churchill to Winston Churchill, 20 December 1955. Churchill Archives, CHUR 1/56.

3 Celia Sandys interview, 21 January 2020.

4 'Question and Answer', Sarah Churchill, *The Empty Spaces*, p. 71.

5 Jock Colville to Mary Soames, 1 October 1982. Mary Soames Family Correspondence, Churchill Archives, MCHL 5/7/77.

6 Mary Soames to Prince Charles, 26 January 1981. Mary Soames Literary Papers, Churchill Archives, MCHL 5/7/76.

7 Mary remained great friends with Sally Mugabe until her death in 1992. She attended Sally's funeral in Zimbabwe as the queen and Prince Philip's representative. However, she did not condone Robert Mugabe's later actions and she felt the subsequent violence of the new regime to be a personal betrayal.

8 'Lady Soames Obituary', 1 June 2014, *The Telegraph*.

9 Robert Hardy, 'We Will Treasure Her all Our Days', in *Finest Hour: The Journal of Winston Churchill*, Special Edition, No. 164 (September 2014).

10 'Obituary Mary Soames', 11 June 2014, *The Stage*.

11 The famous British actor.

12 6 June 2014, 'Interview with Emma Soames', BBC Radio 4, *Last Word*.

13 6 June 2014, 'Interview with Sir Richard Eyre', BBC Radio 4, *Last Word*.

14 'Lady Soames Obituary', 1 June 2014, *The Guardian*.

15 Laurence Geller, 'Foreword: What We Have Lost', in *Finest Hour: The Journal of Winston Churchill*, Special Edition, No. 164 (September 2014).

16 'Lady Soames Obituary', 1 June 2014, *The Telegraph*.

17 'Lady Soames Dies at 91', June 2014, *International Churchill Society.*

18 John Pearson, *Citadel of the Heart*, p. 427.

19 Celia Sandys, 'The End of an Era', in *Finest Hour: The Journal of Winston Churchill*, Special Edition, No. 164 (September 2014).

20 Minnie Churchill, 'She Created Her Own Sunshine', in *Finest Hour: The Journal of Winston Churchill*, Special Edition, No. 164 (September 2014).

21 Interview with Emma Soames, 19 February 2020.

22 Mary Soames, '"Let Us Command the Moment to Remain": Winston Churchill as Father and Family Man', Inaugural Meeting, North Texas Chapter, International Churchill Society, 19 February 1986.

Index